The b... ...nique comparative study of two of the greatest figures in modern architecture – Alvar Aalto and Le Corbusier. By assessing the historical, personal and intellectual influences on their attitudes to nature and the creative direction of their work, this study offers a new understanding about the diversity at the heart of modernism. Through an analysis of the architects' own personalities and their philosophies and ideas about the metaphysical, a better understanding is gained of their ideas for modern urban living. By looking at their most widely known work, the authors analyse the architects' intentions to build nature into the heart of their architecture. In addition, this book is able to offer a unique insight into the lives and creativity of the two men by requisitioning the psychological theories of Donald Winnicott. The authors argue that although there are many similarities between their attitudes towards nature, at heart the two architects have a fundamentally different conception of it.

Sarah Menin studied architecture before researching a PhD on parallels in the life and creative works of Aalto and Sibelius. She has published articles on this subject, as well as other analyses of Aalto, Le Corbusier, the construction of place, psychology and patterns of creativity. In 1999 she was awarded a Leverhulme Special Research Fellowship to study parallels between Aalto and Le Corbusier's interests in nature and patterns of creativity, from which this book has arisen. She is a lecturer in the School of Architecture, Planning and Landscape at the University of Newcastle-upon-Tyne, UK, teaching architectural history and theory, and design. Menin also continues to practise architecture.

Following her training at Cambridge and Princeton, where she held a teaching fellowship, **Flora Samuel** practised as an architect for some years before writing her PhD on Le Corbusier's scheme for La Sainte Baume, where he hoped to create a 'radiant' community in harmony with nature. A lecturer in architectural history as well as design, she has published articles in a number of academic journals on Le Corbusier, psychotherapy, literature, theology and philosophy. She currently runs the second year at the Welsh School of Architecture, Cardiff University, UK.

Nature and Space:

Aalto and Le Corbusier

Sarah Menin and Flora Samuel

Routledge
Taylor & Francis Group

LONDON AND NEW YORK

First published 2003 by Routledge
11 New Fetter Lane, London EC4P 4EE

Simultaneously published in the USA and Canada
by Routledge
29 West 35th Street, New York, NY 10001

Routledge is an imprint of the Taylor & Francis Group

Text design and typesetting by Ninetyseven+, Islington, London
Printed and bound in Great Britain by St Edmunsdbury Press,
Bury St Edmunds, Suffolk

British Library Cataloguing in Publication Data
A catalogue record for this book is available from the British Library

Library of Congress Cataloging in Publication Data
Menin, Sarah.
    Nature and space : Aalto and Le Corbusier / Sarah Menin and Flora Samuel
        p. cm.
    Includes bibliographical references and index.
    1. Aalto, Alvar, 1898-1976–Criticism and interpretation. 2. Le Corbusier,
1887-1965–Criticism and interpretation. 3. Architecture–Environmental
aspects. I. Samuel, Flora. II. Title.

NA1455.F53 A2349 2002
720'.92'2–dc21

                                        2002069882

ISBN 0-415-28124-5 (hbk)
ISBN 0-415-28125-3 (pbk)

This book is dedicated to David Feige and Alex Ojeda

Contents

Illustration Credits

The authors and publishers gratefully acknowledge the following for permission to reproduce material in the book. Every effort has been made to contact copyright holders for their permission to reprint material in this book. The publishers would be grateful to hear from any copyright holder who is not acknowledged here and will undertake to rectify any errors or omissions in future editions of the book.

© Fondation Le Corbusier, FLC/ADAGP, Paris and DACS, London 2002: Plates: 1, 3, 6, 9/JH, 11/SCM, 13/MR, 16/SCM, 17/FS, 19/SCM, 21/SCM, 24/SCM, 26/SCM, 27/SCM, 29/SCM, 30/SCM. Figures: 2.1, 2.2/SCM, 4.1/SCM, 4.2, 4.6, 4.7, 4.8, 4.9, 4.11, 4.12, 5.1, 5.2, 6.1, 6.3, 6.4, 6.5, 6.6, 6.7 / LH, 6.14/LH, 7.1, 7.2, 7.3, 7.4, 7.5, 7.6, 7.7, 7.8/RB, 7.9/RB, 7.10, 7.11, 7.12, 7.13, 8.1, 8.2, 8.3, 8.4.

© Alvar Aalto Foundation, Helsinki (AAF): Plates: 4, 5, 14, 28. Figures: 2.3, 2.4, 2.5, 4.4, 4.10, 5.3, 5.4/EM, 5.5, 5.6, 5.7/IT, 6.2, 6.8, 6.11, 7.14, 7.16, 7.18, 8.6, 8.8, 8.9, 8.10/MIT Press, 8.12, 8.13, 8.14, 8.15.

© Sarah Menin (SCM): Plates: 7, 8, 10, 11, 12, 15, 16, 18, 19, 20, 21, 22, 23, 24, 25, 26, 27, 29, 30. Figures: 1.1, 2.3, 2.6, 2.7, 4.1, 4.3, 5.5, 6.9, 6.10, 7.15, 7.17, 7.19, 7.20, 8.5, 8.7, 8.11; © Lucien Hervé, Paris (LH): Figures: 6.7, 6.14; © René Burri, Magnum (RB): Figures: 7.8, 7.9; © Ezra Stoller / Esto (ES): Figure 6.13; © Flora Samuel (FS): Plate 17; © Jude Harris (JH): Plate 9; © Marc Riboud, Magnum (MR): Plate 13; © Iittala Glass, Finland: Plate 2; © Museo Diocesano, Cortona/Alnari, Firenze: Figure 4.5; © Eino Mäkinen (EM) /AAF: Figure 5.4; © Italo Martinero (IT) / AAF: Figure 5.7.

Acknowledgements

We would like to acknowledge the debt to scholars who have paved the way for this research.

Our research led us often to France and Finland, and we thank scholars, writers, curators and archivists who facilitated this work. We would particularly like to thank the Alvar Aalto Foundation and the Fondation Le Corbusier for their help and provision of excellent archives. In particular were are grateful to Mia Hipeli, Arne Heporauta and Marjaana Launonen from the Alvar Aalto Foundation, Anna Hall of the Mairea Foundation, Madame Evelyne Trehin and Stephane Potelle at the Fondation Le Corbusier for their assistance and co-operation. Kati Blom, Sharon Jones, Meg Parque, Mary Kalaugher, Elizabeth Warman and Wolfgang Weileder are to be thanked for freely giving their help with translations. Closer to home Sylvia Harris has also provided much-needed assistance in obtaining books for this project, and Peter Hill and Nick Pears have given invaluable assistance with challenging computer matters.

We would also like to thank those who have supported this research. In particular Andrew Ballantyne, Peter Carl, Peter Carolin, Robert Coombes, James Dunnett, Suzanne Ewing, Gareth Griffiths, Charles Jencks, Peter Kellett, Sylvia King, Stephen Kite, Mogens Krustrup, Judi Loach, Frank Lyons, Jo Odgers, Juhani Pallasmaa, C.A. Poole, Christopher Powell, Colin St John Wilson, Göran Schildt, Henriette Trouin, Russell Walden, Nick Weber, Richard Weston, and Simon Unwin who have offered assistance at various stages. We particularly acknowledge the support of the late Dr Anthony Storr for his inspiration, his encouragement, his tireless belief in the process of gaining understanding about personality and the creative drive, and his support of the thesis that underpins this book.

We acknowledge the support of those institutions, foundations and trusts that have supported us individually during our doctoral research which led towards the writing of this book: the Leverhulme Trust who funded a Special Research Fellowship which provided the impetus for this book, the British Academy, the Harold Hyam Wingate Foundation, the RIBA Research Trust, and a Dorothy Stroud Bursary from the Society of Architectural Historians of Great Britain.

We want to acknowledge the considerable debt to those people who have assisted us during the writing of this book in practical ways; in particular Caroline Mallinder and Michelle Green at Routledge for supporting our work and guiding us through the publishing process.

Thanks are also due to the many friends who offered friendship and support during the research and writing, including Kati Blom, Prue Chiles, Liisa and Jan Hellberg, Esa Fagerholm, Gisela Loehlein, Adam Sharr, Kostia and Ilona Valtonen and Edmund de Waal.

We would like to thank our children, Anna, Amos, Alice and Otilia for their patience, and finally our husbands, David Feige and Alex Ojeda, to whom we are most indebted for their unfailing support, and to whom we dedicate this book.

We are grateful to the British Academy for funds to cover the copyright fees involved with this publication.

Preface

This book is the outcome of ten years of detailed research into the lives and creativity of Aalto and Le Corbusier. It results from quite independent discoveries of the character and effect of the two men's deep-rooted experiences of nature, their consequent fascination with the processes of nature, and their translation of these passions into their architecture and their art. Discussions between us resulted in the realisation that therein lies a bond which unites seemingly disparate architectural forms, and what is more, explains something of the friendship of the two as men, rather than as architects.

The literary theorist George Steiner has recently written of the persistent existence of God in 'so many unconsidered turns of phrase and allusion' in spite of twentieth-century pretensions towards rationalism. He described Him as 'a phantom of grammar, a fossil embedded in the childhood of rational speech. So Nietzsche and many after him'.[1] The presence of God is felt in this way in the writings of Le Corbusier and Aalto through their use of such words as spirit, harmony, truth, unity and, it will be argued, nature.

Rather than seeking to catalogue their works or formulate a critique of one by the standards of the other, our book seeks to explore the passion both men had for nature and how they allowed this to imbue the heart of their ideas and work. In setting the nature of their interests side by side we seek to illuminate the nature of each individual, and allow this in turn to illuminate the nature of the work of both.

[1] George Steiner, *Real Presences*
London: Faber, 1989, p.3.

Introduction

Nature provided a vital source of inspiration for Le Corbusier and Alvar Aalto. In this book we will explore its influence upon the two men in terms of both their intellectual and their psycho-spiritual development, an area that remains largely unexplored. This is not possible without examining aspects of their own lives and the generation of their interest in the realm of nature. We will also explore the nature of the friendship between the two men and the similarities and differences between their ideas.

Technology and Art: A Natural Unity?

Le Corbusier and Aalto held strong ideas about the ways in which the physical environment could create links with the realm of metaphysics. They drew and painted incessantly, recognising the value of this activity in providing inspiration and resolution of compositional problems for their work. At the same time they were highly innovative in terms of their use of technology, both recognising that it was necessary to draw together the practical and the spiritual to create an uplifting architecture that would be capable of reuniting man with nature, healing a schism that they felt acutely. Le Corbusier was to observe that 'Art, product of the reason–passion equation, is for me the site of human happiness'.[1] It was of central importance in the pursuit of spiritual wellbeing. He believed that painting was a 'miracle' achieved when body and spirit worked in unison.[2] Thus, both men appear to have believed that art played a central role in achieving a state of inner balance.

In this book we will dwell upon the metaphysical, even the spiritual aspects of the two men's work, but this is not to deny the importance of their interest in technology and their wish to create efficient buildings. To achieve this efficiency both called on ideas of natural selection and the 'laws of biological diversity'.[3] Le Corbusier's faith in nature, his belief in evolution was clearly allied to his faith in science and his desire to believe in an overall pattern governing all things.

Indeed, both Aalto and Le Corbusier invested a great deal of energy honing innovative solutions to the functional problems arising in both traditional and new building typologies. The advances in environmental technology that they

[1] Le Corbusier, *Precisions*, Cambridge, MA: MIT Press, 1991, p.68. Originally published as *Précisions sur un état présent de l'architecture et de l'urbanisme*, Paris: Crès, 1930.

[2] Le Corbusier, *A New World of Space*, New York: Reynal & Hitchcock, 1948, p.14.

[3] A. Aalto, 'The Reconstruction of Europe is the Key Problem of Our Time', *Arkkitehti*, 1941, 5, pp. 75-80, in G. Schildt, *Alvar Aalto in his Own Words*, New York: Rizzoli, 1977, p.153.

made, such as Le Corbusier's *brise soleil* and Aalto's circular roof-lights, can be said to have been motivated by a keen sense of how a building's fabric should in no way impede the relation of human life to the natural environment. In their attitudes to technology there is a sense of a passion for nature that motivated a very deep desire to find functional solutions that would allow, for instance, the free passage of light, air, and the control of the sun's energy. Their creative approach to these issues was technically innovative and poetically astute.

Nurturing Natura

Aalto spoke of seeking to avoid the creation of 'psychological slums' through the sensitive adaptation of settlements to the 'surroundings and terrain'.[4] Le Corbusier similarly associated darkness and squalor with poor inner health. In *The Decorative Art of Today* he speculated about what would happen if people were made to whitewash their homes by law:

> There are no more dirty, dark corners. *Everything is shown as it is*. Then comes *inner* cleanness, for the course adopted leads to refusal to allow anything at all which is not correct, authorised, intended, desired, thought-out: no action before thought. When you are surrounded with shadows and dark corners you are at home only as far as the hazy edges of the darkness your eyes cannot penetrate. You are not master in your own house. Once you have put Ripolin on your walls you will be *master of yourself*.[5]

It is clear that he believed, rightly or wrongly, that by changing people's homes, he would be able to change the way that they thought.

In addition to defining a role for the subconscious, Aalto suggested that 'A mystical element is needed' if the whole complex of problems facing society generally, and architects in particular, was to be solved 'in a positive way from a human viewpoint'.[6] He seems to have felt that the mystical level facilitated the empathy that then ensured the outworking of love for 'little man'. Such mysticism, he believed, acted as a guardian against mechanisation that he saw might 'strangle the individual and organically harmonious life'.[7] Indeed, Aalto's association of the search for harmony, organicism and love is important, drawing on his key influences of the wisdom of ancient Greece, and his experiences and knowledge of nature. The role of public servant, instilled in him by his father, seems to have become a crucial element in Aalto's life, as if morally directed creativity could do love's healing (or at least maintenance work) for others and even within himself. These together offered Aalto a template of intent in his work that was equally important for his life.

The interest in ancient Greek thought, shared by both men, was intricately bound to their common interests in nature. Indeed, the etymology of the word 'nature' helps define the terms of this investigation, and the exploration herein of their ideas concerning this realm. In ancient Greek nature was 'physis', meaning 'to bring forth, produce, make to grow'.[8] The English word nature is

4   Aalto, 'The Reconstruction of Europe', in ibid., pp.155 and 150.
5   Le Corbusier, *The Decorative Art of Today*, London: Architectural Press, 1987, p.188.
6   A. Aalto, 'Centenary of Jyväskylä Lycée' in G. Schildt, *Alvar Aalto Sketches*, Cambridge, MA: MIT Press, 1985, p.162.
7   Ibid., p.163.
8   L. Brown (ed.) *Oxford English Dictionary vol.VI*, Oxford: Clarendon, 1933; E. Klein, *A Comprehensive Etymological Dictionary of the English Language*, London: Elsevier Publishing Co., 1971; H.G. Liddell and R. Scott, *A Greek-English Lexicon*, Oxford: Clarendon, 1961.

rooted in the Latin for nature, 'natura', which also meant instinct and birth. 'Natura' thus offers a beginning, and is closely linked to 'nascor', meaning to be born, to grow or arise.[9] From these classical beginnings we allow our investigation to grow from the germ of a child's life in their familial environment, in certain geographical contexts, through the development and education of the individual personality. In this we seek to explore natural growth and creativity, both personal and artistic, involving this investigation in the process of the development of the persons, Aalto and Le Corbusier. This is crucial because any understanding of their own adult conception of 'nature' is undoubtedly affected by their individual, personal developmental processes, as much as any subsequent intellectual enquiry. In this book we argue that the manner in which Aalto and Le Corbusier constructed their architectural places is inextricably linked to how they construct 'nature' in their own minds and hearts. We seek to demonstrate that central to these constructs was their sense of their own identities in relation to the rich experiences of the natural environment, primarily of their youth, and subsequently in their adult pursuit of physical health. Their pursuance of both sentient stimulation and psychological space in the natural environment is also crucial, both to their perception of what nature was, and concomitantly to their conception of what it could be in their architecture. Indeed, both architects addressed nature in a number of different ways at the levels of the practical (physical), the compositional (conceptual) and the symbolic (metaphysical). Herein we will follow their cue.

Central to Aalto's and Le Corbusier's architectural challenge (the questioning of the very conception and meaning of space) is a determination to allow nature to defy the boundaries of building. They encouraged vegetative growth to engulf their human interventions in the environment. Aalto believed that 'the purpose of a building is to act as an instrument that collects all the positive influences in nature for man's benefit, while sheltering him from the unfavourable influences that appear in nature'.[10] For this reason he drew light, sun and greenery into the heart of interior space, as we will demonstrate.

Growing Environments in the 'Gap'

The impression of Le Corbusier given by historians is of a serious and driven man determined to impart to the world his vision of a new architecture appropriate for the machine age. Aalto, on the other hand, is generally remembered as a convivial and carefree character, who, according to his friend and biographer Göran Schildt, while being a flatterer, also had something of a drink-facilitated drive. It will become apparent that Aalto and Le Corbusier were actually more similar than might at first appear. In both cases there were aspects of their personalities that played important roles in their lives and in the direction of their creativity. There is no doubt that both men needed to be creative to remain balanced. The character of this balance will be explored herein.

Both architects had strong ideas about improving the lives of others, arguably because they were so aware of deficiencies in their own. While

[9] Brown, *Oxford English Dictionary*, pp.1889–90.
[10] Aalto, 'The Reconstruction of Europe', 1941 in Schildt, *Own Words*, p.153.

accepting, with other scholars, that psychology cannot completely explain art, here we will address Le Corbusier's and Aalto's life-condition, and the emergence of any psychological breaks or deprivations in it, because such 'gaps' can be shown to have contributed to the make-up of their personalities.[11] It is our thesis that nature played an important role in repairing or compensating for such deprivations. For this reason the psychological framework of the psychiatrist Donald Winnicott, who began his career in the 1950s working with Melanie Klein, will be engaged to draw out something of the reality of their own lives within the language and imagery of natural growth. Unusually for his time, Winnicott believed that experience and environment played an important role in mental health. He championed the effect of the life-condition, those cultural and environmental factors so important to the human growth process, writing, 'When one speaks of a man one speaks of him along with the summation of his cultural experience. The whole forms a unit.'[12] Nature and architectural space were intrinsic to Aalto's and Le Corbusier's reading of this human unit.

Designing to fill a 'gap'

According to Winnicott breaks or 'gaps' which develop in the primary holding environment (the relationship with the mother or other primary carer) are not understood by the infant, and are experienced as episodes of 'primitive agony'.[13] The withholding of affection or the absence of attention prevents the child interacting with its 'Mother' and thus impedes psychic development. This is because the self, like a plant, requires a nurturing environment. In the gaze of the mother the infant sees the reflection of itself and its feelings. The environment (mother) makes the becoming self of the infant feasible. However, Winnicott observed that if the mother is preoccupied, she reflects herself, and the infant will not get something of itself back from the environment, being forced instead to perceive her mood rather than his or her own.[14] This is also known as narcissistic disturbance.[15]

To grow physically and psychologically, Winnicott believed, a human's natural creativity is at work, rejecting, challenging and ultimately integrating the fragments of order experienced into personal inner worlds. Breaks, deprivations or 'gaps' impede this creativity.[16] Health, on the other hand, has a relationship with living, inner wealth and the capacity to have cultural experience.[17] Winnicott saw the relationship with mother as central to this process of creativity, since she is the infant's primary environment in which the child lives creatively.[18]

Winnicott developed this idea into the concept of 'transitional phenomena' in which the child may play with fantasy. This is an intermediate area between his inner world and the world beyond in which transitional or play phenomena can be established. In the opinion of Anthony Storr: 'There are good biological reasons for accepting the fact that man is so constituted that he possesses an inner world of the imagination which is different from, though connected to, the world of external reality. It is the discrepancy between the two worlds which motivates creative imagination.'[19]

[11] D. Winnicott, 'Transitional Objects and Transitional Phenomena' 1951, in D. Winnicott, *Playing and Reality*, Harmondsworth: Penguin, 1971, p.26.

[12] D. Winnicott, *Playing and Reality*, p.116.

[13] D. Winnicott, *Collected Papers: Through Paediatrics to Psychoanalysis*, London: Tavistock, 1958, p.145.

[14] Winnicott, *Playing and Reality*, pp. 130–8.

[15] Broadly this concerns the failure of the child to have its emotions, sensations and expressions reflected back in the mother's eyes, and thus to recognise itself. This early narcissism is legitimate, the fulfilment of which is vital in healthy child development and individuation.

[16] Winnicott, *Playing and Reality*, p.26.

[17] Winnicott, 'The Concept of a Healthy Individual', in D. Winnicott, *Home is Where We Start From*, Harmondsworth: Penguin, 1986, p.36.

[18] Winnicott, *Playing and Reality*, pp.130–8.

[19] A. Storr, *Solitude*, London: Harper Collins, 1997, p.69.

Creative potential involves constantly bridging the 'gap' between inner and outer worlds, and is often facilitated by a 'transitional object' in childhood, be it a favourite cloth or teddy. These objects facilitate the transition between attachment to mother and attachment to later objects – in other words people that the child comes to love and depend on. Such transitional phenomena mediate between the known and the unknown, the inner and the outer worlds for the child. This, Winnicott believed, is the child's first creative act. When the child has had at least some love she can project that on to an 'Other', such as a favourite toy, as a transition to being able to dispense with the actual presence of 'Mother'. Extrapolating from this, it can be said that those who retain a need to cling to mother beyond infancy are unable to form other healthy attachments. Winnicott would suggest that such individuals still long for the comfort and safety of the early environment, one that failed in some way to provide for adequate psychic growth to independence. It is not unreasonable to suggest that such individuals seek mother substitutes, or recreate maternal environments again and again within their lives in one form or another.

Potential Space for Creativity

Winnicott also developed the notion of 'potential space' which is very interesting in the architectural context, being a place that facilitates explorations of the interplay between inner and outer worlds.[20] The notion of this haven-like place grew from his idea that play and creativity are linked in the transitional world (between subjectivity and objectivity).[21] It is a place that Winnicott felt was central to both human and artistic creative development, a psychological zone in which the child feels it can explore otherness – things beyond the safe zone of 'Mother'.

Winnicott argued that the disruption of the environment (or the 'gap') interferes not only with the growth of the individual, but also with the 'potential space' the individual might occupy.[22] He defined potential space as the carving out of a 'place' without impingements. This, he believed, was 'a potential space between a child and the mother when experience has produced in the child a high degree of confidence in the mother, that she will not fail to be there if suddenly needed'.[23] In his opinion cultural experience starts with play. This is the entering of potential space. Aalto demonstrated this in his essay 'The Trout and the Stream',[24] where he discussed his way of playfully sketching ideas, then spontaneously breaking off and playing with his children to free his ideas, before returning to design. Le Corbusier made a more conscious effort to divide his time between periods of work and leisure. As cited, both men sketched and painted ceaselessly, fully aware of a need to allow free flow of, sometimes irrational, ideas from the subconscious.[25]

When the capacity to invest life with play disappears, the joy disappears too, and despair may engulf the individual. Storr has observed that this often happens with particularly creative individuals who have invested so much significance in the work that they can no longer play with it. If, for instance, the

[20] Winnicott, *Playing and Reality*, pp.2–10.
[21] This idea strongly challenged Freudian assumptions of sublimation, wherein creativity is a substitute for instinctual expression.
[22] Winnicott, *Playing and Reality*, pp.2–10.
[23] Winnicott, 'The Concept of a Healthy Individual', in *Home is Where We Start From*, p. 36.
[24] Aalto, 'The Trout and the Mountain Stream', 1947 in Schildt, *Sketches*, pp.96–8.
[25] This is demonstrated in the abstract art that both architects created. For example Plates **4,5** and **6**.

creative work is addressing the 'gap' (consciously or unconsciously), the individual may be 'playing' close to a great deal of unassimilated pain and sorrow. Often there is a sense that if the work (of whatever sort) succeeds life will be good, and concomitantly if it fails the individual experiences the 'gap' anew.

Psychiatrist Frank Lake created a model of the dynamic life cycle of a relatively well-functioning personality,[26] wherein acceptance leads to sustenance, from which status is naturally forthcoming, leading, in turn, to achievement without striving or anxiety. However, often this psycho-dynamic model works in reverse, in which case expectancy of failure and rejection are a great source of anxiety. From achievement we seek status, which gives us sustenance and, we hope, acceptance.[27] It will become apparent that both Aalto and Le Corbusier lived with an intense reverse dynamic life cycle.

With sufficient trust in the environment (initially 'mother'), there can be potential creative space that may facilitate exploration of the interplay between inner and outer reality. Individuals often seek to revisit failed environments through both destructive behaviour and creative activity. Both these modes of 'return' to the 'gap' will be illustrated here through accounts of patterns of positive creativity and of negative personal behaviour in both Aalto and Le Corbusier.

Winnicott thus observed that in situations where a child is placed in an early environment that is less than fully nurturing its development is sometimes inhibited, often resulting in psychosis. This happens by degrees, so if the environment is acutely dysfunctional the child's psychic growth is concomitantly severely impeded. If the deprivation is less acute, so the child's impediment is equally diminished. Alternatively the child may grasp hold of a system of order from beyond their unpredictable environment, internalise it, and use it to seek to bring some order to the interior chaos: seeking to 'structure a world' through creative evolution.[28] This acts like a refuge, and can be an important ingredient in the future direction of a creative journey.[29]

Ecology of Imagination

An investigation into Le Corbusier's and Aalto's drive to utilise nature to improve the lot of humanity calls for a notion of human growth that brings the isomorphic processes of psychology and biology together. For this reason Winnicott's ideas will be augmented by those of Edith Cobb, who profoundly addressed the correlation between human creative growth and natural biological growth in her book *Ecology of Imagination in Childhood*.[30] Cobb believed that, as an alternative to retreating into psychosis, children may engage in 'world-building' in an attempt to structure their lives in analogy with an external system.[31] This is a way, she believed, of seeking to structure unpredictable environments through a process of internalising an external structure or system (such as systems of growth in nature or musical form), and borrowing from it some experience or perception of order. Cobb explored the ways in which mental, psycho-social and psycho-physical health lies in the spontaneous creativity of childhood, be it imaginary play or artistic scribbles.[32] Indeed, some

[26] This is explicated in F. Lake, *Tight Corners*, London: DLT, 1981 and F. Lake, *The Dynamic Cycle*, Lingdale Paper no. 2, Oxford: CTA, 1986. Lake extrapolates from A.H. Maslow's model of Being and Deficient Psychologies demonstrated in *Towards a Psychology of Being*, New York: Van Nostrand Reinhold, 1968.

[27] F. Lake, *Clinical Theology*, London: DLT, 1986.

[28] E. Cobb, *The Ecology of Imagination in Childhood*, Dallas: Spring Publications, 1993, p.17, and H. Bergson, *Creative Evolution*, London: Macmillan, 1911. Cobb's final chapter borrows Bergson's wording, 'Creative Evolution: A Process of Compassion', p.97.

[29] It is suggested that 'creators typically suffered some deprivations and distress in childhood.' R.E. Ochse, *Before the Gates of Excellence: The Determinants of Creative Genius*, Cambridge: Cambridge University Press, 1990, p.81.

[30] Cobb, *Ecology of Imagination*, p.16.

[31] Ibid., pp.17 and 53. This is close to Eriksen's notion of the 'natural genius of the child'. E. Eriksen, *Insight and Responsibility*, New York: Norton, 1964, p.45.

[32] Ibid., pp.15, 17 and 53.

research suggests that 'creative individuals' are much more likely to have suffered trauma, specifically the loss of a parent, in childhood than those who are not creative.[33] It will be argued that both Le Corbusier and Aalto learnt as children to dislocate feelings and expression, resulting in a persistent sense of inner weakness and inadequacy. In both men the sensitive artist seeking approval from a mother figure finds a nemesis in more brutal behaviour (be it their attitudes to and conquering of women, or what might be seen as their flirtation with the elements of Fascism). This was countered by a developing interest in nature and a determination to understand the natural system in which they both spent increasing time in their youth. As well as this deep emotional need for nature, both men shared a northern Romantic view of the natural world, in common with their peers.

As the psyche perceives innumerable parallels between its activity of structuring the inner and outer worlds, and the structures of the actual outer natural world in which it finds itself, so continuation of emotional 'gaps' may fuel the need for the natural environment to be a refuge, even if the gaps are slight. In her introduction to Cobb's book, Margaret Mead suggests that 'human beings need to take in, reshape, and give out, in some altered form, their perceptions of the natural world, the cosmos'.[34] Such an assimilation of varied, even opposing, experiences (such as chaos and order, joy and pain) is vital for the development of a realistic world-view.[35] It is interesting here to note that any opposition between cosmos and chaos is a purely modern invention.[36]

Many psychological studies reveal that the nature and direction of a person's creativity are rooted in key aspects of their early experience, as the work of Anthony Storr, Richard Weisberg and Ellen Winner has demonstrated.[37] If, as Winnicott believed, childhood deprivations ('the death, the absence, the amnesia')[38] result in emotional 'gaps', and individuals revisit these 'gaps' in their creativity, it is our suggestion that Le Corbusier and Aalto directed their creative missions to ameliorate such defects in both themselves and in others. Indeed, as Le Corbusier and Aalto wove threads of their unrecorded reality into their artistic cosmos (in other words their created constructs), they enriched the growth of those very creations. In this way they would make known the unknown, at the level both of their own psyche and that of many other people, often ineffably and sometimes both positively and negatively. 'Realising how much our world was convulsed by the birth pains of the machine age, it seemed to me that to achieve harmony ought to be the only goal. Nature, man, cosmos: these are the given elements, these are the forces facing each other,' wrote Le Corbusier.[39] Drawing together the ideas of Winnicott and Cobb it is possible to suggest that in expressing a desire to address the need for 'order' and 'harmony' he and Aalto were actually articulating an inner need (and thus aspects of the 'gap').

Undoubtedly for both Le Corbusier and Aalto architecture offered a phenomenon through which they could address problems facing humanity and art, and indeed evinces that they believed that these problems were intrinsically related. Both saw art and architecture as a way of addressing the metaphysical realm, a realm they felt was too often ignored. As Aalto affectionately, if a little messianically put it, he sought to 'bring into balance the whole milieu that

[33] A. Storr, *The Dynamics of Creation*, Harmondsworth: Penguin, 1991, and Ochse, *Before the Gates of Excellence*.

[34] Cobb, *Ecology of Imagination*, p.8.

[35] Pre-Socratic thought and ideas, for example, were not conceived in terms of what are now understood as oppositions, but rather both/and notions which tended towards a whole or a cosmos.

[36] W. Jaeger, *The Theology of the Early Greek Philosophers*, Oxford: Oxford University Press, 1947, p.13. Concurring with Hesiod, an early Greek poet who followed Homer, McEwan believes that there is no opposition between kosmos and chaos, believing, with Ovid in mind, that it is a Roman invention. Indra Kagis McEwan, *Socrates' Ancestors*, Cambridge, MA: MIT Press, 1993, p.62.

[37] For example, Storr, *Dynamics of Creation*; R.W. Weisberg, *Creativity: Beyond the Myth of Genius*, New York: W.H. Freeman & Co., 1993, and E. Winner, *Invented Worlds*, Cambridge, MA: Harvard University Press, 1982.

[38] Winnicott, 'Transitional Objects' 1951, in Winnicott, *Playing and Reality*, p.26. Winnicott has been observed as seeking to elucidate the control he believed Melanie Klein had on the direction of the British Psychoanalytical Society (BPS). A. Phillips, *Winnicott*, London: Fontana, 1988, pp.131–2.

[39] Le Corbusier, *A New World of Space*, p.11.

surrounds us', thereby offering 'a true sign of culture ... that serves man in the proper way'.[40]

Aalto was emotionally unstable. At times he was vulnerable as a child, and yet was often manically driven. Le Corbusier meanwhile stuck doggedly to his quest, but not without periods of gloom, particularly late in life, at the lack of acceptance of his work, as he demonstrated clearly in his last testament, 'Mise au point'.[41] Originally named Charles Édouard Jeanneret, he created a persona, Le Corbusier – the architect, strong and impervious to criticism, who was an outsider and a disinterested witness. He also made a conscious effort to create a balance between the subjective and objective, the artist and the engineer, in his life and work. He described painting as 'a battle between the artist and himself' and used it to resolve those inner conflicts that threatened to overwhelm him.[42] This 'Artist Corbu', in whom the humanist flourished, has emerged through the research of, amongst others, Peter Carl, Stanislaus von Moos, Richard Moore Mogens Krustrup and Russell Walden.

Just as a person cannot be fully understood through the physical realm alone, so the physical place-making does not live fully if the metaphysical nature of the created place (be it specifically psycho-social or the spiritual) is ignored. The same may be said of a constructed place when its intended state is somehow 'wounded', an example being Le Corbusier's Unité complexes which, when bereft of surge of their life blood, the free shared social facilities that formed such a central part of their conception, ceased to function properly.

Natural Holding Space

Generally in a 'good enough environment' there would be no 'gaps'; the 'mother' facilitates rather than prevents primary human creativity, both physical and emotional. Here a connection between 'mother' and the 'gap' emerges, one that is important in this context as the 'environment' quickly broadens out from 'mother' to the wider influences. Thus, the first part of the book is devoted to an examination of the ways in which nature became such an important part of the two men's thinking. In Chapter 1 the nature of the 'gap' in the lives of the two architects will be addressed and what is known of their early life-condition described. We will illustrate the ways in which both natural and creative sojourns were central to both their childhoods. In Chapter 2 the historical, personal and intellectual influences on their attitudes to nature in adulthood will be examined. This will lead to an examination of their role in the Modernist mainstream in Chapter 3 wherein the growing relationship between the two men is described. In Chapter 4 an exploration of the place of nature in the ideas and philosophies of Le Corbusier and Aalto as expressed through their writings will take place.

Drawing from their own personal experiences of inner anguish, Le Corbusier and Aalto perceived a great imbalance in the lives of men in the machine age. For this reason they felt a need to create spiritually revivifying environments in which man could live harmoniously within nature. It is this drive that provides the focus for the second part of this book. In Chapter 5 we

[40] Aalto, 'Art and Technology', 1955, in Schildt, *Sketches*, p.127.
[41] Le Corbusier, 'Mise au Point', in I. Žaknić, *The Last Testament of Père Corbu*, New Haven: Yale University Press, 1997, pp.83-101.
[42] Le Corbusier, *Sketchbooks Volume 4*, 1957–1964, Cambridge, MA: MIT Press, 1982, sketch 506.

will examine the personalities of the two men and the ways in which they were manifested in their own personal retreats at Cap Martin and Muuratsalo. The intention at the heart of these two schemes was to refresh and heal through a submersion in nature. This may also be said to be the main driving force behind their religious buildings at Ronchamp and Vuoksenniska, churches that provide the focus for Chapter 6. Having addressed the way in which the two men blurred the boundaries between nature and mystical experience we are then better able to examine the ways in which they approached the design of dwellings, which were, for both men, inherently sacred spaces.

In the third part of this book this idea will be extended into our discussion of their designs of dwellings for other people, whether individual homes, discussed in Chapter 7 or mass housing, discussed in Chapter 8.

Rather than intending to provide a comparative critique of the two men's work, we aim to describe the ways in which both men sought to restore mankind to the 'conditions of nature', growing their own definitions of nature and applying them to their work, and to some extent to themselves. It will be seen that whilst both men shared this common aim it manifested itself in their work in rather different ways.

Chapter 1

The Human Side[1]

The lives and creativity of both Le Corbusier and Aalto are riddled with (and enriched by) paradox and contradiction. The acceptance and relation of these is vital to a mature understanding of the two men and their work. It is also a position that allows penetration of the live force behind the creativity of the two[2] – one that was rooted not merely in intellectual artistic enquiry about form, but in a deeper personal struggle to actualise and reconcile aspects of themselves, their past, and the world-view which arose from their early experiences. In this chapter we will place particular emphasis on seeking an understanding of their early emotional experiences, their experiences of nature, and the role these played in the establishment of their particular interests and creative direction.

Although one of the polemic impressions Le Corbusier promoted to the world was of a man who wanted to start from zero, he readily acknowledged the importance of the past, observing that 'any reflective man thrust into the unknown of architectural invention cannot base his creative spark on anything but the lessons taught by past ages'.[3] Aalto's work is peppered with allusions to the classical past, and in an early essay, 'Motifs from the Past' (1922), he wrote of how rare stylistic details from the past are precious and 'signify a great deal more', being in some way 'in total harmony with their surroundings'.[4] However, he also often quoted Nietzsche's notion that 'Only obscurantists look back', perhaps in part because of a desire to avoid having to dwell on uncomfortable aspects of the past, both history's and his own.[5] One context for this comment was a discussion of primitivism versus technology, but he followed it with a more general version: 'It doesn't help to turn back towards the past; we must look forward if we are to solve our problems.'[6] This suggests that, at least consciously, he did not want to face certain difficult threads of past reality, hinting at a preference to attempt to move on regardless. Generally speaking such denial prevents the mastering of painful memories and therefore assimilation and restoration of emotional balance.

Aalto did not however completely deny his past. He often allowed it to the fore in the creative sphere, mediated in part through a concern to build relationships between nature and man and in part through a concern to bring

[1] Reference to a journal Aalto sought to launch in the early 1940s. Outlines of this project are in the Alvar Aalto Foundation, Helsinki, hereafter referred to as the AAF.

[2] S.K. Langer explores this in *Feeling and Form: A Theory of Art Developed From Philosophy in a New Key*, London: Routledge, 1953, p. 98.

[3] Le Corbusier, *Le Corbusier Talks with Students*, New York: Orion, 1961, p.57.

[4] Aalto, 'Motifs from the Past', 1922, in G. Schildt, *Alvar Aalto Sketches*, Cambridge, MA: MIT Press, 1985, p.2.

[5] Aalto citing Nietzsche, 'Interview for Finnish Television', July 1972, in G. Schildt, *Alvar Aalto in his Own Words*, New York: Rizzoli, 1997, p.274.

[6] Ibid.

architectural functionalism to the borders of psychology and beyond. In this way he was able to work from a place in which his awareness of his own psychological vulnerability was not denied. Writing of Aalto's 'unassimilated sorrow', Göran Schildt suggests that, 'Instead of accepting the tragic law of annihilation, he tried in his architecture to create a lasting, objective world, above all a world of deep cosmic harmony'.[7] These words could equally well be applied to Le Corbusier, and offer a telling juxtaposition of the psychological, the objective and the cosmic.

Mother and the 'Good-enough' Environment

In seeking to explore Le Corbusier's and Aalto's childhoods, and the nature of their endeavours to address any subsequent 'gap' in their lives, it becomes immediately apparent that their mothers played an important role in their emotional and therefore their creative development, both artistic and personal.

Marie, Mother and Maternal Deprivation

The young Le Corbusier, then known as Charles Édouard Jeanneret-Gris, was born in 1887 in the small town of La Chaux-de-Fonds in the Swiss Jura. His father, Georges Édouard Jeanneret-Gris, was a cultured watch enameller by trade and his mother, Marie Charlotte-Amélie Perret, a piano teacher.

Apparently Édouard, a complicated boy, was contradictory in his behaviour, at times sociable, at others introspective. Kenneth Frampton writes that 'he was socially inept and yet blessed with a boisterous sense of humour. He was fiercely loyal in friendship and yet, at times, blatantly opportunistic. He oscillated throughout his teens and early twenties between flaunting his artistic ability and suffering bouts of extreme insecurity.'[8] It will be seen that these were traits that he was to retain throughout his life. For example, he wrote to his mother in 1954, 'I will always wake up every morning feeling in the skin of a fool ... old nitwit Corbu is a funny guy who will snuff it in a madhouse.'[9]

Édouard was born into a middle-class family rooted in the history of the La Chaux-de-Fonds, which had rationally imprinted itself upon the pastoral landscape during the nineteenth century. The social structure of small workshops was central to the international watch-making identity of the settlement. The town defied its geographically peripheral position, being exposed to leading political and cultural forces, drawn in by the successful watch business. The tradition of religious freedom and political rebellion is vital in the socio-economic character of the town, giving it its individual reputation.

Édouard and his brother Albert were given religious instruction by their aunt Pauline, a very religious woman. Their mother was less religious. They went to the local Independent Protestant church regularly, their parents attending only on religious holidays. At the age of sixteen Édouard received six weeks of formal religious instruction but was soon to reject the faith within which he was raised, spending the rest of his life searching for an alternative spiritual ideal.[10]

Within the family it seems that Édouard's mother Marie was the greatest

[7] G. Schildt, *Alvar Aalto: The Early Years*, New York: Rizzoli, 1984, p.71.

[8] K. Frampton, *Le Corbusier*, London: Thames & Hudson, 2001, p.8. Édouard's birth father notes in his diary, 'Mrs Grattiker, the nurse took charge of him. All went well, he was put immediately on cow's milk and he drinks his bottle like a man', cited in Brookes, *Le Corbusier's Formative Years*, Chicago: University of Chicago Press, 1997, p.9.

[9] Le Corbusier, letter to his mother, 10 November 1955. Fondation Le Corbusier (hereafter referred to as FLC) R2 (2) 171.

[10] H. Allen Brookes, *Le Corbusier's Formative Years*, Chicago: University of Chicago Press, 1997, p.20.

inspiration in moral and educational terms. H. Allen Brookes notes that Édouard was more proud of his bourgeois maternal ancestors than of those of his father, who had been artisans and farmers.[11] Indeed the Lecorbesier name upon which he would forge his new identity, came from his mother's side of the family. Through Marie came the strong Protestant principled discipline, characterised by her advice, borrowed from Rabelais, and adopted as a motto by Le Corbusier that, 'Whatever you set out to do, make sure that you do it'. Perhaps it was her musicianship that made his mother value precision, but also urged her to encourage the more abstract artistic goals to which Édouard was to be drawn. Le Corbusier was to reminisce: 'It was a matter of occupying a particular square on the social chessboard: a family of musicians (music heard all through my youth), a passion for drawing, a passion for the plastic arts, purity, acuity, a character which wanted to get to the heart of things, harmony.'[12] While the family as a whole prized technical, intellectual and aesthetic work, Marie appears to have felt more attachment to Albert, whose musical talents were closer to her own.[13] This state of affairs did not escape Albert, who evidently tried to make amends by drawing his mother's attention to his younger brother: 'didn't you love Édouard when he made you stop before each flower, each different texture, each tint'.[14]

Marie was to suffer a miscarriage when Édouard was four years old. Brookes notes that this, 'coupled with a worsening depression, terminated the family's growth', suggesting that times were hard and that she may well have been preoccupied with things other than the care and attention of her youngest son.[15] Indeed Brookes gives an account of Édouard's mother being dominant at home, talking incessantly, contradicting others and ordering them about. She also seems to have been inconsistent: one minute possessive and brisk, and another extremely tender – contradictions that are extremely confusing to a child. It is our thesis that Le Corbusier spent much of his life seeking the approval of his strong-willed mother (who lived to be more than a hundred) in an attempt to fill the 'gap' opened by the apparently inadequate expression of her love. Flowery and flattering letters from Le Corbusier to Marie, at various stages in his life, suggest something of the intensity of his relationship with her.[16]

Selma, Sadness and Substitutes

Alvar Aalto's relationship with his mother seems to have been extremely affectionate, but was tragically severed, resulting in a more acute 'gap' than that suffered by Le Corbusier. Alvar was born in 1898 in the small Finnish town of Kuortane in Southern Ostrobothnia. He enjoyed a very close relationship with his mother, Selma Mathilda Hackstedt, who came from an educated Swedish-speaking family. Selma and her sisters were considered radical, being keenly interested in issues of women's emancipation, and becoming financially independent through a vocational training of some sort. For this reason Selma chose to work as a post mistress and her sisters, Flora and Helmi, trained as teachers. Aalto often described his mother in 'Ibsenian' terms, trail blazing in her views about female emancipation, writing about the feminist calibre of those (including herself and her sisters) who, like Hedda Gabler, dared to challenge

[11] Ibid., p.8.
[12] Le Corbusier, *Modulor*, London: Faber, 1954, p.182.
[13] Brookes, *Formative Years*, p.16.
[14] A. Jeanneret, letter to his parents, 24 November, 1908. Cited in ibid., p. 152.
[15] Ibid., p.9.
[16] See for example letter to his mother dated 18 August 1940, FLC R2 (4). Le Corbusier wrote to his mother about an encounter that he had with an American psychiatrist, who told him that judging from his paintings, Le Corbusier evidently had some problems with his mother that he had not managed to resolve. Letter, Le Corbusier to his mother dated 19 February 1937, FLC R2.1.149
[17] We are grateful to Nicholas Weber who is currently completing the research for a biography on Le Corbusier for further verifying this impression.

the status quo.[17] Selma bore five children, of which Alvar was the second. She died suddenly after contracting Meningitis when he was eight. Her first child died in infancy, the last (a girl also called Selma) remained weak throughout childhood, and Aalto's youngest brother, Einar, who had become a soldier at his father's insistence, killed himself in terror of the start of the Winter War, when the Russians invaded Finland, in the autumn of 1939.

Alvar described having enjoyed close physical intimacy with his mother beyond his infancy, sleeping in her bed while his father was away on surveying expeditions until her death; later in life he often made tender references to his mother's beauty and even her underwear.[18] Soon after Selma's death, his aunt Flora married his father, a relationship described by Schildt as a marriage of convenience that grew into one of affection.[19] Aalto was never able fully to admit the degree of the deep trauma of his mother's death, preferring instead to fuse his mother and his aunt into one happy memory. He seems to have been unwilling to work through painful memories, preferring instead to bury them alive. A number of his friends report that his wives were not only life companions, but were the 'security and substitute for his lost mother'.[20] It is surprising then that his biographer can describe this extrovert character as having a 'basic sense of security … he never seems to have doubted his own worth and ability', adding only a page later that 'he could not bear to be alone'.[21] This does not add up, and leads us to suggest that his fear of being alone holds more truth than the idea that Aalto was a secure individual.

As cited above, early separations (or lack of continuation) in the contact relationship with mother may be experienced as episodes of primitive agony. Add to this the complete severance of this relationship and the psychic shock that Aalto may have experienced becomes clear, and may at least be described as traumatic. It is therefore feasible that the subsequent 'gap' is perennial, being something to which a person returns again and again, either to fall into, in illness or depression, or alternatively to address with vital determination in the creative sphere. Undoubtedly these repeated bereavements left Aalto permanently scarred, with a pathological dread of anything that touched on death. They also resulted in him withdrawing into what has been described by friends and observers as long bouts of hypochondriachal illness, depression and even periods of psychosis, as his son-in-law (the psychiatrist Yrjö Alanen), has described it.[22] Yet, that Aalto somehow requisitioned his 'tragedy' and ran with it, so to speak, to address the needs of the 'little man' in his work is of central import.

The outworking of these key mother-shaped 'gaps' will be explored in the discussion of the feminine in the work of Aalto and Le Corbusier in later chapters, yet the influence of the fathers is also crucial in the development of the two architects.

Fastidious Favouritism

The two main sources that shed light on Édouard's father are his own descriptions and his father's diaries, recently brought to light by Brookes. Georges Édouard Jeanneret-Gris was a meticulous craftsman, whose skill was to

[17] Selma Hackstedt, cited in Schildt, *Early Years*, p.32.
[18] Ibid., p.48.
[19] Ibid., p.49.
[20] Ibid., p.71.
[21] Ibid., p.69.
[22] G. Schildt, *Alvar Aalto: The Mature Years*, New York: Rizzoli, 1992, p.14. J. M. Richards wrote that Aalto 'was completely disorientated, lost his customary ebullience and drank until his friends despaired of his future!' *Memories of an unjust fella*, London: Weidenfeld & Nicholson, 1980, p.203.

enamel watches, and who valued the personal outworking of creative endeavour. He worked in a workshop for watch decorators which formed part of the town's famous horology industry. He participated in all aspects of town life, at the heart of which was the work ethic: one lived to work, and one did not flaunt wealth or possessions, if one was fortunate enough to have them.

The biographical work of Brookes suggests that Édouard's father took great pride in caring for his sons and helping them develop a sense of self-worth. Their capacity to work, study and hike was frequently noted in his diaries, with emphasis in favour of Albert.

> *April 6, 1895* Our Albert just passed his spring examination with success, 110 out of 110 – maximum. The boy gives us great pleasure. His brother is less conscientious.
>
> *July 13, 1895* Our two sons both took first prize in their class; this pleased us greatly.

But in 1899 Édouard's father pens a telling diary entry.

> *February 6 1899* At home great undertakings; our Albert, who makes great progress in music, will play on Wednesday in a concert ... We have great hopes of success. This dear little child gives us great pleasure, whether in his musical or his scholarly studies ... His brother [Édouard, the black sheep of the family][23] is usually a good child, intelligent, but has a different character, susceptible, quick-tempered, and rebellious; at times he gives us reason for anxiety.[24]

This is interesting because it sheds light on the parental priorities for the boys: intelligence and good behaviour. He places a 'but' in his description of Édouard's 'different' character, painting a picture of the challenge the younger son posed. Albert was greatly pressured to do well in his studies, particularly music. Brookes speculates that his bad stutter, and psychosomatic symptoms that later prevented him from practising his violin and taking up further study in 1907, may have been a manifestation of excessive compulsion to achieve, and his consequent lack of confidence. Unsurprisingly Albert failed to meet his parents' expectations, and was later judged to be 'too serious' by his father, who himself was not exactly a light-hearted individual.[25]

It is against this background of intense pressure that Édouard developed a need to seek solitude, almost as an escape. He reminisced that as a child he had 'always drawn by the light of the family table', the pencil and paper and the circle of light offering quiet refuge.[26] The suggestion from his father's diary, that the parents favoured Albert, did not cause a rift between the two brothers, and they remained devoted to each other, close confidants throughout their lives.[27] Brookes notes that when a number of architects met Marie, and congratulated her on having such a talented son, she 'thanked them for their kind remarks concerning Albert'. It seems that she never fully appreciated the talents of her youngest.[28] Although Brookes concludes that there was no lack of love for Édouard,[29] the youngster would undoubtedly have recognised the inequality of his parents' attentions. However, their attention seems eventually to have

23 These parentheses are Brookes'. Brookes, *Formative Years*, p.13.

24 Diary entry of G.É. Jeanneret-Gris. Ibid., pp.12 and 13.

25 Diary entry of G.É. Jeanneret-Gris December 1905. Ibid., p.41. In a letter to Ritter Le Corbusier writes, 'The truth is that my father is absolutely convinced that his sons will never be any good. Up till now he has been justified, but damn it, he is in such a hurry!' Letter Le Corbusier to Ritter, early summer 1911, FLC quoted in J. Lowman, 'Le Corbusier 1900–1925: The Years of Transition', unpub. PhD thesis, University of London, 1979, p.46.

26 Le Corbusier, *A New World of Space*, New York: Reynal & Hitchcock, 1948, p.10.

27 J. Loach evinces this in her critical review of Brookes' book, 'Jeanneret becoming Le Corbusier: Portrait of the Artist as a Young Swiss', *Journal of Architecture*, 5, 2000, pp.91–9.

28 Brookes, *Formative Years*, p.16.

29 Ibid., p.42.

rendered Albert inactive, and to have resulted in both boys lacking in confidence. Indeed, perhaps Édouard actually had the easier of the two experiences of this dysfunctional home.

Brookes suggests that the warmth and affection expressed by Édouard's father in his diary is touching, yet he seems to have been a reserved character, sitting quietly absorbed in his own thoughts, rather than having been demonstratively affectionate towards his children. He paints a picture of how, at home, his wife dominated and he moderated, coming alive and animated in his realm, the mountains. Le Corbusier wrote: 'Nature was the setting where, with my friends, I spent my childhood. Besides, my father was passionately devoted to the mountains and river which made up our landscape.'[30] His father was president of the local Swiss Alpine Club, and passionate about experiencing nature. Thus perhaps his strongest influence was the intensity of the manner in which he introduced Édouard to nature pursuits, such as climbing, trekking and close observation of natural history in the Jura mountains. Édouard was certainly encouraged to look hard at nature. Apart from the excitement of such sojourns, Brookes describes Édouard's infancy as 'uneventful'. Nevertheless he continued to traipse the Alps with his father: 'We were constantly on mountain tops: the vast horizons were familiar.'[31]

Le Corbusier went on to recall that 'Adolescence is a time of insatiable curiosity. I knew flowers inside out, the shapes and colours of birds, how a tree grows and how it keeps its balance even in the eye of a storm.'[32] In this way he learnt an appreciation of the landscape from his family. This was coupled, later, with the cultural and political significance of such alpine landscapes. His body, often described as 'frail' by his father,[33] was physically challenged, he was mentally stimulated and, it appears, spiritually uplifted. Importantly these were experiences in which his father was animated. Le Corbusier later reminisced that: 'from childhood my father used to take us on walks through the valleys and up the mountains pointing out what he admired most: the diversity of contrasts, the staggering personality of objects, but also the unity of laws'.[34]

Here he unashamedly projected personality upon natural objects, and to some extent introjected aspects of the natural world into himself. Speaking from hindsight Le Corbusier might well be mythologising his youth, but it is clear from the analytic drawings and landscape paintings that he produced during this period that a yearning to discover and demonstrate 'the unity of laws' began to stir within him at an early age. Charles Jencks suggests that it was on these trips that he developed a taste for being alone in nature.[35]

As the watch-making industry modernised, Édouard's father found that his very specific skills were becoming redundant. He wrote: 'Little by little I retire from civic life in order to become more and more cloistered and ignored. Soon I shall disappear completely!'[36] It seems very peculiar that he and his wife should have decided to apprentice Édouard to the same dying trade. Their move could be seen to demonstrate a disregard for their son's future, but this seems unlikely. The town's complete dependence on crafted watch-making up to this date may have contributed to something of a denial about the coming of the machine. Édouard was brought up in a society of craft workshops, masters and apprentices.

[30] Le Corbusier, *The Decorative Art of Today*, London: Architectural Press, 1987, p.194.

[31] Ibid., p.194.

[32] Ibid.

[33] Diary entry of Georges Édouard Jeanneret-Gris. Brookes, *Formative Years*, p.12.

[34] Le Corbusier, *Modulor 2*, London: Faber, 1955, p.297.

[35] C. Jencks, *Le Corbusier and the Continual Revolution in Architecture*, New York: Monacelli, 2000, p.20.

[36] Diary entry of Georges Édouard Jeanneret-Gris, December 1893. Brookes, *Formative Years*, p.18.

It was through the practice of master and apprentice that he developed his architectural skills. He subsequently practised the same mode of work in his atelier.

Aalto, Ego and the Stiff Upper Lip

Such a fear or denial of progress did not characterise Aalto's forebears. His father was a land surveyor, working to map the vast expanses of forest in Central Finland. Yet the line of succession from father to son was also an issue in Aalto's home. Late in life, Aalto recalled, even fantasised about the fecundity of his father's work environment for him, through memories of his drawing table:

> The white table is big. Possibly the biggest table in the world, at least in the world and the tables I know ... The table had two storeys. In the lower storey, I lived from the moment I learned to crawl on all fours ... until I was ready to be moved up to the upper storey, the white table top itself ... On that table maps were drawn of large parts of Finland ... vast forests and unending wilderness ... The white table of my childhood was a big table. It has kept growing. I have done my life's work on it.[37]

This may have been as close as he could get to participating in his father's occupation or having his father's attention.

If the women of the Hackstedt family were largely responsible for instilling the importance of culture into Alvar, the men offered a clear, if archetypically masculine, image of the importance of rational action. Aalto's father, J.H. Aalto as he was known, was caring but cold.[38] He was an active, pragmatic gentleman, who seems to have felt dis-eased in the emotional realm, preferring, like Édouard's father, to dwell in the rational world, but was certainly not without appreciation of cultural issues. He was, by all accounts, serious about his work, which he bore as a weight upon his shoulders. He was known for being 'extremely reserved in his manner',[39] even taciturn, and yet at the same time sociable. Thus Aalto's father comes across as having been something of an enigma. Undoubtedly he believed in providing a safe and stimulating environment for his children, although his reserve would have rendered him inadequate to provide compensation for his children in terms of the necessary physical and emotional warmth when his wife died. It may have been his own self-knowledge of this that persuaded him to encourage, or perhaps accept, Flora's wish to step into her sister's shoes. Indeed, it was she who asked the children if they had anything against her becoming their new mother.

The Aalto family was one of the many emerging middle-class families in a society where it was a great struggle to rise from subsistence existence through the meagre opportunities for education. J.H. Aalto was born in 1869, from peasant stock in the parish of Vanaja, in the Finnish province of Häme. His father's water mill business was failing in the wake of steam, so he was encouraged to learn the alphabet from an itinerant teacher, and began to trudge four miles to and from the lyceum in Hämeenlinna, which the composer Sibelius was also to attend. Eventually, after much academic travail, he graduated from

37 Aalto, in conversation with Schildt, July 1972, in Schildt, *Own Words*, p.274.
38 It was the fashion in late nineteenth-century Finland for the educated class to be known by their initials.
39 Schildt, *Early Years*, p.25.

the grammar school when he was twenty-two, much older than his peers, and went on to train as a land surveyor in Helsinki. J.H. Aalto was very proud of having risen, against all odds, from the peasantry to the educated class of public servants. His parting words to his son as he left home to study architecture were 'Alvar, always remember you're a gentleman'.[40] Interestingly Aalto always described his father's role as one of the greatest importance, although, as Schildt points out, J.H. Aalto was deputy surveyor for nineteen years before being promoted to junior surveyor and only became a senior surveyor after a further three years.[41]

In 1903 Alvar's father felt life in Kuortane was too isolated for his young family, from whom he had to be away for long periods, as he surveyed distant parts. The family thus moved to Jyväskylä, soon becoming an establishment at the forefront of intellectual and creative activity there.[42] As part of his job J.H. Aalto continued to undertake work trips into the depths of the forest, surveying, hunting and fishing. Alvar accompanied his father on such excursions into the wilds from an early age. These would sometimes last some days, and seem to have increased in frequency after his mother died. Such times close to his father in the forest may have ameliorated his sense of loss more because of increasing familiarity with the vitally nourishing context of the forest than because J.H. Aalto shared his grieving with his sons. Certainly, in terms of the influence on his future, something in the nature of the forest seems to have fostered Alvar's imagination. Like Édouard, he introjected aspects of the natural world into himself, or at least into his imagination, to revive them through the creative act of designing.

Added to this was his experience of participating in his father's work staking out land for a railway. Making inroads into wilderness, and forging progress in this way, was not questioned in Alvar's milieu. This became for him the basic model of interaction between civilisation and nature.[43] Aalto recalled this a few years before his death.

> Surveying was a tradition in my family on both my father's and my mother's side. And so it was natural that even as a school boy I should work for my father during summer holidays as a cartographer's assistant. As for the Finnish landscape, it was there all around me, all the time. That experience of a working balance also gave me an idea of how man should treat his surroundings. You [Schildt] have written in your books that man's activities in nature are like a cancer in a living body. But it doesn't have to be like that. We can instead seek a balance with our environment and concentrate on healing the scars we have caused.[44]

If read in the light of Aalto's deep personal scars, his love of nature and the fecundity of the imagination in creativity, the latter part of this quotation is a moving explanation of his oeuvre.

Like most middle-class families of the time, the Aaltos sought even closer contact with nature during the summer, renting rooms in Rottola Farm near Alajärvi from 1910, and often visiting their aunt Helmi who had moved to Lovisa on the Baltic Coast from 1911. Schildt suggests that exposure to the rural milieu of Rottola gave Aalto the ability to adopt a *vox humana* when necessary,

40 Ibid., p.26.
41 Ibid., pp.24-5.
42 The Aalto household played host to many of the intellectuals and artistic elite of the time, such as poet Eino Leino, writer Juhani Aho and painter Akseli Gallen-Kallela, who passed through on their way to and from Karelia – the creative Mecca of the time.
43 Ibid., p.59.
44 Aalto, from a conversation with Schildt, *Own Words*, p.274.

countering his more usual self-important tone, one which he may have inherited from his father.[45]

Aalto's strongly rationalistic streak grew from the influence of the objective worlds of both his surveyor father and his forester grandfather. This was accompanied by the latter's inventiveness, and the cultural interests of his aunts, the Hackstedt sisters. Like Le Corbusier, from early on Aalto seems to have had an urge to synthesise a rational, unsentimental objectivity, and a longing for emotional comfort and the subjective realm. Aalto had an insatiable yearning for physical affection, probably relating back to severance of the early relationship with his mother.[46] He covered this vulnerability and sensitivity with something of his father's military bearing, authoritative gait and pompous manner, often telling his subordinates 'You don't give orders to an Aalto'.[47] Schildt describes the contrast between the establishment figure of his father and Aalto's more bohemian existence as being less important than the similarities between the architect's office, the strong desire 'to work objectively' for the greater good, and the experience of working on the large 'white table'.[48]

Forest and Rock: Education of Matter

The early formal education of both Le Corbusier and Aalto seems to have had less influence on the direction of their lives than that which they received at home. That both spent a great deal of time in the natural environment, exploring, hunting, trekking, playing or studying nature is certain and may have been crucial to their future outlook (Fig.1.1). Later Le Corbusier recalled how his youth was enveloped by an interest in the natural world:

> Our childhood was illuminated by the miracles of nature. Our hours of study were spent hunched over a thousand flowers and insects. Trees, clouds and birds were the field of our research; we tried to understand their life-curve, and concluded that only nature was beautiful and that we could be no more than humble imitators of her forms and her wonderful materials.[49]

Indeed, Loach suggests that to understand Le Corbusier's early sensibility, it is essential to understand the mountain landscape and the place of the mountains in the psyche of the Swiss, as that nation's prime unifying and distinguishing factor.[50] Without question, the same applies to Aalto.

Meadows and Mountains

Le Corbusier was most at home in the Jura mountains, a system of Alpine forelands surrounding the grid-iron streets of La Chaux-de-Fonds.[51] The winter climate is very cold, as pools of cold air slump in the high valleys. The mountains do not reach the bare heights of the high Alps, and the forest vegetation therefore comprises oak groves and beech forest at lower altitudes, with higher elevations covered with firs. The crests above the tree line are covered with Alpine grasses, with occasional isolated moors. Although wildlife is now

[45] Schildt, *Early Years*, p.63.

[46] Viola Wahlstedt-Guillemaut (Viola Markelius as was) spoke openly to Schildt about her erotic relationship with Aalto, indicating that 'He always tried with everyone', and that he was somehow child-like in his 'incredible longing for tenderness'. Next to the sketch of an unknown naked woman Schildt alludes to Aalto's innumerable affairs. G. Schildt, *Alvar Aalto: The Decisive Years*, New York: Rizzoli, 1986, p.50.

[47] Schildt, *Early Years*, p.27.

[48] Ibid., p.27.

[49] Le Corbusier, *Decorative Art of Today*, p.132.

[50] Loach, 'Jeanneret becoming Le Corbusier', p.93.

[51] The Jura mountains were named for their dense forestation, *jura* meaning 'forest' (from the Gaulish *jor, juria*; ultimately related to Slavic *gora*, 'mountain').

practically extinct, this was not the case in Édouard's youth.

In those days farming varied from the dairy economy to the vineyard zone of the western and southern faces of the Jura. Villages are found in abundance, especially in the valleys, while larger cities have grown almost entirely on the margins. In his watercolours Édouard depicted the high plateau valleys in which the forested hills open on to pristine, grazed meadows.[52] Indeed, the name of the town, La Chaux-de-Fonds, means 'meadow at the end of the valley', its coat of arms carrying the image of a beehive.

Having grown up around the watch-making industry, the town has also been a famous haven for revolutionaries throughout history – an association Édouard was happy to adopt. There was an immense symbolic dichotomy between this ordered town and the mountains. This was challenged by the development of the Pouillerel district, in which his first villas were built, nestling on the side of the mountain, reaching out to both nature and civilisation, and softening the grid-iron nature of the town. Yet Édouard spent his youth not in this suburban context, but in a rather sombre apartment block in town.

[52] For example: G. Baker, *Le Corbusier: The Creative Search*, London: Spon, p.17, fig. 1.7 and p.20, fig. 1.13.

Spruce, Pine and Small Town Radicals

Alvar was five when the Aaltos moved to the provincial town of Jyväskylä. The town was young, founded only in 1837, and as its name suggests it had grown up from humble beginnings as a 'grain village'. The area is characterised by 'infinitely vast, deserted forests'[53] punctured by innumerable expanses of water. It is located at the head of Lake Päijänne, which runs over 150 kilometres south to Lahti. At the beginning of the twentieth century, however, the lake was no longer the main traffic artery, as the railway was coming (staked out in part by Alvar and his father). Jyväskylä was quickly becoming industrialised, with a population of some 3,000.

At this time Jyväskylä was already nationally known as the Athens of the north, largely because of its Finnish-speaking cultural life during the second half of the nineteenth century. Aalto wanted it to become the Florence of Finland.[54] It was partly this that attracted his father to the town, but the decision to move was mainly due to the establishment in 1858 of the first Finnish-language folk school (which Alvar later attended). The town then hosted the first meeting of folk-school teachers in Finland, in 1863. This year also marked the opening of the teacher training college (which Aalto was later to redesign). The first Finnish-speaking girls' school was established the next year.[55]

Although the topography was different, the height of the Jura mountains and the latitude of central Finland meant that the flora and fauna that Le Corbusier and Alvar experienced was not dissimilar. In common with much of Finland, the area in which Alvar traipsed as a youngster is dominated by conifers (mainly pine and spruce), although silver birch is also widespread. More than 1,000 species of flowering plants have been recorded (a practice learnt at school to this day). The place is still relatively rich in wildlife, with elks, wolf, wolverine, lynx and the occasional bear, and a variety of waterfowl on lakes. In Alvar's day wild reindeer were still seen. For this reason he was a keen hunter and fisherman, able to poach salmon, trout, whitefish, pike, char and perch.

As in Switzerland, the natural environment was crucial to the young nation's self-image. Thus understanding the nature of the forest was tied up with a strong determination to resist the threat of Russia to the East.[56] Indeed, in a romantic tone Schildt suggests that the forest was 'the common denominator' between Alvar, his father and grandfather – 'the experience of nature as a spontaneously growing, ever-changing environment, which bestows its gifts on man, but which man must tend with expert knowledge and love'.[57] Aalto's passion for the natural environment is palpable in both his writing and his creative work.

Conclusion

Two themes arise from this investigation. The first concerns the fact that both Aalto and Le Corbusier grew out of childhood with what can be loosely described as a mother-shaped 'gap' and a longing for relationship with mother or mother substitutes. Certainly, as will become increasingly apparent, definite themes of

[53] J.L. Runeberg, 1832, cited in Kalevi Riikinen, *A Geography of Finland*, Lahti: University of Helsinki, 1992, p.121.

[54] Schildt, *Early Years*, p.252.

[55] Until these establishments were opened schools in Finland were Swedish-speaking, reflecting the language of the wealthier minority.

[56] Finland had been a Grand Duchy of Russia since 1809, having been part of Sweden. She became independent for the first time during the Russian Revolution, in 1917.

[57] Schildt, *Early Years*, p.34.

the feminine and the mother figure can be demonstrated in the lives and work of both Le Corbusier and Aalto.

The second theme concerns the degree to which Le Corbusier and Aalto undertook a great deal of physical and imaginative activity in the natural environment. Indeed their early experience of nature seems to have infiltrated the psyches of the two boys in the form of a fundamental and unchanging order. This knowledge of the processes of nature was to inform everything that they did in later life.

Chapter 2

Natural Growth, Natural Contract:
From Pattern to Principle

The need to establish absolutes often seems to have been at the centre of Le Corbusier's work, be they Purist absolutes or natural laws. However, the forms of his architecture that greet us are often far from absolute, and indeed defy a single reading. As William Curtis writes, Le Corbusier's inventions were often triggered by 'analogical leaps of thought between disparate phenomena'.[1] As for Aalto, created artistic forms were as active and vital to him as natural form. They were elements of the desired re-infiltration of the concept of cosmos (or natural order) into the reality of the modern world, of human life and of nature.

The two paths to architectural practice taken by Le Corbusier and Aalto differed markedly. In this chapter we will focus upon the major influences that made up their education, in the broadest sense, by making an assessment of the historical, intellectual and personal influences on their developing attitudes towards nature as they matured into adulthood. It is our aim to understand whether nature acted as an agent of integration, or whether there was a discrepancy between it and their other philosophies.

Brookes subdivides Le Corbusier's education into three phases. The first covers his basic state education and the second his five years spent at the École d'Art in La Chaux-de-Fonds. The third phase consisted largely of self-directed study, travel and apprenticeships with two influential architects, Auguste Perret and Peter Behrens.[2] Aalto's education divides into his schooling in Jyväskylä and his more conventional architectural training in Helsinki.

[1] W. Curtis, *Le Corbusier: Ideas and Forms*, New York: Phaidon, 1986, p.11.

[2] H.A. Brookes, *Le Corbusier's Formative Years*, Chicago: University of Chicago Press, 1997, p.24.

A Self-Mastering Nature

Careless Infancy?

The two Jeanneret boys began school at a private kindergarten using the Froebel method of instruction in August 1891. Much has been written about the influence of the Froebel method on the work of Frank Lloyd Wright, and one might speculate that it may have had a similar influence on the infant Le Corbusier. Édouard transferred to the local state school in 1894, where he was consistently ranked first in a class of forty-four boys. Both he and Albert were to receive first prize in their respective classes in July 1895.

Édouard entered secondary school, the École Industrielle, in 1899 (it was upgraded to gymnase status while he was there) and quickly settled in academically, being ranked third out of thirty-five students in his report of April 1900. At about this time, Jeanneret senior wrote of the roles that the rest of his family were taking in a local production of *Snow White and Rose Red*: 'Marie accompanies, Albert plays in the orchestra, Édouard is the gnome "Le Sarcasme"'.[3] Édouard was already practising to be a comic outsider, a role in which he later revelled, here outside the close relationship between Albert and his mother.[4]

Édouard's father regarded him as usually being a 'good' and 'intelligent' child, but he expressed concern that he had a 'difficult character, susceptible, quick-tempered, and rebellious' sometimes giving 'us reason for anxiety'.[5] This was an opinion corroborated by one of his teachers, who described him as 'careless and negligent'.[6] Indeed his performance at the Gymnase began to show a marked deterioration, and because of this he transferred to the École d'Art at the age of fourteen and a half.

From Negligence to the Planting of Enthusiasm

This move seemingly positioned Édouard ready for a move into his father's realm of work (ornamental engraving was the speciality of the school), but actually instigated a move away from the family circle of concern completely. Its importance would not become apparent until the change of vocation into architecture arose. The most crucial influence at the École d'Art was that of his teacher and early mentor Charles L'Eplattenier, who instilled in him a quasi-religious appreciation of nature and with whom he was to form an intense friendship. Le Corbusier later wrote of the experience:

> My master said: Only nature is inspiring and true and should be the support of human endeavour. But do not make nature in the manner of landscape painters who show nothing but the exterior. Scrutinise the cause, the form, the vital development and make a synthesis in creating ornaments. He had an elevated conception of ornament – which he conceived as a microcosm.[7]

It was as if the young Le Corbusier was able then to integrate the influence of

3 Ibid., p.14.
4 Later in life Le Corbusier was to enjoy dressing up either as clowns or convicts when the opportunity for fancy dress arose. M. Bacon, *Le Corbusier in America*, Cambridge, MA: MIT Press, 2001, p.218.
5 Diary entry for 6 February 1899 by Georges Édouard Jeanneret-Gris. Brookes, *Formative Years*, p.12.
6 School report by Édouard's algebra teacher. Ibid., p.21.
7 Le Corbusier, *The Decorative Art of Today*, London: Architectural Press, 1987, p.198.

these two men, his father and L'Eplattenier. He wrote, 'My master was an excellent teacher and a real man of the woods, and he made us men of the woods'.[8] Meanwhile L'Eplattenier required them to study nature's 'cause, forms and vital development ... to study passionately our immediate environment'.[9] For this reason many of Jeanneret's early excursions into watchcase design take nature as their theme.[10]

Like many of his contemporaries, L'Eplattenier adhered to the Romantic idea that a close observation of nature would reveal larger truths.[11] He helped to focus Le Corbusier's appreciation of nature into a more cohesive theory. While reinforcing the interest in nature first initiated by his father, L'Eplattenier also instilled in him a thirst for books by introducing him to the writings of John Ruskin[12] and Owen Jones, amongst others.[13] Le Corbusier later wrote, 'Ruskin spoke of spirituality. In his *Seven Lamps of Architecture* (1849) shone the Lamp of Sacrifice, the Lamp of Truth, the Lamp of Humility'.[14] From Owen Jones's *Grammar of Ornament* (1856), referred to as the student's 'bible',[15] he learnt of the importance of close observation and drawing as a means to access the lessons of nature. The implication was that the cellular structures of nature were repeated throughout the universe on both a small and a large scale, united in a great chain of being. 'Everything is arranged according to principles consistent with the whole: ... every organism is a kind of link in the chain of variants around the axis between two poles,' Le Corbusier was to observe.[16] The outer forms of nature, he believed, could reveal inner truths.

Jones's thesis was that 'man appears everywhere impressed with the beauties of Nature which surround him, and seeks to imitate to the extent of his power the works of the Creator'.[17] For Jones 'the savage' was better able to recreate a 'true balance both of form and colour' because he was 'accustomed only to look upon Nature's harmonies'.[18] Further, 'if we would return to a more healthy condition, we must even be as little children or as savages; we must get rid of the acquired and artificial, and return to and develop natural instincts'.[19] Jones was in this way an important influence on Le Corbusier, the superiority of seemingly untainted cultures, closer to nature, being a continuing theme in his work.

Le Corbusier drew constantly in his childhood and his youth. Later sketches bear a close relation to Ruskin's, in terms of both what he chose to draw and the ways in which he chose to draw it. In his analysis of Le Corbusier's sketchbooks, Geoffrey Baker concludes that 'it was through drawing that he understood the world'.[20] He learnt on the one hand about the moods of nature and on the other hand about structures inherent to nature. Indeed, his early sketchbooks are dominated by landscapes.

L'Eplattenier took a great interest in the idea of the garden city, writing a paper to a local town-planning conference in which he drew heavily on the ideas of the Austrian theorist Camillo Sitte. He was quick to convey his enthusiasm to Le Corbusier, who set about writing a history of town planning, using the model of this theorist.[21] Just as nature provided essential inspiration for his work on the small scale of decoration, nature would provide inspiration on the large scale, that of town planning.

8 Ibid., p.194
9 Ibid.
10 See Brookes, *Formative Years*, pp.24-40.
11 See for example the discussion of the artist Paul Klee in R. Rosenblum, *Modern Painting and the Northern Romantic Tradition*, London: Thames & Hudson, 1994, p.154.
12 See M.P. May Sekler, 'Le Corbusier, Ruskin, the Tree, and the Open Hand', in R. Walden (ed.) *The Open Hand*, Cambridge, MA: MIT Press, 1982, pp.42–95.
13 G.H. Baker, *Le Corbusier: The Creative Search*, London: Spon, 1996, pp.26–8. Jean-Petit quoted Le Corbusier: 'We had as our Bible that large and magnificent folio by Owen Jones, *Grammaire de l'Ornement*, a most splendid enumeration in color of the Egyptian, Asiatic, Greek, etc styles ... up to those of the middle ages.' Jean Petit, *Le Corbusier lui-même*, Paris: Forces Vives, 1970, p.25.
14 Le Corbusier, *Decorative Art of Today*, p.132.
15 Cited by Petit, *Le Corbusier lui-même*, p.25.
16 Le Corbusier, *Decorative Art of Today*, p.175.
17 Owen Jones, *The Grammar of Ornament*, London: Dorling Kindersley, 2001, p.31.
18 Ibid., p.36.
19 Ibid., p.38.
20 Baker, *Creative Search*, p.16.
21 T. Benton, 'Urbanism' in T. Benton (ed.) *Le Corbusier Architect of the Century*, London: Arts Council of Great Britain, 1987, p.200.

Analysing Organisms

All these pursuits were continued as passions in adolescence and into adulthood, although they were pursued less in physical terms than they were in the realm of intellectual enquiry. In the region of the Swiss Jura there is a saying that nature is like a well-regulated clock.[22] This clearly says more about the projection of the fastidiousness of watch making onto nature, than it does about the natural environment itself. Indeed Le Corbusier was to write, 'I took from my father observation and from my mother enthusiasm'.[23]

Brookes believes that L'Eplattenier alone determined that Le Corbusier should become an architect despite the misgivings of many, including some of his own. The change of vocation, proposed in 1905, had already been suggested as Le Corbusier's engraving workload was reduced as a result of a deterioration in his sight in 1904. He may also have seen it as a useful lever to create some distance between himself and his family whatever tension this created, and however painful this seemed. By this time he had excelled in his studies and demonstrated a passion for fulfilment in work in a way that had not been seen to date. His father described him as 'a real slugger', referring to the driven manner of his pursuance of learning.[24]

At this time Le Corbusier encouraged his parents to buy land and build a house out of town even though his father's business was failing – a move that brought conflict between husband and wife. The project did not proceed until 1912.

2.1
Evergreen fir tree covered with snow, pencil and india ink, 15x17 cm. E. Jeanneret, 1906.

The fir-tree became an important influence upon Le Corbusier during this period (Fig. 2.1). He used it as a motif in his designs, Baker suggests, to compensate for a lack of local visual traditions. In this case, as Baker puts it, 'Analysis of an organism becomes a springboard for creative action'.[25] Subsequently Le Corbusier's preoccupation with trees became more universal, as will be demonstrated below.

[22] Aymon de Mestral citing Louis Loze in *Daniel Jean Richard: Founder of the Jura Watch Industry* (1672–1741), Zürich: The Institute of Economic Research, 1957, pp.50–1.

[23] Le Corbusier, cited without source in Baker, *Creative Search*. p.13.

[24] Diary entry of Georges Édouard Jeanneret-Gris,. December 1905. Brookes, *Formative Years*, p.42.

[25] Baker, *The Creative Search*, p.xvi.

Le Corbusier had begun to see the world in terms of patterns, of lines and of geometry that would, ideally, be linked together in a cohesive whole, that unity that he perceived in nature. This may explain why he took such a great interest in the chapter on Pythagoras in Édouard Schuré's book *Les Grands Initiés*, another gift from L'Eplattenier. Subtitled *Esquisse de l'histoire secrète des religions*, it records in turn the lives of a number of great spiritual leaders: Rama, Krishna, Hermes, Moses, Orpheus, Pythagoras, Plato and Jesus. Pythagoras, a follower of the mystery cult of Orphism, founded a religious order at Croton in the late sixth century BC. The Pythagoreans were ascetic in their approach to life and looked upon Apollo as a figure of veneration.[26] Pythagoras took it upon himself to discover a way to express his view of the cosmos rationally, by means of mathematics.[27] It seems more than likely that the young architect was influenced by Pythagoras's belief that the contemplation of harmony and order in the universe would encourage the development of harmony and order within the soul.[28] Mathematics would provide the means to create a link between man and nature. Evidently Schuré's book made a great impression on the young Le Corbusier who wrote to his parents January 1908:

> I have just finished reading *Les Grands Initiés* a fortnight ago ... This Schuré has opened horizons to me which have filled me with happiness. I foresaw this – no, that's going too far. More accurately I struggled between, on the one hand, rationalism, strongly imbued in me by an active real life and the little bits of science which I picked up at school and on the other hand, the innate, intuitive idea of a supreme being, which is revealed to me at every step by a contemplation of nature. This struggle prepared the ground to receive that noble harvest with which this 600 page book is full. I am now more at ease, I am happier although I have no solution and hope one day to glimpse it so that I can throw myself into resolving it.[29]

He was to begin a quest which was to last him for the rest of his life.

At approximately the same time as he read Schuré, Le Corbusier also read Henri Provensal's *L'Art de Demain*.[30] In Paul Turner's opinion some of the ideas to be found in Provensal can be found almost intact in Le Corbusier's work.[31] Drawing upon ideas of German Idealism and using examples from nature, science, philosophy, history and religion, Provensal created a theory of life. Put simply, Provensal believed that the structures of such natural phenomena as crystals could be emulated in both art and architecture to create links between the works of man and those of nature which he described as a 'supreme intelligence' sometimes called 'Destiny, Providence' and, ultimately, 'God'.[32] Provensal also suggested that the balance of masculine and feminine elements found in nature should act as a natural law to which artists should aspire.

Le Corbusier also read Nietzsche's *Thus spoke Zarathustra* at this time. The book did not become what Jean-Louis Cohen calls 'bedside reading material', indeed he was not to return to the book until 1961, when, as an embittered old man he began fully to recognise its worth. Cohen writes that 'the traces of the architect's concrete interest for Nietzsche's philosophical project are more latent than manifest'.[33]

26 W.K.C. Guthrie, *Orpheus and Greek Religion*, London: Methuen, 1935, p.220.

27 Ibid., p.217.

28 Ibid.

29 Letter 31 January 1908. In the archives at La Chaux-de-Fonds (CdF LCms 34, transcription supplied by Mlle Françoise Frey). Quoted by T. Benton, 'The Sacred and the Search for Truths,' in Benton (ed.) *Architect of the Century*, p.239.

30 P. Turner, *The Education of an Architect*, New York: Garland, 1977, p.10.

31 Ibid.

32 H. Provensal, *L'Art de Demain*, Paris: Perrin, 1904, p.60 in Fondation Le Corbusier hereafter referred to as FLC.

33 J.-L. Cohen, 'Le Corbusier's Nietzschean Metaphors', in A. Kosta and I. Wohlfarth (eds), *Nietzsche and 'An Architecture of Our Minds'*, Los Angeles: Getty, 1999, p.311.

The Flowering of Potential

In 1905, aged eighteen, Le Corbusier joined L'Eplattenier's course on the design of architecture and decoration. His teacher found him work with a local architect, René Chapallaz. Their design for the Villa Fallet appears to have its origins in the arts and crafts movement as well as the local vernacular (Fig. 2.2). At that time Le Corbusier was working on stylised images of pine trees, translating them into design motifs. These can be seen, for example, in the trellised work of the balconies.[34] The repeated geometric motifs in the gables are also significant, suggesting repeated patterns within nature, an idea that Le Corbusier may have developed from Owen Jones. Jones wrote that 'flowers or other natural objects should not be used as ornaments, but conventional representations founded upon them sufficiently suggestive to convey the intended image to mind, without destroying the unity of the object they are employed to decorate'.[35]

Le Corbusier's next most significant commission in La Chaux-de-Fonds was to be the Villa Schwob (1916–17), by which time his attention had moved away from decoration towards geometrical games. Here he plays with the combination of circle and square, a union of opposites, that was to continue to fascinate him throughout his life. Already ideas about geometrical harmony were in evidence in his work.

Le Corbusier read constantly, seeking, Curtis believes, to augment his intuition with the precedent of the thoughts of others.[36] He attached himself to one mentor after another while his ideas and experience of architecture grew. Yet beneath this search he, like his brother, experienced the constant battle with a lack of self-confidence.

Le Corbusier left La Chaux-de-Fonds in June 1907, at the age of twenty, to pass several months travelling in northern Italy, spending the winter months in Vienna before travelling to Paris for the first time.[37] Turner records that during this period Le Corbusier was reading the works of Ruskin extensively. In Turner's opinion it is likely that he was impressed by Ruskin's 'theory of two temperaments, the one Northern European, the other Southern or Mediterranean' – the Northern being active, domestic, practical and level-headed' and the Southern being 'contemplative, monastic, mystical and what Ruskin calls "insane"'.[38] Although Ruskin suggested that the greatest arts combined elements of both temperaments Turner observes that he clearly favoured the latter, as did Le Corbusier, which is strange considering his Northern background. It will be seen that Le Corbusier's idealised vision of nature was Southern in character, epitomised by the interaction between sun and sea. In *When the Cathedrals were White* he wrote, 'I have felt myself become more and more a man of everywhere with, nevertheless, one strong root: the Mediterranean, queen of forms under the play of light'.[39]

Paris, Perret and the Practice of Architecture

Early in the twentieth century a re-evaluation of the role of nature and religion was taking place in a number of European countries, most significantly in the Bauhaus in Germany through the work of the theosophist Madame Blavatsky.

2.2
Gable of Villa Fallet, La Chaux-de-Fonds. E. Jeanneret, 1905-7.

34 J. Jenger, *Le Corbusier: Architect of a New Age*, London: Thames & Hudson, 1996, p.14.
35 O. Jones, *Grammar of Ornament*, p.25.
36 Curtis, *Ideas and Forms*, p.22.
37 Turner, *Education of an Architect*, p.30.
38 Ibid., p.35.
39 Le Corbusier, *When the Cathedrals were White: A Journey to the Country of the Timid People*, New York: Reynal and Hitchcock, 1947, pp.29–30.

Julia Fagan-King has noted that there was a 'pervasive quasi-religious belief in a high mystical ideal for a new era' among artistic circles in Paris at this time. In her opinion:

> That the arts were a channel to the divine or the Absolute, that the aesthetic creative or appreciative experience was comparable to the ecstasy of mystics or prophets with an equivalent divine power, was a deep rooted belief reaching far back beyond their immediate predecessors, the symbolists, to the mystically orientated exemplars of Michelangelo and Leonardo da Vinci – even to Plato himself.[40]

Le Corbusier went to Paris in 1908 to spend sixteen months working for Auguste Perret. He was eventually to make it his home in 1917. During this time he made aquaintance with a number of different artists and authors whose work would make a lasting impression on him, for example Josephin Péladan, Guillaume Apollinaire, André Breton, André Gide and Jean Cocteau. Each of these men was strongly influenced by the ideas of ancient Greek religion and philosophy, most notably those of Plato. Le Corbusier's interest in such matters would have been fuelled by his enthusiasm for their work.

In 1907 Apollinaire wrote a collection of poems, *Bestiare ou Cortège d'Orphée*, in which he incorporated the figure of Orpheus as a symbol of the poet and the artist in general.[41] Apollinaire was instrumental in identifying and defining the early twentieth-century art movement known as Orphism, which counted among its members Robert Delaunay, Francis Picabia, Marcel Duchamp and Fernand Léger, who was also to become a close friend of Aalto's.[42] A collection of Orphic paintings was put on display at the *Salon des Indépendants* in March 1913. In his review of this exhibition in the Orphic magazine *Montjoie!* (29 March 1913) Apollinaire exclaimed, 'If cubism is dead, long live Orphism. The kingdom of Orpheus is at hand'.[43] Orphic artists took inspiration from Orpheus's ability to create harmony through his music.[44] They wanted to achieve a similar state of harmony through painting, using colour and form to affect the emotions and communicate meaning.[45] This was to become perhaps the central aim of Le Corbusier's work.

Journey to the East

Le Corbusier augmented the knowledge gained through reading with periods of travel, like the one which took place in 1911 and was encapsulated in his book *Journey to the East*. His companion on this trip was his close friend William Ritter, an influential writer and artist.[46] Ritter was homosexual, though whether he and Le Corbusier were in a relationship together is not known.

It is a characteristic of Le Corbusier's writing at that time to be both passionate and effusive when writing to both men and women, so little can be determined from the tenor of his letters. Le Corbusier's personal life is a subject that has been assiduously avoided by his biographers thus far. Whatever their relationship, it should be noted that sexuality was a subject of great interest to writers and artists at that time and for this reason it might have been an area that Le Corbusier wished to explore. In *Journey to the East* Le Corbusier wrote of 'the

[40] J. Fagan-King, 'United on the Threshold of the Twentieth Century Mystical Ideal', *Art History*, 11, 1, 1988, p.89.

[41] G. Apollinaire, *Le Bestiaire ou Cortège d'Orphée* in M. Décaudin (ed.) *Oeuvres Complètes de Guillaume Apollinaire*, Paris: André Balland et Jacques Lecat, 1966, p.17.

[42] V. Spate, 'Orphism', in N. Stangos (ed.) *Concepts of Modern Art*, London: Thames & Hudson, 1997, p.194.

[43] J. Turner (ed.) *The Grove Dictionary of Art*, London: Macmillan, 1996, p.569.

[44] V. Spate, *Orphism: The Evolution of Non-figurative Painting in Paris in 1910–14*, Oxford: Clarendon, 1979, p.61.

[45] Ibid., p.2.

[46] The correspondence between Jeanneret and Ritter is held at Swiss National Library in Berne.

thrill which we may experience when we dare a word or gesture toward something we adore, who excites us and to whom we must express it', suggesting that he had some experience in matters of the heart – as might be expected of a twenty-four-year-old who was to utilise his libido so carefully in his creative work.[47] Le Corbusier wrote of the temptations of the monastic life, 'in the evening, hands dangling between the thighs, eyes, guided by thoughts, would be cast ... on the brothers, ah torment', though the seriousness of his words cannot be taken for granted.[48]

In the opinion of Adolf Max Vogt, Ritter fulfilled the role of father figure for Le Corbusier.[49] He reflected back upon his time with Ritter in the preface to the first volume of the *Oeuvre Complète*:

> In the confused period when one begins to throw oneself with confidence into the great game of life ... I found an older friend who accepted willingly my insecurity and my puzzlement ... His heart was overawed before the phenomena of nature and the battles that tear people asunder. Together we wandered through these great landscapes that are filled with historical significance – the lakes, the high plateaus, the Alps.[50]

The journey culminated with a visit to the Parthenon, a building which exercised a very particular fascination for Le Corbusier, presumably because of his interest in ancient Greek philosophy and myth and his belief in the power of number and proportion to create an architecture in tune with nature.

Le Corbusier also augmented his education through hours of meticulous study in museums. He later reminisced in *The Decorative Art of Today*:

> I put my questions only to what is not called great Art. Of course I went on Sundays to see the Cimabues, the Breughels, the Raphaels, the Tintorettos, etc. But to work, to draw, to understand the full richness that one give's one's work, and the degree of concentration, of transposition, of invention, of re-creation that is required, I settled where no one at that time put his easel – far from the Grand Galerie. I was always alone.
>
>> At the Musée Cluny, for the tapestries, miniatures, Persian plates.
>> At the Guimet, for all the deities in bronze, wood or stone.
>> At the gallery of M. Pottier, for the Etruscans and Greeks.
>> At the Trocadero, for the portals of the French cathedrals.
>> At the museum (of Natural History) to learn many lessons.
>> The Etruscans in the ethnographic Museum of Florence.
>> Antique decorative art in the Museum of Naples, and at Pompeii.
>> What lessons, what lessons! What drawings, conscientiously putting and then answering questions with the precise outline of an eloquent form![51]

These investigations provided the raw material for much of his later work.[52] Through them he began to learn about the early religions and iconography of Europe and elsewhere; simultaneously he learnt about natural history and the patterns within nature.

[47] C. Green, 'The Architect as Artist' in Benton ed., *Architect of the Century*, p.126.

[48] Le Corbusier, *Journey to the East*, Cambridge: MIT Press, 1987, p.206.

[49] A.M.Vogt, *Le Corbusier: The Noble Savage*, Cambridge, MA: MIT Press, 1998, p.122.

[50] Le Corbusier and P. Jeanneret, *Oeuvre Complète Volume 1, 1910–1929*, Zürich: Les Éditions d'Architecture, 1995, p.8. Translation Vogt, *Noble Savage*, p.124.

[51] Le Corbusier, *Decorative Art of Today*, pp.198–200.

[52] Édouard Trouin marvelled at Le Corbusier's extensive knowledge of art history. 'Rapport du Secrétaire Général (Édouard Trouin) sur nos projets en cours', 8 February 1955, FLC 13 01 390.

Educating Aalto

It is apparent that Aalto had a more conservative education at the local lyceum and the architectural school in Helsinki, although his extracurricular activities were similar to those of Le Corbusier.

Dyslexia and the Free Play of Imagination

Schildt gives an important account of Aalto's schooling, which began at a small preparatory school after he arrived in Jyväskylä. From the age of ten, Aalto attended the Finnish-language grammar school (or lyceum as it is sometimes known) in the town from the age of ten. Working around what seems to have been dyslexia, Aalto flourished at school, demonstrating a brightness and creativity but no academic diligence. He is reported to have been an avid reader, who loved 'book culture',[53] picking up concepts and ideas with ease, but being interested in neither dogma nor detail. Perhaps because he had some dyslexic problems languages always floored him, but in mathematics and biology, those subjects in which he was tutored at home, he excelled. However, at school, if the spelling was ignored, his essays were successful, especially those in which he was allowed to be creative. Most importantly his creative drawing skills were exceptional, winning a competition, and finding publication on one occasion.

Schildt describes Aalto's school as 'bilingual, internationally oriented and sceptical in matters of religion', but with a progressive faith in development.[54] In a speech marking the centenary of the lyceum Aalto recalled that his French teacher, a certain Gabriel Gideon Ronimus, had been particularly influential on him, further nurturing a philosophy of doubt and scepticism in the student's mind that was planted at home. This doubt encouraged the architect to challenge the inhumanity, as he saw it, of over-emphasising mechanisation.[55]

Aalto was a good sportsman and was elected head of the sports club, a sure sign of his popularity. His physical education teacher, Store, strengthened Aalto's interest both in physical activity and the competitive spirit. Importantly Schildt reports that Store encouraged a balance of academic and physical exercise, a model of the ideal of 'universal man' which would have rendered the Renaissance idea fruitful when he came across it in his cultural studies.[56] Such a synthesis between experience and learning, between the everyday and cultural or historical, always appealed to Aalto. Le Corbusier would similarly believe it important to cultivate the mind and body simultaneously, an idea possibly derived from his reading of Plato.[57]

Here it is appropriate to mention the character of Aalto's maternal grandfather, Hugo Hamilkar Hackstedt. This patriarch worked in forestry as a teacher at the Evo Forestry Institute, the first forest school in Finland, founded in 1862.[58] The Institute's aims were to initiate forest research and educate forest officers, to requisition and indeed invent technical methods of forestry, to encourage extremely wide-ranging study of forest life, including nature healing, hydrotherapy, the theory of felling, and the importance of founding saving banks in small communities; it also went beyond this to promote a broad

53 Schildt, during a film interview Y. Jalander (dir.), E. Tuovinen (ed.) *Alvar Aalto: Technology and Nature*, New York: Phaidon Video, PHV 6050.

54 G. Schildt, *Alvar Aalto: The Early Years*, New York: Rizzoli, 1984, p.163.

55 A. Aalto, 'Centenary of Jyväskylä Lycée', in G. Schildt, *Alvar Aalto Sketches*, Cambridge: MIT Press, 1985, pp.162–4.

56 Schildt, *Early Years*, p.56.

57 For Plato the body played an important role in giving access to the divine. Plato, 'The Republic III', in S. Buchanan (ed.) *The Portable Plato*, Harmondsworth: Penguin, 1997, p.402.

58 Aalto was very proud of the position of Evo in the development of Finland's forest culture. From his youth Aalto had a deep love for the reality of Finland (what Schildt describes this as un-dogmatic nationalism, *Early Years*, p.164). He was drawn to the image of the ethnologist Elias Lönnrot on his tireless expeditions to gather the last fragments of the oral tradition in the backwoods of Karelia. The pluralism of his home encouraged him to challenge the brand of Finnish Nationalism of the leading nineteenth-century Finnish thinker J.W. Snellmans. However, Aalto did admire Snellman's appraisal of the Enlightenment philosophers, Aalto, 'The "America Builds" Exhibition, Helsinki, 1945', *Arkkitehti*, 1, 1945; repr. in G. Schildt (ed.) *Alvar Aalto in his Own Words*, New York: Rizzoli, 1997, p.132.

education embracing, for example, the work of Goethe, Dickens and Darwin. The influence of this diversity is crucial to Aalto's development, whose inventor-forester grandfather fostered progressive ideas such as the notion that great artists were guides that should be followed. Like that of his father, his grandfather's influence was thus both one of ingrained scepticism and inventive pragmatism. Both worked on the basis of Goethe's notion of the purposeful interaction with nature, and indeed, according to Schildt, Aalto shared Goethe's view that man is an integral part of nature's cycle, something that is also likely to have influenced Le Corbusier.[59] Importantly too, the influences of father and grandfather were both bound to the practice of forest-based livelihoods. In 1904 Hackstedt resigned as chief instructor at Evo and moved to Jyväskylä, where he died in 1909, only three years after the sudden demise of Aalto's mother. His influence on the boy's ideas, as well as that of Evo, may be said to have been embroidered around the stories that were told rather than memories of actual visits, but were none the less potent for this.

Alvar spent a great deal of time really playing – be it theatrical shows, physical games or playing out fantasy roles. Indeed, his daughter Hanni Alanen has said that he felt more at ease with children and enjoyed being childish later in life.[60] In childhood he seems to have also spent time practising and performing music, drawing and painting, or being in the wilds in one way or another. He took lessons from a painter in Jyväskylä named Jonas Heiska, and claimed also to have had lessons with the famous National Romantic painter Eero Järnefelt in Helsinki during his student days, although there is no evidence of this. Aalto's teenage paintings have the air of Järnefelt's Romanticism, and are not dissimilar to Le Corbusier's early efforts in their Romantic celebration of nature (Fig. 2.3).

Rehabilitating Happy Hellas

Aalto had broad literary interests in his youth, and later. He was influenced by his mother's interest in Goethe, Ibsen and the Finn Zacharias Topelius but had his own boyish books too. Indeed, in later years he would still return to the literary heroes of his youth, Jules Verne, Anatole France (in particular Abbé Coignard) and H.C. Anderson. In his adolescence he read Prince Kropotkin, Albert Engström and August Strindberg. He was, by all accounts, an avid reader. Alongside these literary excursions Aalto cherished an important seven-volume tome that had been his grandfather's. Its name, translated from Swedish, is *Book of Inventions – Survey of the Progress of Industrial Work in all Fields*.[61] The first volume, now in tatters, despite being re-bound in his old age, has chapters on 'The history of civilisation of the human race', 'Architectural techniques and the various types of buildings', 'Construction of towns' and 'Communications'. It was probably used by his grandfather to teach the basic principles of architecture at Evo, and handed on to Aalto when he died. Covering a number of complex issues in simple ways, this remained a lifelong companion for the architect.

That Aalto was influenced by this book is undoubted, but the separation of its influence from that of his grandfather is less certain. The well-thumbed pages about the proportioned buildings enjoyed by 'the art-loving, cheerful

59 Le Corbusier aquired a copy of Goethe, *La Faust*, (Lausanne, 1895) in 1916.

60 Hanni Alanen during an interview for the film, *Alvar Aalto: Technology and Nature*.

61 *Uppfinningarnas Bok, Öfversigt af det industriella arbetets utveckling på alla områden*. Swedish translation 'edited by O.W. Åland in collaboration with experts', Stockholm, 1873, cited by Schildt, without further bibliographical details, *Early Years*, pp.194-8.

inhabitants of happy Hellas', and about the homes built by Romans and the importance of social and practical needs of the user for architects, might well have been the blueprint for his architecture. In some of his early designs, Villa Väinö for his brother (Fig. 4.4) and the Jyväskylä Funeral Chapel (both from 1925) for instance, there are interior sketches that seem to be clearly inspired by the etching of a Roman atrium illustrated in the *Book of Inventions*.

Coupled with the influence of his father and grandfather the book's significance grows – be it in the appeal of information about practical details or the declaration of universal truths. It is Darwinian in tone, projecting progress into both the organic and social spheres of life. Some of the ideas from the book, characterised by what Schildt calls 'the naïve progressive optimism of the nineteenth century', find expression in Aalto's later writing.[62] It did not, however, control him. He allowed nothing, save perhaps the trauma from childhood, to control him, since his scepticism determined that he simply resisted or ignored dogma.

Aalto's home environment in Jyväskylä was a busy one. Many people mingled there, be they immediate or extended family, friends, visiting cultural figures or tenants. The buildings were complex too. The family home was at the bottom of Harjukatu (Ridge Street). It occupied a large sloping site on which were a collection of buildings and a two-level 'garden' space. The buildings included a large single-storey main building, a smaller house comprising two apartments, and lower down the site, some minor buildings. The description of a courtyard surrounded by varying architectural forms might allude to many of his later buildings, the spirit of each responding to their particular community of needs. Indeed, there is a certain community spirit in the Aalto house, a certain chaotic feel that never took over completely.

Later in life Aalto stated that he was clear by the age of ten that he wanted to be an architect, stimulated, he said, by having seen Eliel Saarinen's watercolour interiors of the Hvitträsk Studio complex in 1907.[63] Schildt projects that the profession of architecture allowed Aalto to remain 'faithful' to both the family tradition of the white table (and its associated objectivity) and his own creative instincts.[64]

While Le Corbusier was determined to hunt down an appropriate architectural education, Aalto accepted the pedagogical system on offer in a more conventional manner, but with no less enthusiasm and, perhaps, no less drive. Through his lectures and articles Aalto does come across as being far less academic than Le Corbusier, perusing the classics rather than studying with the driven intent. Although as cited Schildt describes how Aalto loved 'book culture',[65] he comes across as being at heart an imaginative intuitive. A friend of Aalto's from the United States, Harmon Goldstone, has gone as far as to say that Aalto was 'inarticulate with words. He could communicate wonderfully with drawings, with intuition, with gestures', for instance when giving lectures in America before he had learnt to speak English.[66] Schildt, however, suggests that Aalto's talks were theatrical experiences in which great truths were demonstrated by a flowing tongue. Aalto certainly seemed to see himself as both a deeply cultured public servant and a bohemian for whom the intricacies of financial management and etiquette, for instance, were unimportant.

[62] Compare 'All nature, the universe, consists of innumerable units, of which not a single one can be wrested from its context in relating to the others without unsettling the harmony of the totality' from *Book of Inventions* with 'Nature, biology, offers profuse and luxuriant forms; with the same constructions, same tissues, and the same cellular structures it can produce millions and millions of combinations', Aalto, 'Rationalism and Man', 1935; repr. Schildt, *Sketches*, p.51.

[63] Aalto wrote a detailed account of having been overwhelmed by these images in his introduction to A. Christ-Janer's biography of Saarinen, published in 1948 (*Eliel Saarinen*, Chicago: Chicago University Press, 1979). Aalto and Saarinen were friends at this time.

[64] Schildt, *Early Years*, p.66.

[65] Schildt, during an interview for the film *Alvar Aalto: Technology and Nature*.

[66] Harmon Goldstone during an interview. Ibid.

Anarchy, Nihilism or the National Romantics

Aalto's studies of architecture in Helsinki began in 1916, while the last of the Jugendstil vegetation of the Hvitträsk trio of Herman Gesellius, Armas Lindgren and Eliel Saarinen was growing in granite form in the capital of the Grand Duchy. Aalto was initially taught by Usko Nyström,[67] whose idiosyncrasy made a great impression on him. Schildt reports that Nyström 'had contempt for everything conventional and ready made. He wanted all problems to be solved in a new and unique way'.[68] For instance Nyström explored gluing layers of cardboard to make chairs, from which Aalto may have gleaned the principle behind the idea for bent and laminated wooden furniture. Importantly for Aalto's development, Nyström criticised aspects of Saarinen's work, preferring the unaffected and the intimate over the massively monumental. Nyström, it seems, was Aalto's first architectural mentor.

Aalto described how 'the department was one great family, never subjugated, but given a cultivated inner discipline by a paternal authority'.[69] Part of this ambience came from Aalto's later student days when he was taught by Lindgren. When this teacher died, in 1929, Aalto wrote of how he had represented the idea of 'the architect' almost as a colleague, rather than model professor, which was important to the students, and how Lindgren coped with the unruly students by having 'an ocean of self-control and Homeric humour'.[70] Lindgren's influence was equally important as that of other tutors but also quite different, since it offered a discipline that might have been anathema to Nyström, and a proximity to the ideas of Jugendstil and thus to the importance of nature in design.

Whilst Aalto was loath to acknowledge the influence of others upon his work at times he did recognise the influence of Saarinen, whose work had first impressed him at the tender age of nine,[71] although he would repudiate the architect's importance on certain occasions.

Although later, both in Helsinki in the 1930s and in the United States in 1946, Saarinen and Aalto were to meet as equals, for the young student architect to acknowledge the influence of the prominent Hvitträsk trio, the generation against whom he sought to protest, was perhaps difficult. Romantic Classicism rather than Art Nouveau was, after all, Aalto's chosen starting point.

Historical Enquiry and a Passion for Italy

Lindgren's lectures had instilled in Aalto a love of Ancient Greece, Italy and the Italian Renaissance (particularly Brunelleschi), aspects of which were to remain central to his compositional outlook and his favour for a 'Southern' attitude to life. It was not until 1933 that Aalto would visit the Acropolis, but its significance should not be underestimated. Lindgren also introduced Aalto to the writing of Jacob Burckhardt, through whom he inhabited Renaissance buildings. He was already familiar with Goethe, and used the German cultural mediator in his studies and indeed later in his journeys into the past. Yet, as has been suggested, Aalto seems to have been motivated to bring order from the chaos of his deep personal loss – that psychological 'gap' that threatened to, and did on occasion,

[67] Not to be confused with the earlier classicist Gustaf Nyström who designed neoclassical buildings such as the house of Estates, Helsinki, 1891. Gustaf Nyström taught only the senior students. He died in 1919 and was replaced by Armas Lindgren.

[68] Schildt, *Early Years*, p.79.

[69] Aalto, in 'Armas Lindgren and We', *Arkkitehti*, 10, 1929; repr. Schildt, *Own Words*, pp. 241–2.

[70] Ibid.

[71] Aalto, 1948, introduction to A. Christ-Janer's book, *Eliel Saarinen*, Chicago: Chicago University Press, 1979.

engulf him. Such a drive seems to have acted like a magnet, drawing to itself ideas that addressed natural order and the potential for the growth towards a precarious harmony. Although, as suggested, Aalto rarely acknowledged the ingenious vegetative styling of Finland's Art Nouveau, in Chapter 4 we will demonstrate how he began to develop his own notion of organic growth in his early articles; a notion that generated ideas and forms rooted in both his nature studies and his need to be part of a community of people.

Veering to the Vernacular

As part of the campaign of nation building, Finland's architectural heritage was in the process of being studied, measured and recorded at the time Aalto completed his education. He played his part in this process, coming to hold a respect for the vernacular forms through such analysis. 'Here we met with architecture', as he put it.[72] He held the Niemelä Farmstead, moved from Konginkangas (a village near his home town of Jyväskylä), to the Seurasaari folk museum in Helsinki, to be 'the highest goal architecture could aim for' (Fig. 7.15).[73] This collection of buildings manifested something of 'the authority of the ancients' he felt – those belonging to Finland not Greece.[74] In 'Motifs from the Past' (1922) Aalto explained that international stylistic impulses 'coming from outside' were transformed by local conditions, making the architecture: 'as Finnish as one could possibly hope for. The architect's faithfulness to themselves and Finland's harsh conditions is proved by the fact that, even at their first appearance these motifs seem to be completely at home in their new surroundings.'[75]

Aalto expressed his deep desire to see architecture rooted in both human activity and the natural context. 'Motifs from the Past' is also an early expression of his notion of the integration, or even the internalising, of borrowed elements which offered an idea of stylistic assimilation that requires education and maturity. The montage of Villa Mairea some fifteen years later comes to mind (Plate 20). Not all of his earlier compositions were so successful. There was a world of difference, Aalto felt, between learning from these humble forms and seeking, as the National Romantics had done, to reproduced aspects of them.

It is important here to understand that the small urban scene of Helsinki, which at the time had a population of only 150,000, was fertile ground for young intellectuals and artists. Finland only became independent of Russia at the moment of the Russian Revolution, when Aalto was studying in Helsinki, and therefore compared to other capitals it was small and relatively little cultivated, and could host much creative outpouring from the small circle of artists and intelligentsia there. Although his studies at school were in Finnish, Aalto entered into a largely Swedish-speaking intellectual circle, and flourished.[76]

Life (or Death) and Nature

Another teacher, Carolus Lindberg, seems to have been extremely important to Aalto. Cara, as he was known, was an assistant to the professors and a friend of the lively students at the architecture school in Helsinki.[77] In a Christmas article

[72] Aalto commenting on the importance of measuring Naantali's old convent church, 'Motifs from the Past', *Arkkitehti*, 2, 1922; repr. Schildt, *Own Words*, p.33.

[73] Aalto, cited by repr. Schildt, *Early Years*, p.163.

[74] Aalto, 'Motifs from the Past', Schildt, *Own Words*, p.33.

[75] Ibid.

[76] Aalto wrote many humorous articles in the *Keberos* journal.

[77] An example of Lindberg's view of the past is demonstrated in his introduction to Finnish architecture, 'Architecture', *in Finland: The Country, its People and Institutions*, Helsinki: Otava, 1927. In this piece he concludes with the need to cast 'a backward glance at the road already traversed', p.9.

he wrote for *Kerberos* in 1921, Aalto envisaged an imaginary conversation between Cara, Lindgren and C.L. Engel (the neoclassical architect who designed Senate Square in Helsinki) in which Cara repeated the words 'Organic – organic'. This was challenged by 'La Notre', in other words Engel, saying 'Clipped clipped, that's how it must be'.[78] Whether or not Aalto considered the 'organic line', as he was later to call it,[79] the answer at this stage, there was certainly a clear notion that it was *a way*. Any teaching that led to this notion would have confirmed Aalto's own experience, which was strongly rooted in the harsh reality of the backwoods, rather than a romantic idyll. Schildt suggests: 'The forest calls for another kind of adaptation; it is not irrational, but a much more complicated biological unit, in which parts work on one another and combine to form a more organic whole than a field.'[80]

Elsewhere in this *Kerberos* piece Aalto expressed something of his early ideas about unity, giving one of his characters these words:

> We are gathered here ... we whose task it is ... dream of the impossible ... of perfection ... each one believes he carries the spark in him ... but we understand, we realise that we are only one part ... when will he come who unites it all? He who is both humourist and tragedian, he who both builds and tears down. He who loves the spirit of matter like no-one before. He who can and cannot ... the mystery of the world ... the synthesis ... and ladies ... to him bottoms up![81]

This light-hearted passage is typical of Aalto's humour, the tone and creative fluency of which demonstrates an important aspect of his belief, his approach, and his experience. On a more serious note, amidst the new Functionalism of the Stockholm Exhibition in 1930, he suggested, 'The artist thus steps in among the people to help create a harmonious existence with the help of his intuitive sensibility'.[82] Yet this too leaves his statements about architecture feeling insubstantial, unless what he said and wrote is seen in the light of his personal experience. It thus becomes a veiled explanation of how, in general, to work around the reality of a broken human life: 'the comedy and tragedy – both', as he put it later.[83] Suddenly the explanation of how he generated rich architecture from lack and deprivation appears more profound.

Aalto was not a political idealist, nor was he motivated to address social problems at this stage. His home town, to which he returned to establish his first practice, was a solidly right-wing environment, with a conservative peasantry in the surrounding environs. His family's liberalism was radical in comparison; he therefore had the language and sceptical outlook that allowed him to converse happily with those of left and right.

Aalto was to break his studies while spending a short time in custody under suspicion of being part of the Jaeger Movement (supported by Germany) that was resisting Russian authority.[84] In the complicated civil war that followed the Russian Revolution, Finnish society was in total upheaval amidst Rightist fears of a Soviet takeover if the Communists gained power.[85] Aalto chose to support the Whites against the Reds, although he seems to have had some sympathy with aspects of the Left's agenda, and later had many Communist

[78] Aalto, writing as Ping, 'Benvenuto's Christmas Punch', *Kerberos*, 1–2, 1921.

[79] Aalto, letter to Gropius, 1930, AAF, cited in G. Schildt, *Alvar Aalto: The Decisive Years*, New York: Rizzoli, 1986, p.66.

[80] Schildt, *Early Years*, 1984, p.34.

[81] Ibid.

[82] Aalto, 'Stockholm Exhibition 1', *Åbo Underrättelser*, 22 May 1930, in Schildt, *Sketches*, p.16.

[83] Aalto, 'Instead of an Article', 1958, *Arkkitehti – Arkitekten*, reprinted in ibid., p.161.

[84] Finland had been an unwilling Grand Duchy of Russia since 1809, when it was taken from the Swedish realm.

[85] Interestingly the immense Finnish resistance against the Russian invasion in 1939 (the Winter War) suggests that the 'workers' would not have wanted to be taken over by the Soviets.

friends. He made his way north, to the White held zone, and fought for Finland's independence, as the Whites saw it.

This experience of active service haunted Aalto, who would not recount the details except to express his disgust at the execution of Red officers. He knew he did not have the nerves for war, and later avoided a call up in dramatic style.[86] Aalto coped through both denial and playfulness, retelling the experiences as what one friend described as 'deliciously plausible lies'.[87]

Aalto returned to his studies after the civil war. Displaying his real priorities he wrote to his father in 1918, 'I'm a hell of a liberal and an opportunist in theory, in practice I'm an architect and a generally top man'.[88]

Aalto's Early Renaissance

After military service, as 'regimental architect' during 1922–3, Aalto's concerns became more wide-ranging. He had visited Gothenburg to experience the newest ideas in architecture and planning, to see the work of Ragnar Österberg. He hoped to work with Gunnar Asplund, who declined even to receive the young visitor.[89] In Gothenburg Aalto was felt to be 'surprisingly countrified', 'unkempt' but with a 'lively intelligence' and an astonishing 'facility in expressing himself'.[90] He then returned to Jyväskylä to establish himself in practice.

While in Jyväskylä Aalto became interested in the radical movements in art.[91] He was keenly aware of Cézanne's renunciation of rigid perspective, and, as cited, claims to have regularly visited Eero Järnefelt's studio in Helsinki to paint in 1918. He also took from his friend, the Finnish painter Tyko Sallinen, a certain primitivism and rendering of the normal and everyday, which he composed into a theme of unorthodox balance in his work.

Aalto was hugely strengthened and grounded by his marriage to Aino Marsio in 1924. Aino was older than Alvar. She was herself an architect with a deep concern for social issues, to which her husband was gradually drawn. The couple started their honeymoon to Italy by aeroplane, and Aalto described the flight as 'the first Hellenic day of my life'.[92] This was Aalto's second flight, and a statement of his belief in progress. There was no contradiction for him between progress and classicist passion. The trip also confirmed his love of Venice, Tuscany and particularly 'architettura minore'.

Aalto saw himself as one of the 'Young architects of the North, who dream of a cool, classical linear beauty'.[93] Indeed, early in his career, Aalto wrote that 'Jyväskylä must act the role of Central Finland. As the capital, it is a stage on which the intellectual forces of the region confront each other.'[94] He believed that 'The holy unity of art is by no means a dead Renaissance ideal',[95] and set out to persuade the local establishment that 'The slope of Jyväskylä ridge is almost like the mountain vineyards of Fiesole'. Here he displayed both his vivid imagination and his determination to yank the town into the cultural ambience of the Italian civitas and, as always, back to the natural environment. Through his preoccupation with the Mediterranean, which undoubtedly he shared with Le Corbusier, he wanted to create a northern reflection of the Italian and Greek environment. At one level this seems to be a ludicrous fantasy, but in a deeper

[86] Schildt, *Early Years*, p.96.

[87] Sten Branzell's description of Aalto, recounted in ibid., p.97. Letter held in the Anna Branzell Archive, Gotheburg.

[88] Aalto, letter to his father, J.H. Aalto, 27 November 1918. AAF. Cited in Schildt, *Early Years*, p.107.

[89] Aalto and Asplund became good friends later.

[90] Anna Branzell, to Schildt, *Early Years*, p.123.

[91] He was interested the Fauvist work of the Swede Isaac Grünewald – and well versed in the art movements in Finland, having become close to many artists while in Helsinki.

[92] Aalto, in letter to his assistant, Ypyä, October 1924, cited in Schildt, *Early Years*, p.136.

[93] Aalto, in *Iltalehti*, 1923, in ibid., p.113.

[94] Aalto, *Keskisuomalainen*, 30 November 1924, in ibid., p.253.

[95] Aalto, 'Painter and Mason', *Jousimies*, 1921, and *Keskisuomalainen*, December 23, 1923.

2.4
Perspective of Muurame church,
near Jyväskylä. Pencil on paper.
Aalto, 1926–9.

sense it demonstrates his determination to underpin the young, nature-saturated Finnish towns with borrowed cultural heritage. He suggests something of this in his perspective of Muurame Church design (1926, Fig. 2.4). Here he sought to tie the architecture to the topography – Italian hill-towns clinging to remnant volcanic cores, draped with vines – even if this required a sleight of hand by which pine bowers became cascading vine branches.

Alongside this love of the neoclassical form sat what Schildt has drawn as Aalto's anarchist tendency, one that seemed to counter any sense of classical 'order'. Certainly one of his perpetual literary enjoyments came from Prince Peter Kropotkin's *Memories of a Revolutionist*, from 1901, in which there is an account of a childhood in feudal Russia. Schildt is sure it was the humorous recollections of the last days of the Czarist Russia, and the humane, moral attitude of the author, and not Kropotkin's theories that attracted Aalto – the emotional anarchist.[96]

The seeming contradiction between classical order and anarchist chaos is also undermined by the ancients' sense of the natural scheme of things and Heraclitian flux to boot. The philosophies of natural harmony and humanism

[96] Incidentally Aalto's anarchism meant he did not vote in elections and distrusted all ideological groups. Connar has challenged Schildt's reading of Aalto as an anarchist in *Aaltomania*, Helsinki: Rakennustieto, 2000.

that underpinned ancient Greek civilisation were an important inspiration for Aalto,[97] and he was a great admirer of the vitality of ancient Greek culture.[98] Very often in his speeches he would refer to ancient ideas of culture or nature as a way of drawing the subject towards the profound. He was not interested in abstract mental constructs, but rather discussion of that which was close to human experience generally, and, it shall be argued, his experience personally.

As the example of Jyväskylä indicates, Aalto would requisition the Renaissance and transfer it to the northern context with Mannerist twists to suit the brief and the environment. In his mind this was a healthy unsettling of the 'order' of classicism. Here we see an example of Aalto's anarchistic streak at work.

Other than his honeymoon, Aalto's only foreign visit during his Jyväskylä years was to Stockholm and Denmark in 1926. He admired both the simplicity and the oblique placing of elements in Asplund's work. From this point on he ceased to use so much ornament in his own work, as the pared-down Renaissance basilica form of Muurame Church illustrates (Fig. 2.4).[99] Perhaps the most important outcome of the trip was his contact with Sven Markelius, an architect who had worked with Österberg, and through whom Aalto was then to learn of the moderns of Europe.

Purism, Paimio and the Art of Aphorism

Paris and Purism

At this time Le Corbusier was naming the journal that he established with the artist Amédée Ozenfant *L'Esprit Nouveau* after an essay entitled 'L'Esprit nouveau et les poètes' in which Apollinaire, its author, stated that modern poets were prophets for whom Plato was a primary source of inspiration.[100] Le Corbusier had met Ozenfant in 1918 at the instigation of Auguste Perret.[101] During the war Ozenfant had founded the periodical *L'Élan*, the goal of which was propaganda for French art and ultimately the 'French spirit'.[102] Ozenfant encouraged his friend to paint – a revelation for Le Corbusier, who wrote:[103]

> I then recognised that art – broader and deeper than anything else – is the means by which the individual may count completely. Realising how much our world was convulsed by the birth pains of the machine age, it seemed to me that to achieve harmony ought to be the only goal. Nature, man, cosmos: these are the given elements, these are the forces facing each other.[104]

This yearning to address aspects of the self through art recalls Winnicott's famous suggestion that 'Through artistic expression we can hope to keep in touch with our primitive selves whence the most intense feelings and even fearfully acute sensations derive, and we are poor indeed if we are only sane'.[105]

Late in 1918 Ozenfant and Le Corbusier held an exhibition together, shortly

[97] Aalto discussed the origin of the Greek word for architecture in his speech marking the centenary of Helsinki University of Technology, 5 December 1972. Schildt, *Own Words*, pp. 281–5.

[98] In a speech setting out his *Aims as Chairman of SAFA* (SAFA archives, 1963), Aalto refers to the vitality and importance of Greek civilisation. Ibid., p.163.

[99] The distinction between Jyväskylä Funeral Chapel and Murrame Church illustrate this change in detailing. G. Schildt, *Alvar Aalto: The Complete Catalogue of Archiecture, Design and Art*, London: Academy Editions, 1994, p.43, fig. III.2.4 and p.44, fig. III.2.5.

[100] G. Apollinaire, *L'Esprit nouveau et les poètes*, Paris: Jacques Haumont, 1946, p.24. On 26 November 1917 Apollinaire set up a conference on the subject of l'Esprit Nouveau.

[101] C.S. Eliel, *Purism in Paris*, New York: Harry N. Abrams, 2001, p.15.

[102] Ibid, p.12.

[103] Le Corbusier, *A New World of Space*, New York: Reynal Hitchcock, 1948, p.10.

[104] Ibid.

[105] D. Winnicott, 'Primitive Emotional Development' (1945), in *Collected Works*, London: Tavistock, 1958, p.150.

after which they published *Après le cubisme* and then, in 1920, the first edition of *L'Esprit Nouveau*. 'We founded *L'Esprit Nouveau* in order to open paths' towards the 'laughing clear and beautiful sky' wrote Le Corbusier.[106] This journal, 'an international review of contemporary activity', was to become the mouthpiece of Purism, the art movement created at their joint instigation in which they attempted to achieve maximum poetic effect by using a very limited range of subject matter, consisting in the main of bottles, glasses and books (Plate 1).

It was within the pages of *L'Esprit Nouveau* that Le Corbusier and Ozenfant were first to publish many of those ideas that eventually found their way into the highly influential book *Vers une Architecture*. The journal also contained articles on a wide range of other subject matter including archaeology, science, psychoanalysis, sexuality, medicine, alchemy, art and literature. The nineteenth issue of the journal included an article entitled 'Nature and Creation' by the two men. The links between this diverse journal and their cool Purist canvases has never been fully explored. In *Après le cubisme* the two men liken a painting to an equation. In their words everything can be expressed through number. Art, for Ozenfant and Le Corbusier, must comply to a set of rules. These, it becomes apparent, derive from nature and owe much to ancient Greek and Egyptian thought. They wrote: 'The ancient canons, widely thought to be artificial codes, templates, were based exclusively on precise knowledge of the universality of the natural laws that govern the exterior world and condition works of art.'[107] Through these it would be possible to link disparate elements into a cohesive whole in harmony with nature.

It was in 1920 that Édouard Jeanneret started to use the name Le Corbusier. Ostensibly he began writing under this name in order to prevent confusion with his cousin Pierre Jeanneret, with whom he was to work in partnership, but there are a number of other possible reasons for the change. In particular it enabled him to differentiate in his mind between Jeanneret the man and Le Corbusier a heroic figure with a mission.[108] He recorded in *A New World of Space* how, in the beginning, he would sign his paintings Jeanneret and his architecture Le Corbusier.[109]

By the end of 1918 the collaboration between Ozenfant and Le Corbusier was so close that Ozenfant was later to write that from that point until 1925 the two artists became 'we': Le Corbusier-Saugnier, their joint *nom de plume*. The professional and intellectual relationship between them became such that Ozenfant felt the need to divorce his first wife, Zina Klingberg, and begin what Carol S. Eliel has called 'a new, more physically pared down chapter of his life, which he later called – using an aptly machine-oriented metaphor – the "period of Vacuum-cleaning"'.[110]

Le Corbusier's father's diaries over this period indicate that his parents were worried about his health both mental and physical: 'He is reduced by fatigue ... he has thrown himself into all sorts of undertakings ... he aims too high'.[111] It seems that Le Corbusier's parents felt indebted to Ozenfant for looking after their son.[112] Eliel makes the observation that Le Corbusier was concentrating so hard on his work with Ozenfant that he built nothing between 1918 and 1922, a testament to the importance of the intense relationship between the two men. Their collaboration was to finish abruptly with the twenty-

[106] Le Corbusier, *New World of Space*, p.11.

[107] Ozenfant and Jeanneret, 'After Cubism' in Eliel, *Purism in Paris*, p.157.

[108] It is significant that he chose a name so similar to the word *corbeau* meaning crow or raven in French. He is likely to have been fully award of the significant role of the crow in alchemy, a portentous figure that flies over the blackened world, the bringer of change. Le Corbusier thought of himself as a witness or observer. He would on occasion draw a picture of the bird in preference to his signature, as he did on a letter to Aalto. Le Corbusier's letter to Aalto 5 August 1954 (AAF).

[109] Le Corbusier, *New World of Space*, p.13.

[110] A. Ozenfant, *Mémoires*, 1886–1962, Paris: Seghers, 1968, p.103 quoted in Eliel, *Purism in Paris*, p.22.

[111] Entry in Le Corbusier's father's diary 2 April 1919, Bibliothèque de la ville de La Chaux-de-Fonds. Quoted in Vogt, *Noble Savage*, p.125.

[112] Le Corbusier, 4 September 1919. Ibid., p.125.

eighth edition of *L'Esprit Nouveau* in 1925. Eliel observes that 'Tellingly, Ozenfant remarried in 1926; clearly his primary psychological and intellectual allegiance of 1918–25 to Jeanneret, had ended'.[113]

Not long after his break with Ozenfant Le Corbusier began a relationship with Yvonne Gallis, a 'model' from the south of France. They married in 1930. Anecdotal evidence suggests that Le Corbusier lived with her for a number of years, before marrying her because of familial pressure.[114] When Yvonne came into Le Corbusier's life his paintings went through a transformation. He began to experiment with new kinds of subjects, including a variety of what he called 'objets à réaction poétique' – bones, shells and other natural objects. Women too became a favoured subject for his artistic explorations (Plate 3). At the same time his work went through a radical change, as shall be seen in Chapter 7.

Towards Paimio

In the early days of his practice in Jyväskylä and then Turku, Aalto had a number of much older Finnish mentors from whom he learnt and on whom he leant. Chief amongst these was the Finnish critic Gustav Strengell, author of *Staden som konstverk* (The City as a Work of Art).[115] This book, with which Aalto was clearly familiar, addressed the importance of 'wholeness'.[116] The progressive architect Sigurd Frosterus, who was another leading light in the new Society of Finnish Architects (SAFA), also began to foster Aalto's career at this time. Importantly Frosterus had worked with Henri Van de Velde and brought home a keen determination to build progressively in the backwoods of the north. He also brought to Aalto's attention the ideas of the Swedish art critic Gregor Paulsson regarding social responsibility.[117] Influenced by the social commitment of his wife Aino, Aalto championed Paulsson's agenda against the conservative grain of the times, becoming a friend of Paulsson himself. It was through these contacts that Aalto became increasingly interested in new developments in architecture. Later Aalto was to become very close to Van de Velde himself, a friendship he valued greatly.[118]

After winning the competitions for the Agricultural Cooperative Building for Turku, Finland's most westerly city, in 1927, Aalto decided to move there, closer to the forces of change that were massing new forms in Sweden. Soon afterwards he began to collaborate with the sensitive architect Eric Bryggman, seven years his senior and already established in practice in there.

Aalto was at this time beginning to think in terms of ascetic Functionalism, but continued a few projects in the neoclassical style of their conception.[119] Having secured the commission for the Viipuri Library in 1927 through a neoclassical competition entry, he redesigned the scheme in January 1928, stripping it of its neoclassical ornament, long before its site was completely changed.[120] At the same time he was boldly conceiving other projects in purely Functionalist terms, most notably the Turun Sanomat Building. Aalto was already conversant with the ideas behind Le Corbusier's early constructional and aesthetic experiments. Indeed, on meeting the owner of the Turun Sanomat, in 1927, Aalto had actually not yet seen a Functionalist building; nevertheless he

113 Eliel, *Purism in Paris*, p.64.
114 C. Jencks, *Le Corbusier and the Continual Revolution in Architecture*, New York: Monacelli, 2000, p.191.
115 Strengell was influenced by Camillo Sitte's *Der Städtebau* (1888) which concentrated on the organic growth of social needs of a society, from which German medieval town aesthetics developed, and by Brinckmann who addressed the Renaissance, Baroque and eighteenth century.
116 Aalto puts forward similar arguments in an article, 'Urban Culture', *Sisä-Suomi*, 12 December 1924. Schildt, *Own Words*, pp.19–20.
117 Paulsson was a Swedish art critic. Frosterus reviewed Paulsson's book *Den nya arkitekturen* (New Architecture, 1916) in *Arkkitehti* journal.
118 Letters from Van de Velde to Aalto, AAF.
119 Some projects, such as the Agricultural Cooperative Building completed in 1929 and hailed as 'the first Functionalist theatre in the North', had been stripped of their early neoclassical friezes.
120 At this stage the entry drew closely on Asplund's Stockholm City Library.

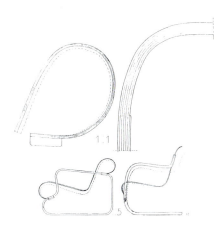

2.5
Paimio chair drawings. Aalto,
c.1932.

quickly persuaded the owner to commission a new building on Corbusian lines. Only a year later he had begun to compose buildings, like Paimio Sanatorium (1928–33) with even greater Modernist confidence, but therein greeting visitors with his characteristic iconoclasm, combining the tropes of Modernism with his own: the flexing, almost accommodating gesture of the waving entrance canopy and the Paimio Chair (Fig. 2.5).

In this way Aalto juggled his commitment to the calm neoclassical image of a Renaissance town like Jyväskylä and to the new architecture with ease. In his hands the aesthetic distinction between the two seems to have been subtle.

The run-up to the great Functionalist exhibition in Stockholm in 1930 was important for Aalto, further familiarising him with the revolutionary ideas of the Gropius and the Bauhaus, J.J.P. Oud and Le Corbusier. He and Bryggman decided to pre-empt the Stockholm Exhibition by setting up an exhibition to mark the seven-hundredth anniversary of the City of Turku in 1929.[121] To be seen to be at the forefront of European Modernism was crucial to Aalto, and after the Turku Exhibition he marched on to new realms of Functionalism and the quiet character of Bryggman moved sideways into his own, profound but little publicised realm.

Ancient Greek Cosmology in an Epoch of Technology

The foregoing experiments at the cutting edge of the modern epoch were not to the exclusion of correspondence with Daidelus and the nature of ancient form and ideas. Both Le Corbusier and Aalto acknowledged the importance of ancient Greece in their thinking about their role as architect and their conceptions of society and life.

Le Corbusier and the Architectural Phenomenon

Le Corbusier observed that 'it was only in 1919 – at the age of 32 – that I was really able to see the "architectural phenomenon"'.[122] By this stage in Le Corbusier's career his philosophical and spiritual viewpoint was already well developed. In the earlier discussion of Le Corbusier's reading of Schuré it was seen that he looked to ancient Greek philosophy, the views of Plato and Pythagoras, as a source of spiritual ideas. He also turned to the ideas of those who were influenced by these philosophers such as the medieval church builders and those early scientists the alchemists. Annotations to Le Corbusier's copy of *Escalarmonde de Foix*, a book on the Cathars about the fourteenth-century mystical heretics from Languedoc who sought to achieve purity through the renunciation of the body, show that Le Corbusier took a close personal interest in the sect. The notes also suggest that he believed the Cathars to be in receipt of knowledge derived from that of Plato,[123] which they then passed on to the troubadours of fourteenth-century France.[124] Further annotations suggest that he may have believed the traditions of courtly love and veneration of the feminine

[121] It was also to be the Third Finnish Fair.
[122] Le Corbusier, *Modulor 2*, London: Faber, 1955, p.267.
[123] See annotations to C. Saint Palais, *Esclarmonde de Foix: Princesse Cathare*, Toulouse: Privat, 1956, p.27 in FLC.
[124] Ibid., pp.28–9.

promulgated by the troubadours were also based on the ideas of Plato[125] and of the Egyptian Hermes Tresmigistus, the so-called father of alchemy.[126] The significance of these influences upon Le Corbusier's attitude to nature will become further apparent in later chapters. Le Corbusier's friend and client Édouard Trouin was to call this tradition of wisdom Orphism, referring back to the ancient mystery religion of that name and, simultaneously, the art movement instigated by Apollinaire.[127]

According to the Neoplatonist philosopher Pico della Mirandola, much admired by Le Corbusier,[128] the Orphics had 'a secret doctrine of number' that was understood and utilised by the ancient Egyptians, Pythagoras, Plato, Aristotle and Origen.[129] Le Corbusier underlined a section referring to this continuous thread of knowledge in the book *Nombre d'or* by his friend Matila Ghyka, and alluded to it in *Modulor 2*, extending it into the twentieth century.[130]

The ancient Orphics were highly syncretic in their approach to religion; they were prepared to see all religions as manifestations of one and the same thing. Having been so influential in ancient times, Orphism could be linked to the history of a number of world religions and for this reason it could be used as a means to cross boundaries between race and religion.

Focusing upon the paradoxical god Orpheus, this religion, adhered to by both Plato and Pythagoras, encompassed those dualisms, of light and dark, day and night, masculine and feminine, that played such an important part in Le Corbusier's thinking. Such dualisms were key to Aalto's thinking too, but did not have an Orphic heritage.

Orpheus was said to be the prophet of a particular type of mystery religion that W.K.C. Guthrie describes as 'a modification of the mysteries of Dionysos'[131] and a 'species of the Bacchic'.[132] Dionysos, who appeared to his followers in the guise of a bull (a favoured theme in Le Corbusier's paintings),[133] was, according to the scholar, worshipped under many names including Pan and Apollo.[134] Such was the beauty of Orpheus's music that he was able to persuade the gods to allow him access to the Underworld in pursuit of Eurydice, his love. He thus had a special role in the propagation of musical harmony – a subject that, as we have seen, held a particular fascination for Le Corbusier.

Orpheus was thus unique in having made the journey in death and back again. His sojourn into the land of death meant that he alone had knowledge of the secrets of Hades and could tell his followers the best way to prepare for Afterlife.[135] The Orphic goal was to obtain knowledge of a secret doctrine of number, to allow the soul to leave the body at the point of death and move up through the heavenly spheres to be reunited with god, in Le Corbusier's terms nature.[136] Number would give access to the divine. For Daniel Naegele the way in which Le Corbusier ordered space 'testified to the existence of another reality, a higher order, a space that the poet sees and strives to recreate'.[137] Here an art critic unveils in Le Corbusier's work that which gives creative substance to Winnicott's notion of Potential Space. It is as if Le Corbusier's notion of creating the 'ineffable' space is an urge to seek to manifest a refuge for the non-verbal nature of humankind, if not specifically the pre-verbal.

[125] Ibid., p.27.

[126] Ibid.

[127] Trouin, 'Table provisoire' for book entitled 'La Sainte Baume et Marie Madeleine,' n.d., FLC 13 01 396.

[128] Le Corbusier, *Sketchbooks Volume 3 1954-1957*, Cambridge, MA: MIT Press, 1982, sketch 1011.

[129] Pico della Mirandola, *On the Dignity of Man*, Indianapolis: Hackett, 1998, pp. 30–1.

[130] M. Ghyka, *Nombre d'or: rites et rhythmes Pythagoriciens dans le dévelopement de la civilisation Occidental*, Paris: Gallimard, 1931, p.57 in FLC.

[131] Guthrie, *Orpheus*, p.39.

[132] Ibid., p.41.

[133] Ibid., p.114.

[134] Ibid., p.41.

[135] Ibid., p.29.

[136] G. Filoramo, *A History of Gnosticism*, Oxford: Basil Blackwell, 1991, pp.52–3.

[137] D. Naegele, 'Photographic illusionism and the "New World of Space"' in M. Krustrup (ed.) *Le Corbusier: Painter and Architect*, Aalborg: Nordjyllands Kunstmuseum, 1995, p.134.

Aalto, the Antique and the Ideal

One thing that becomes apparent from a reading of *Journey to the East* is Le Corbusier's fascination with what he calls 'Sweet Death'.[138] He is repeatedly drawn to sketch in cemeteries and burial grounds and he comments on the funeral customs of different cultures. Death, 'she' in Le Corbusier's terms, is feminine in character.[139] It will be argued that for Le Corbusier death and nature were almost synonymous. To die was to be restored to a state of unity with all things, an idea to which Aalto could not subscribe. Death had a devastating and even paralysing hold on the Finn, suspending him over the 'gap' of his mother's sudden demise. He was never able to address death directly as Le Corbusier did in *Mise au Point*,[140] yet he would process the notion of *Sterben und Werden* (dying and becoming) from nature into the architectural realm with ease throughout his oeuvre.[141]

Death was thus inherent to ideas of life and growth, and was associated closely with the forms and ideas of archaic Greece. In his student days Aalto recorded his excitement about ancient Greek form in a rare letter to his parents. 'My studies are progressing rapidly. I have almost finished with my stone hut. I've been going hard at the art of ancient Crete and Mycenae for the last couple of weeks, morning and night. Such exciting subjects just won't let you go once you start studying them.'[142]

Indeed, over time Aalto seems to have become deeply interested in the ancient ideas of 'natural order' and form. These and their symbolic, if vestigial, representation in fragmentary form in his work drew him towards an understanding of natural order that was congruent with his experiences of the natural world and human nature.

Demitri Porphyrios and Colin St John Wilson have explored the notion that Aalto was attracted to a form of ordering rooted in *hetera*, the Greek word for 'other'. In their work there is a wealth of material that draws Aalto's compositions and his attitudes to nature together. However, in their analyses, neither of them takes the notion to its natural conclusion, and it will be beneficial to investigate this here.[143]

Porphyrios's analysis of Aalto holds to the notion of heterotopia as 'That order, which western rationalism mistrusted and derogatorily labelled disorder'.[144] He borrows this notion from Michel Foucault's *The Order of Things*, but does not address pre-Socratic sources. Foucault himself explains that heterotopia is 'the state of things laid, placed, assigned sites so very different from one another that it is impossible to define a locus common to them all'.[145] Recently Wilson has used the same appellation of 'other', but without citing the parallel with the Greek word *hetera*, nor connecting with Porphyrios's important thesis. This omission may be due to the fact that Wilson finds what can be recognised as a natural order emerging from the fulfilment and manifestation of function, in other words Hugo Häring's maxim 'allow them to unfold their own forms' or *Leistungsform*,[146] rather than suggesting that he accepts that there is no discernible order.

While broadly concurring with Wilson, here we venture to suggest that the Hellenic root of 'other' is extremely significant since it can refer to an 'other',

[138] Le Corbusier, *Journey to the East*, p.135.

[139] Ibid., p.163.

[140] Le Corbusier, 'Mise au Point', translated and interpreted in I. Žaknić, *The Final Testament of Père Corbu*, New Haven: Yale University Press, 1997.

[141] The old imperative form was *Stirb und Werde*.

[142] Aalto, letter to his parents, 8 October 1918 from Helsinki. Schildt, *Early Years*, p.106.

[143] D. Porphyrios, *Sources of Modern Eclecticism: Studies of Alvar Aalto*, London: Academy Editions, 1982 and C. St. John Wilson, *The 'Other' Tradition of Modern Architecture*, London: Academy Editions, 1995.

[144] Porphyrios, *Sources of Modern Eclecticism*, p.2.

[145] M. Foucault, *The Order of Things*, Bristol: Arrow Smith, 1977, p.xvii.

[146] H. Häring, 'Wege zur Form', in *Die Form*, 1, October 1925, pp.3-5.

differently ordering element within Aalto's search for harmony. Thus it draws the notion of 'harmony'(that which inspired much of Western civilisation) back beyond Aristotle to Sophistry, wherein 'nature-as-coming-to-be' was central, and in which a certain flux was accepted as being inherent in any natural order. This 'other' ordering principle permits some elements of natural growth to dwell at the heart of a natural order, just as it was in the Finnish forest, and as it is in the psycho-anthropological work of Cobb's 'world-building' and Winnicott's primary creativity.

It is our suggestion that Aalto revisited something of the pre-Socratic 'logic of ambiguity',[147] responding to an undefined need to create (the 'inner urge'), exploring a natural order that was simultaneously inherent in himself and apparent in the natural world in which he dwelt. He could adopt this construct of natural order and then reflect it back within himself as a structure for his inner world-building, as a notion of improved psycho-physical human life. After all, he wrote in 'The Trout and the Mountain Stream' of the dialogue of inner and outer realms in the creative process.[148] In other words, rooted in his ineffable and precarious inner balance, there is an idea that takes form in a building, through the pattern of what the building contents want to be (in other words the broadened character of the human elements that in-form the whole). This may have been an image of exactly what he could not be himself, but strove to construct – harmony in human life.

Thus it may be said that Aalto looked to the ancients for enlightenment on this, as much as to his own experience of the ecological system of the backwoods. As suggested, it seems that his grasp of ancient composition and ideas was more intuitive than it was academic, but it was deeply important none the less. Purposeful interaction with nature, that which had been primary at the Evo Forest Institute and in his father's surveying work, was coupled in Aalto's mind with a Darwinian belief in the march of progress. Aalto's sensory experience of survival in the forests was a palpable ingredient in his views about nature, what Schildt calls forest wisdom. This led him to describe Aalto as a 'Goethean in Modernist disguise, an adherent of ancient Greek cosmology in an age of technology'.[149] Aalto's determination to humanise technology may indeed be a modernisation of Goethe, and even a furtherance of the German's ideals, since it accepts technology but seeks to synchronise it with natural solutions.

Schildt suggests that Aalto shared with Goethe a notion that man is an integral part of nature's cycle, and therefore cannot stand outside it.[150] Indeed, in 1956 Aalto wrote of the importance of Goethe's integration of creative thought based on matter in his *Italienische Reise* (Journey to Italy), believing that here there is a rare sign of the integration of art, sciences and practical work.[151] Aalto had been seeking a synthesis of the arts and the sciences since his early years, when the spirit of Evo pervaded life. Again this drawing together of phenomena seems to have been almost natural, as if Aalto were deeply familiar with disorder. He was certainly attracted to the exuberance of the ad hoc in the urban milieu of Italy, and even in the collection of buildings that was home in Jyväskylä. Again, these ideas were closely coupled with Aalto's other fundamental understanding of nature and its sometimes messy, raw order. Closely tied to the ideals of liberal

[147] Vernant uses the expression 'logic of ambiguity' to describe pre-Socratic thinking. J.-P. Vernant, *Mythe et Pensée chez les Grecs*, Paris: La Découverte, 1985, p.250.

[148] Aalto, 'The Trout and the Mountain Stream', 1947 in Schildt, *Sketches*, pp.96–8.

[149] Schildt, *Early Years*, pp.200–1.

[150] Schildt, *Own Words*, p.37.

[151] Aalto, 'Form as a Symbol of Artistic Creativity', 1956, in ibid., p.181.

humanism to which he had been exposed at home, these ideas would have also been confirmed by the writings of his friend, the eminent Finnish philosopher G.H. von Wright, who wrote on the subject of humanism.[152]

Unity, Uncertainty and the Potentialities of Natural Form

Towards Unity – Père Teilhard and Père Corbu

Le Corbusier was meanwhile looking for theories that would bind together those areas of his life that he perceived to be in a state of tension. He spent many years seeking a theory of evolution that would simultaneously reconcile the facts of religious experience with those of natural science. He also sought writers whose ideas would corroborate his own. For this reason, late in life, he developed a strong interest in the work of the priest and palaeontologist Pierre Teilhard de Chardin.[153] The ideas of the Jesuit, much influenced by Goethe, provide an excellent means to access Le Corbusier's own thoughts on the relationship between man and nature.

Teilhard urged his audience to rise up above the 'uncertainties' of the world and look down upon it in order to see phenomena as a whole. By taking the broad view he was able to observe the ways in which improvements in communication and the effects of war and migration have 'stirred the human dough'. He wrote, 'the more we seek to thrust each other away, the more do we interpenetrate', calling for 'ever increasing unification'.[154] His knowledge of evolution, gained through his experience as a palaeontologist, was used to back up his argument for projected developments in the consciousness of man.[155]

It was Teilhard's belief that one of the main catalysts for change was love, primarily love between man and woman. He wrote in *Human Energy* of man's need to complete himself through woman. For Teilhard women played an important role in giving man access to nature and to the divine.[156] This was close to Le Corbusier's own thinking, as will become apparent in the discussion of Ronchamp in Chapter 6. Certain analogies can be drawn between Le Corbusier's buildings and the figures that inhabit his paintings.

Although it might be an exaggeration to suggest that Le Corbusier thought of his buildings as being in some way alive, acting upon us through what he called a 'psychophysiology of the feelings', the implication is that they are not entirely passive.[157] Teilhard posited the idea that 'Consciousness … is a universal property common to all the corpuscles constituting the Universe, but varying in proportion to the complexity of any particular molecule.'[158] In these terms a building would be humming with life at the molecular scale, 'Man, with his billions of interacting nervous cells, finds a natural, cosmically enrooted place in this generalised physical scheme.'[159] Here Teilhard seems to refer to the mythopoetic world of early man when all things were in some sense alive, a time for which Le Corbusier retained a deep nostalgia.

[152] Aalto would have been very familiar with the philosophical writing of G.H. von Wright, the Wittgenstein specialist who taught at Cambridge University for many years.

[153] Letter from Le Corbusier to Andreas Speiser, 22 December 1954. FLC. Dossier Speiser R3 04 369.3.

[154] P. Teilhard de Chardin, *The Future of Man*, London: Collins, 1964, p.125.

[155] See F. Samuel, 'Le Corbusier, Teilhard de Chardin and La planétisation humaine: spiritual ideas at the heart of modernism', *French Cultural Studies*, 11, 2, 32, 2000, pp.163-288.

[156] P. Teilhard de Chardin, *L'Énergie humaine*, Paris: Éditions du Seuil, 1962, p.42.

[157] The phrase 'psychophysiology of the feelings' is used repeatedly by Le Corbusier. e.g. *Oeuvre Complète Vol. 6, 1952–1957*, Zürich: Les Éditions d'Architecture, 1995, p.52.

[158] Teilhard, *Future of Man*, p.130.

[159] Ibid., p.131.

Rousseauesque Suspicions

Le Corbusier, or 'Père Corbu' as he sometimes called himself, turned to what he believed to be the roots of Christianity, Egyptian and Greek philosophy, in an attempt to find a pure religion untainted by the 'hypocrisy' of the last two millennia. Similarly he adhered to Rousseau's belief that man was essentially good by nature, but had been perverted by human institutions, 'the academies' in his words.[160] 'I am attracted to the natural order of things. I don't like parties ... I look for primitive men', wrote Le Corbusier at the outset of *The Radiant City*.[161] Vogt makes the significant point that Le Corbusier, like Rousseau, measured 'the alienation of things and beings' in terms of a 'distance' from their 'point of origin'. In his opinion Le Corbusier, as 'a serious connoisseur and admirer of Rousseau ... aimed at nothing less than transposing Jean-Jacques' body of thought into the language of architecture' and that it became his primary aim to 'preserve or save the innocence of the landscape'.[162] Le Corbusier retained throughout his life a profound nostalgia for a purer past, hence his great interest in the 'primitive' cultures and ancient history.

It should be noted that Le Corbusier was not alone in expressing such sentiments. A revival of interest in alternative forms of spirituality within Parisian artistic circles at the time was fuelled by recent discoveries in the field of archaeology and palaeontology. In particular there was a burgeoning interest in the cave art of prehistoric cultures.

The first notable discovery of Palaeolithic art, that of the painted ceilings in Altamira in Spain, took place in 1879, but many then believed such paintings to be modern forgeries. Subsequent discoveries of other caves in France convinced prehistorians that they were genuine.[163] Nobody had believed that such beauty and sophistication could be possible amongst such a primitive people.[164] It may be that the discovery of these paintings confirmed Le Corbusier's Rousseauesque suspicions about the superiority of early cultures. He and Amédée Ozenfant included a number of images from cave paintings in their journal *Esprit Nouveau* in the early 1920s.[165]

Aalto, Abbé Coignard and the 'Universalist' Agenda

In an important lecture from 1925, which (utilising a character created by the writer Anatole France) he entitled 'Abbé Coignard's Sermon', Aalto had spoken in profound terms of wanting to take Rousseau's idea of the 'natural' further to include the psychological.[166] Like France, who mixed sources such as socialist ideas with the lives of saints, so Aalto mixed beauty of form with the Christian message; 'a well developed heart is a far better instrument than the educated mind'.[167] Aalto continued a discussion about how form can represent something to which we may aspire by quoting Abbé Coignard directly, 'God has laid down something which people do not have the intelligence to seek', before declaring that 'form is nothing but a concentrated wish for everlasting life on earth'. In a part of the text which remains in note form alone, there is a heading that draws in Ruskin's ideas about architecture being the natural art.[168] This dates from the years before Aalto embraced Modernism, when he was still ensconced in

[160] Second letter of Jean-Jacques Rousseau to the Count de Malesherbes. Cited in Vogt, *Noble Savage*, p.125. Letter Le Corbusier to Abbé Ferry, 10 July 1956, FLC E2 02 167.

[161] Le Corbusier, *The Radiant City*, London: Faber, 1967, p.6.

[162] Vogt, *Noble Savage*, p.138.

[163] These were either totally sealed (with deposits from the quaternary period), such as La Mouthe, or where engravings were buried under soil containing Palaeolithic artefacts.

[164] A. Seiveking, *The Cave Artists*, London: Thames & Hudson, 1979, p.55.

[165] See 'L'Angle Droit,' *Esprit Nouveau*, 20, New York: Da Capo Press, 1969, unpaginated.

[166] Aalto, 'Abbé Coignard's Sermon', 6 March 1925 in Schildt, *Own Words*, p.57.

[167] Aalto, untitled lecture, dating from around 1925. Alvar Aalto Foundation, hereafter referred to as AAF.

[168] Aalto, notes for second part of 'Abbé Coignard's Sermon', read 'Architecture – the natural art (Ruskin)' in Schildt, *Own Words*, p.57.

Jyväskylä, suggesting that his ideas about the natural roots of architecture came from his early influences and found no contradiction with the preoccupations of his classical sojourn nor his Modernist aspirations.

As well as calling upon ancient inspiration when discussing profound subjects, Aalto also called on Nietszche and August Strindberg. Aalto often cited the latter's attempts to draw the antithetical together into synthesis, and the capacity to question through one's creativity.[169] He will also have seen in the work of both men an intensity of the tortured self he knew so well, and, what is more, the intense need to draw together disparate experiences. Aalto wrote, 'even things that appear to be completely antithetical can be reconciled somehow or other'.[170] A parallel in his architectural form is so often evident. This notion of forging relationships between the disparate is the root of much of Aalto's thinking, and links his many and varied influences.

From Bauhaus to Bent Wood

Aalto began to be interested in mass-produced furniture at this time, having, up to this point, only designed one-off artefacts. After Asplund's Senna chair of 1925, Aalto produced a 'Folk Senna' in 1928, a simplified, modernised version of his mentor's original. Simultaneously this chair demonstrates the origins of Aalto's work, in Asplund and the neoclassical, and the future of his work, in quality serial production with a curved accent. Replacing Asplund's wooden legs with Bauhaus tubular steel, 'Aalto has left the gnawed bone of doctrinaire Functionalism far behind', observed his English friend, the architect Philip Morton-Shand.[171] He was to go much further in this regard with his innovative bent-wood furniture.

Indeed in 1931, the same year that László Moholy-Nagy drew attention to the importance of experimentation that had been at the very heart of the Bauhaus, Aalto began his wood experiments with Otto Korhonen (Fig. 2.6). Schildt suggests that Aalto conceals his indebtedness to Moholy-Nagy by citing Yrjö Hirn's concept of play as the origin of these experiments.[172] Through such painterly and wooden experiments Aalto discovered more about nature's potential flexibility, producing, for instance, the elegant and flexible chair leg, affectionately called 'the little sister of the column' (Fig. 2.7), acknowledging its

[169] Aalto, 'Art and Technology', 1955 in Schildt, Own Words, p.174, and Aalto, 'The Enemies of Good Architecture', RIBA Discourse, 1957 in ibid., p.203.
[170] Aalto, Art and Technology, lecture at his installation into the Finnish Academy, 1955, in ibid., p.174.
[171] P. Morton-Shand, in a radio lecture, repr. in The Listener, 11 November 1933. Cited in Schildt, Decisive Years, p.39.
[172] Yrjö Hirn was a Finnish aestheticist who became close to Aalto only in the latter's later years.

antecedents in history. This concept was to spawn innumerable other architectural forms and features in his work, yet he felt that both in his own career, and in the developments of great movements of culture, 'it all began with painting'.[173]

Aalto painted almost continually throughout his life. He saw his paintings as a forum for experimenting with the relationship of formal elements; 'Right now I feel that we are looking for Unity ... the holy unity of art is by no means a dead Renaissance ideal', he wrote in 1921.[174] To this end he was close to a number of artists including Fernand Léger, Alexander Calder, Hans Arp and Constantin Brancusi, and greatly admired Braque. Aalto's abstract paintings from 1940 often offer a sideways glimpse at a natural reality, for example a landscape or anatomical detail (Plates 4 and 5), but more often than not they demonstrate an exploration of the relationship of organic and geometric forms, bearing striking relationship to some of his architectural forms.[175] Aalto's paintings, like those of Le Corbusier, were intrinsically linked to his designs but, unlike his Swiss counterpart, he never sought recognition as an artist.[176]

Man the Unknown: Aalto and Uomo Piccolo

Aalto did not specifically seek intellectual justification for his work, but gathered other explorations about man's general condition that were congruent with his pragmatic approach and therefore his experience, hence his repeated reference to "uomo piccolo" or little man in his writings.[177] He became increasingly preoccupied with the reality of building, finding less time and less need to invest in his name abroad. His writings suggest that he was increasingly interested in drawing on the variability at the heart of nature, finding this in cultures as diverse as ancient Greece and modern Japan. In 'Rationalism and Man', from 1935, he mused about Japanese culture, noting that 'contact with nature and enjoyment of its constant variation is a way of life that cannot be reconciled with overly formalistic ideas.'[178] He felt that there was a sympathy between the materiality of the backwoods buildings and those of Japan. 'The houses in the old Karelian area are especially close to my heart. They represent an almost extra-European architecture comparable with that of Japan.'[179]

Alexis Carrel's book *Man the Unknown* (1935) was a source of excitement for Aalto, since it arrived at some of the same conclusions as he had reached with Moholy-Nagy.[180] Carrel, a physiologist and winner of the Nobel Prize, wrote, 'We must listen to Bergson'[181] while setting out to explore unknown realms of humanity in terms of objective science, physiology, psychology, aspects of time intuition and intelligence (largely repeating Henri Bergson), extolling the rise of the gifted individual (in eugenic tones), all towards the goal of 'the remaking of man'. Carrel believed, 'The restoration of man to the harmony of his physiological and mental self will transform his universe.'[182] Carrel's ideas would have been somewhat familiar to Aalto because they came close to those of the Finnish thinker Eino Kaila (with whom Kirmo Mikkola associated Aalto's thinking of this period) and his line of linking biological issues with those of quality of life and progress of society.[183] In essence, Carrel's thesis was that man should lead a biologically well-adjusted life, but many of the associated eugenic

[173] Oft-repeated remark cited by Schildt, *Early Years*, pp.153 and 159.

[174] Aalto, 'Painter and Mason', 1921 in Schildt, *Own Words*, p.31.

[175] Schildt, *Complete Catalogue*, p.275.

[176] Aalto refused to let the French art dealer, Louis Carré, for whom he designed a house, promote his art in Paris.

[177] For example Aalto, 'Culture and Technology', 1947; repr. in Schildt, *Sketches*, p.94.

[178] Aalto, 'Rationalism and Man', speech to the Swedish Craft Society, 1935; Repr. in Schildt, *Sketches*, p.93.

[179] Aalto, letter to Otto Völckers, cited in Schildt, *Decisive Years*, p.114.

[180] A. Carrel, *Man the Unknown*, New York: Harper, 1935.

[181] Ibid., p.155.

[182] Ibid., p.291. Durkin particularly finds Carrel's extensive writing about intuition to be inspired by Bergson. J.T. Durkin, *Hope in our Time: Alexis Carrel on Man and Society*, New York: Harper & Row, 1965, p.24.

[183] K. Mikkola, 'Aalto the Thinker', in *Arkkitehti* 7/8, 1976, pp. 20–5.

[184] In this Bergson resisted the polar opposition of Mechanistic and Finalistic explanations of evolution, although this also invites the accusation that he promotes Finalism, yet falls short of deliberate teleology. In other words he suggests there is a final end, but declines to describe its nature.

Top: 1
Nature morte pâle à la lanterne, oil on canvas,
81 x 100 cm. E. Jeanneret, 1922.
FLC (FLC 209).

Left: 2
Drawing of Savoy vase for Karhula-Iittala glass
design competition. Aalto, 1932. Pencil, chalk,
gouache and paper on cardboard.

Right: 3
La Femme au guéridon et au fer à cheval,
E. Jeanneret, 1928.

Top: 4
Oil painting, 43 x 52 cm. Aalto, 1955.

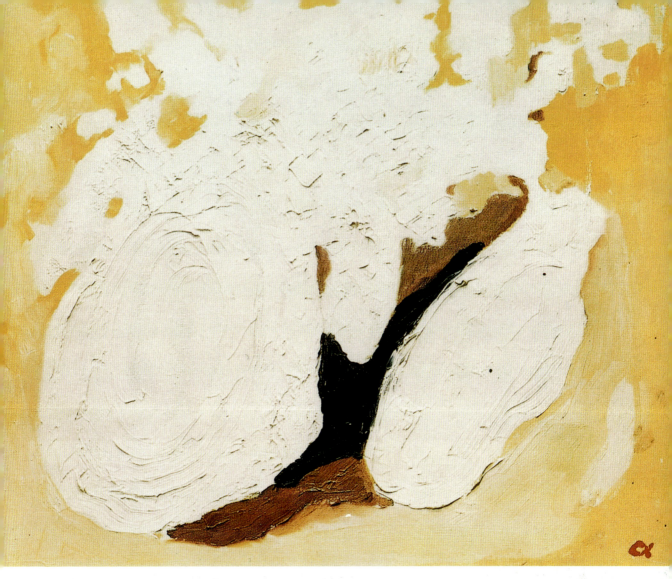

Opposite: 5
Oil painting, 53 x 67 cm. Aalto, 1959.

Below left: 6
Icône, from *Le Poème de l'angle droit*, Paris:
Éditions Connivance, 1989, p.131.

Below right: 7
View towards courtyard of the Summer House,
Muuratsalo. Aalto, 1952–3.

Above: 8
Terracing, Helsinki Technical University,
Otaniemi, Finland. Aalto, 1955-64.

Below: 9
Entrance elevation of Notre-Dame-du-Haut,
Ronchamp. Le Corbusier, 1950–5.

Opposite: 10
View towards chancel of Church of the
Three Crosses, Vuoksenniska. Aalto, 1956–9.

Top left: 11
Stained-glass window in south wall of Notre-
Dame-du-Haut, Ronchamp. Le Corbusier,
1950–5.

Top right: 12
View of clerestory windows and tripartite
detail housing movable wall, Church of the
Three Crosses, Vuoksenniska. Aalto, 1955–8.

Right: 13
Side chapel, Notre-Dame-du-Haut,
Ronchamp.
Le Corbusier, 1950–5.

Top: 14
Oil Painting, 64 x 80 cm. Aalto, 1949.

Above: 15
View of stained glass and crosses, Church of the
Three Crosses, Vuoksenniska. Aalto, 1955-8.

Right: 16
Gargoyle and water cistern, Notre-Dame-du-
Haut, Ronchamp. Le Corbusier, 1950–5.

[185] P. Teilhard de Chardin, *The Appearance of Man*, London: Collins, 1965, p.261.

[186] A.R. Lacey, *Bergson*, London: Routledge, 1989, p.181.

[187] H. Bergson, *Creative Evolution*, trans. A. Mitchell, London: Macmillan, 1911.

[188] H. Bergson, *Mélanges*, Paris: Presses Universitaires de France, 1972, pp.766–7.

[189] Bergson, *Creative Evolution*, p.262.

[190] Aalto, 'National Planning and Cultural Goals', *Suomalainen-Suomi*, 1949. Repr. as 'Finland as a Model for World Development' in Schildt, *Own Words*, p. 167–71.

[191] Mikkola, 'Aalto the Thinker' p.23. Mikkola also believes that Aalto's use of time is similar to Bergson's continuation and duration (*durée*). In *An Introduction to Metaphysics* (1903) Bergson introduced the notion of the fluidity of time through experiences of knowing, relative and absolute. He sought to highlight real existence, *durée*, as opposed to the relative time represented by a clock face.

[192] For example: Aalto, 'Erik Gunnar Asplund Obituary', *Arkkitehti*, 11–12, 1940, in Schildt, *Own Words*, p.242, and Aalto, 'National Planning and Cultural Goals', *Suomalainen-Suomi*, 1949; Repr. as 'Finland as a Model for World Development' in ibid., pp. 167–71.

[193] Moholy-Nagy believed that all art strives for 'timeless biological fundamentals of expression that are meaningful to everyone'. L. Moholy-Nagy, The New Vision, Chicago: Institute of Design, 1947, p.13.

[194] Ibid., p.16.

[195] Ibid., p.17.

[196] D.W. Winnicott, *Home is Where We Start From: Essays by a Psychoanalyst*, London: Pelican, 1987, pp.142–9.

ideas are ideologically unpalatable today. Aalto would have been broadly aware of Bergson's Vitalism, which concerned life energised by a vital force (an *élan vital*) to provide a unity that random variation lacks, by overcoming the potential chaos of change and flux.[184]

Bergson's *élan*, for instance, explained variation, which in Darwinism was understood as pure chance, and which Teilhard de Chardin believed was a tool to explain 'the dynamic rigour of a situation'.[185] The cause of the *élan vital* was psychological, and was thus beyond science and moral 'law'.[186] In a letter of 1908 Bergson admits that his work, *Creative Evolution*,[187] makes God the *source* (his emphasis) of '*élans*' (plural),[188] stating elsewhere that God is 'unceasing life, action, freedom'.[189] Aalto seems to have found this freedom in his experience of nature.[190] Indeed, Mikkola believes that the *élan vital* encompassed the relationship of nature and development inherent in Aalto's work,[191] augmenting ideas from the Bergsonian Carrel, often cited by both Aalto[192] and Moholy-Nagy.[193] This was a suggestion that the basics of art are indeed the basics of life. Indeed, Moholy-Nagy believed that the term 'biological' stood for 'the laws which guarantee organic development' which, if conscious, would protect against damaging influences and promote the goal of 'man's organic function'.[194] He pointed out that if children are not damaged psychologically they will usually act in accordance with biological laws, avoiding what is damaging.[195] These ideas were hugely attractive to Aalto, uniting architecture and life. They also reinforce Winnicott's notion used here that, given a 'good-enough' environment, children will thrive.[196]

Conclusion

From this chapter it can be seen that at the end of their initial schooling and architectural training, both taught and self-driven, the two architects were profoundly influenced, among other things, by the philosophies of the ancient Greeks and the Italian Renaissance, Aalto in a more intuitive way than Le Corbusier who studied the subject with a greater degree of earnestness. Both were interested in the issue of harmony as expressed through the ideas of Plato and Pythagoras. Aalto however seems to have been interested in the roots of the notion of harmony in a more precarious dialogue of the disparate, which allowed 'other' forms of order, such as the organic model, to effect the whole. For both men nature was an agent of integration, allowing them to bring together a number of disparate elements into a cohesive philosophy.

Evidently nature played an important role in the ideas of many artists and thinkers in Aalto and Le Corbusier's circles. Indeed many people at that time were exploring its role in religion and science. Buildings – like people, plants and other natural organisms – were subject to the processes of natural selection, they believed, and thus the laws which govern organic development should govern that of architecture.

Chapter 3

The Meeting of Modern Minds

In the northern periphery of Europe the attraction of progress soon resulted in
a complete shift of gear in Aalto's career. He wanted to be close to those famed
individuals who promoted progress through the modern functional approach.
Initially the focus of this chapter is Aalto's growing contact with mainstream
Modernism, since this draws him towards the sphere in which Le Corbusier
was a central figure, but the focus then shifts towards the newfound friendship
with Le Corbusier, ten years his senior and already a figure of some renown due
to the publication of *Vers une architecture* in 1923. They were soon to develop a
friendship of mutual respect as the sceptical Aalto defied any normative code of
Modernism, and gesticulated an earthy wave (*aalto* in Finnish) towards the heart
of the tendency to be dogmatic (and the wave was in wood). Le Corbusier
evidently felt a deep affinity with this maverick figure. It is the nature of the
relationship between the two men that forms the focus of this chapter.

Modernity Moves North

Aalto was not at the cutting edge of European culture until Modernism turned
towards the architects of the north. His Swedish colleague Sven Markelius had
travelled by car through Europe in 1927 to gather information and influences for
his practice, visiting destinations such as the Dessau Bauhaus and Berlin.
Perhaps more than anybody else, Markelius is responsible for introducing Aalto
to what was happening in the rest of Europe. Aalto's contact with Markelius
deepened once he moved to Turku in 1927 soon after the Swede returned from
his study tour of modern buildings in the summer of 1927. After Markelius wrote
a review of Gropius's housing for *Byggmästaren*, the German agreed to lecture
in Stockholm in March 1928. Markelius was subsequently invited to give a
lecture in Turku, in which, Schildt relates, he admitted that Gropius' socially
oriented agenda had challenged the artistic emphasis of Le Corbusier.[1] This is
important because it positions Aalto closer to Gropius than to Le Corbusier at
this stage and it was Gropus that he first suceeded in making personal contact.

[1] G.Schildt, *Alvar Aalto: The Decisive
Years*, New York: Rizzoli, 1986, p.48.

Indeed, throughout his biography Schildt seems to have a hidden agenda of putting a wedge between the ideas of Aalto and those of Le Corbusier, thus working within the narrow understanding of Le Corbusier's work largely through his early white buildings.[2] In his writings Aalto makes reference to Le Corbusier's work, not to Gropius's, and it is not an exaggeration to suggest that the Finn sought to unite the art of one with the social agenda of the other. However, later in life Aalto seems to have enjoyed contact with the creative soul of Le Corbusier much more than what might be described as the withered soul of Gropius's pedagogy, from whom he was somewhat estranged in later years, even when they were in Cambridge, Massachusetts at the same time.[3] Yet of most significance at this early stage was Aalto's drive to meet and spend time with the leading lights in the architectural world.

While many Markelius and Bryggman buildings seem to foreshadow Aalto's more famous edifices, Markelius's wife recalled that 'Alvar helped Sven to soften down his architecture and taught him the value of wood. Deep inside they were both artists, however socially minded they tried to be'.[4] In the 1930s Aalto switched his attentions back to his early mentor Asplund until the Swede's death in 1940, finding that his concentration on 'man, with all the innumerable nuances of his emotional life and nature' was closer to his own (damaged) heart.[5]

Missing Le Corbusier

In June 1928 the Aaltos undertook a study tour of their own, by plane, with the aim of meeting Le Corbusier in Paris. They travelled via Denmark, where they met Poul Henningsen,[6] and on to Amsterdam, meeting Johannes Duiker, whose Zonnenstraal Sanatorium impacted upon Aalto's Paimio design. In Paris they discovered that Le Corbusier was actually in Moscow, but at his atelier they met Alfred Roth, who remained a life-long friend. They also met André Lurçat and saw his latest work, and it is likely that they spoke with him of the forthcoming gathering of CIAM, the *Congrès Internationaux d'Architecture Moderne*, to be held at La Sarraz three days later.

The Aaltos did not visit Germany, but returned home to design the competition entry for the Paimio Sanatorium, soon considered to be one of the greatest Functionalist buildings. It is interesting that Aalto headed straight for Le Corbusier, not for Gropius. Whether it was because Markelius had not visited Paris, but had met Gropius, or because Aalto felt that Le Corbusier was more important, remains a matter of speculation.

Following the inauguration of CIAM, Karl Moser wrote to invite Markelius to join the group. He in turn invited Henningsen and Aalto, with whom he travelled to Frankfurt for the second CIAM in October 1929.[7] Interestingly at this stage, Aalto had most contact with Gropius, who by then had left the Bauhaus for Berlin. Perhaps as a result of this affiliation with Gropius, Aalto never visited the Bauhaus. In spite of his strong distaste for ideological groupings Aalto was quickly accepted by CIAM. In reality he positioned himself as an adjunct to the main forces, and a dissenter from its themes, while sojourning with its central characters. It was undoubtedly a tendency that was very useful to his career.

[2] Ibid., pp.16–17, 48 and 75.

[3] Letters in the Alvar Aalto Foundation Archives, hereafter referred to as AAF, describe a difficult situation in which Gropius wrote asking Aalto to pay for some phone calls made from his house in Cambridge, Massachusetts, which Aalto thought was particularly mean.

[4] Interview between Viola Markelius and Schildt, 14 January 1979, cited in Schildt, *Decisive Years*, p.49.

[5] Aalto, 'E.G. Asplund in Memoriam', 1940 in G. Schildt, *Alvar Aalto in his Own Words*, New York: Rizzoli, 1997, pp. 242–3. When Aalto first sought out Asplund the architect had no time for the young Finn. However, when established Aalto went straight to the heart of his mentor.

[6] Henningsen's famous PH lamp is thought to have influenced Aalto's subsequent lamp designs, as did his radical journal *Kritisk Revy*, which was pro social and environmental change, anti sterile dogma.

[7] The art critic Gotthard Johansson travelled with them. Later, in 1932, he wrote of the common 'instinctive and assured sense of proportion' that characterised Le Corbusier and Aalto. Cited by K. Mikkola, *Aalto*, Jyväskylä: Gummerus, 1985, p.10.

Sigfried Giedion and the Social Message: The Stockholm Exhibition

The 1930 Stockholm Exhibition confirmed that Modernism was firmly on the architectural agenda in Sweden,[8] with its 'deliberate social message' as Aalto put it.[9] It was a celebration, Schildt believes, of the positive consequences of Darwin's doctrine of the blind struggle for survival, associating this with an anarchistic sense of freedom offered by the show.[10] This is a curious but enlightening interpretation of the Modernist angle, drawing to the fore a yearning for progress that was particularly apt for the young nation of Finland that wanted to raise itself up from subsistence existence, through the window open to Europe. At the exhibition Aalto forged a friendship with Sigfried Giedion, the CIAM secretary, whom he had met at the second CIAM meeting in Frankfurt a year earlier. This friendship flourished despite Aalto's disdain for the organisation's dogma and his own irregular attendance. Giedion admired Aalto for having established a unique way of drawing together history, technology, social concerns and a deep congruence with nature, celebrating and publicising it with gusto (if not a degree of exaggeration) in the second edition of his famous book *Space, Time and Architecture*.[11]

Searching for a Gentler Modernism

Later in 1930 the Aaltos followed up the friendships they had established in Frankfurt and Stockholm by visiting Berlin to stay with Gropius and spend time with Moholy-Nagy. Together this group went to a meeting of some CIAM members, including Gerrit Rietveld, Richard Neutra and Hugo Häring, at Palmgarten on 25 September. This was before Häring was alienated from CIAM as an apostate.[12]

Aalto then went with Giedion and Karl Moser to Zürich, where, it seems he had contact with Hélène de Mandrot.[13] Following his visit to Berlin in 1930 Aalto wrote to Gropius about his mission to 'make buildings for people into whose heads the "organic line" will not fit for another 100 years'.[14] His use of the term 'organic line' suggests something important about Aalto's priority and preoccupation even at this early stage. Ten years later he was to write to Mandrot (for whom Le Corbusier designed the rustic edifice of the villa at La Pradat, Provence in 1931) in moving tones, addressing the humanist agenda that still faced modern architecture, inspired, it seems, by his own tragedy: 'I think people psychologically need security.'[15]

Building Naturally

Moholy-Nagy was a natural teacher, easily sharing his bountiful ideas, introducing Aalto, for instance, to the potential of film, photography and Constructivist theories. That he gave Aalto copies of his own radical books is of interest, but Aalto's own unwillingness to discuss their conversations demonstrates even more. These books, especially *Von Material zu Architektur* (The

[8] This has been analysed by Raija-Liisa Heinonen, *Funktionalismin läpimurto Suomessa*, Helsinki: Museum of Finnish Architecture, 1986, pp. 208–13, and Elina Standertskjöld, 'Alvar Aalto and Standardisation', in R. Nikula, M.–R. Norri and K. Paatero (eds.), *The Art of Standards*, *Acanthus*, Helsinki: Museum of Finnish Architecture, 1992, p.74.

[9] Aalto, 'The Stockholm Exhibition 1930', *Åbo Underrättelser*, 22 May 1930; repr. in Schildt, *Own Words*, p.72.

[10] Schildt, *Decisive Years*, p.62.

[11] S. Giedion, *Space, Time and Architecture*, second edn, Cambridge, MA: Harvard University Press, 1949.

[12] In 1931 Aalto went to the meeting of the inner circle of CIAM, CIRPAC (*Comité International pour la Résolution des Problèmes de l'Architecture Contemporaine*) but spent most of his time with Moholy-Nagy. Although he had been at the heart of the Bauhaus, Moholy-Nagy was an important ingredient in encouraging Aalto's natural instinct to fly beyond the dogma of that agency.

[13] There is an extensive collection of letters from Mandrot in AAF.

[14] Aalto, letter to Gropius, autumn 1930. Cited in Schildt, *Decisive Years*, p.66.

[15] Aalto letter to Mandrot, cited in G. Schildt, *Alvar Aalto: The Mature Years*, New York: Rizzoli, 1992, p.49.

New Vision: From Material to Architecture) from 1929, explain the place of 'organic' thinking in Moholy-Nagy's ideas and art, and therefore it is not unreasonable to suggest that Aalto's reluctance to discuss them was exactly because they were so important to him. In a note of thanks for his copy we see something of its significance when Aalto wrote, it was 'magnificent, lucid and beautiful, perhaps your best book'.[16] Schildt speculates that the Hungarian taught Aalto about the opening up of space within buildings and the need to use nature as a model for architecture. Aalto was however already familiar with the use of space in Rietveld's Schröder House and in Le Corbusier's work, and had already written about how nature should inhabit architecture in 'From Doorstep to Living Room', in 1926. Here he had drawn on the ideas of both Gustav Strengell's *The House as a Work of Art*,[17] and Le Corbusier's *Vers une Architecture*, as will be demonstrated in Chapter 4.[18] Aalto himself had written about the place of nature in architecture as early as 1925 in a piece on the 'Temple Baths on Jyväskylä Ridge'. 'Build naturally,' he instructed here.[19]

Moholy-Nagy's articulation of the need for the psychological and the biological to be the roots from which architecture found its own order was undoubtedly important to Aalto, but more in the form of a confirmation than as the cause of a shift in the Finn's work. Such confirmation may have stimulated Aalto to listen to his own instincts more, to create Paimio, in part, in response to his own experiences of life.[20] This experience may have moved Aalto away from the more formulaic practice of Gropius towards the free, deeply nature-inspired artist in Le Corbusier.

The Paimio Punch

Although Frosterus and Strengell were at this time seeking to promote his work, Aalto's buildings were finding a frosty reception amongst the conservative establishment in Finland. Asplund visited Paimio on his way to lecture at the Nordic Building Congress in Helsinki in July 1932 and, as a result, he decided to concentrate his lecture on the theme of architecture in the environment, emphasising Aalto's first major Modernist building, to the disdain of many. Colleagues of a conservative taste were disdainful of this 'progress' and publicly accused Aalto and Asplund of being Bolshevik. Aalto's response was to box the ear of the accuser. This incident resulted in an uproar in architectural circles, healed only by the intervention of Aalto's old teacher Carolus Lindberg.

In 1933 Aalto moved to establish himself in Helsinki. After a period of psychological and physical crisis which followed on from pneumonia in 1935, Aalto took a break, meeting colleagues in Brussels for a CIAM planning committee before going on to Switzerland to spend time with the Giedions. Aalto took home a deep sense of personal recuperation and a revitalised principle of humanising Rationalism, and more importantly, an intuition about manifesting it in architecture.

[16] Cited in Schildt, *Decisive Years*, p.77.

[17] Gustav Strengell, *Byggnaden som Kunstverk* (The House as a Work of Art), Stockholm: Bonnier, 1928.

[18] Aalto illustrated his article with Fra Angelico's *Annunciation*, a Pompeiian villa and Le Corbusier's Esprit Nouveau Pavilion, amongst others. Schildt, *Own Words*, pp.49–55.

[19] Aalto, 'The Temple Baths on Jyväskylä Ridge', *Keskisuomalainen*, 22 January 1925; repr. in Schildt, *Own Words*, pp. 17–19. See also Aalto, 'Architecture in the Landscape of Central Finland', *Sisä-Suomi*, 26 June 1925; repr. in ibid., pp. 21–2.

[20] See for example Aalto, 'Rationalism and Man', Speech to the Swedish Craft Society, 1935; repr. in ibid., pp.89–93.

The Personable Personas of Prophets

At this stage it is helpful to demonstrate what is known about the relationship between the two men. Having missed Le Corbusier during the Paris trip in 1928, Aalto was able to meet him at the second CIAM in Frankfurt a year later, a gathering 'over which the spirit of Le Corbusier hovered' as one of his Scandinavian friends put it.[21] Aalto's letter home suggests he spent most of his time cultivating contacts with the German-speaking contingent, having no French himself.[22] Aalto and Le Corbusier were to meet again at the Brussels CIAM in 1930.

Aalto, Athens and the Prophet of Functionalism

In a clear expression of the importance of ancient Greek thought to the work of Modernism, Le Corbusier, Giedion and their CIAM colleagues travelled across the Mediterranean, from Marseille to Athens in 1933, where they were joined by others. At this stage, however, Aalto was making waves, so to speak, at the heart of the cause, and his studio was so busy that he missed the cruise, but flew to join the gathering in Athens.

The congress is described by Aalto's protégé Nils-Gustav Hahl, who was sent to catch the cruise in Aalto's stead. Reporting on the Congress for Hahl in *Hufvudstadsbladet* describes how, in the absence of Gropius, Le Corbusier was dominant:

> ... the renowned father and prophet of Functionalism ... two enormous loud speakers convey his words to a few hundred listeners ... He varies on his favourite theme 'air, son (sic), lumière' ... It goes without saying that Le Corbusier is one of the foremost figures ... He is known as a Classic Functionalist, but in his speeches he is its most passionate Romantic. His figure is thin and bony, behind the large goggles his eyes have the confidence of the unshakable fanatic.[23]

Hahl also reported in *Tulenkantajat* on a lecture by Léger about colour in architecture, to which Le Corbusier and Aalto had added their enthusiastic opinions: 'both of them typically considered only the physiological effect colours have on people, and almost wholly disregarded their aesthetic qualities.'[24] Certainly for Le Corbusier colour, like sound and space, could be manipulated to bring people into a harmonious relationship with nature. To this end he himself designed a range of colours based on those of the sky, sand and so on, marketed by the Italian firm Salubra. It was 'a system which makes it possible to establish a strictly architectural polychromy in the modern dwelling, one in accordance with nature and with the deep needs of each person'.[25]

Aalto had lunch with Le Corbusier on arrival in Athens, having come too late to join an island cruise. Le Corbusier had noticed Aalto and, as Schildt puts it, 'honoured the young Finn with his friendly camaraderie'.[26] Aalto missed a great deal of the business of the congress, preferring to explore the Acropolis drawing and photographing, and spending time with his friends Léger and

[21] Gotthard Johansson, 'The 1930's in Memoriam', cited in Schildt, *Decisive Years*, p.61.

[22] Aalto, letter to Aino, 25 October 1929, AAF.

[23] Schildt, *Decisive Years*, p.91-4

[24] Hahl, in *Tulenkantajat*, cited in Schildt, *Decisive Years*, p.95.

[25] Le Corbusier, 'Claviers de couleurs' from the trade literature for Salubra in L. M. Colli, 'Le Corbusier e il colore'. *Storia dell'arte*, 43, 1981, p.283.

[26] In a letter to his friend the painter Fernand Léger, Le Corbusier sends his special greetings to Aalto, who was also a close friend of Léger. Letter Le Corbusier to Fernand Léger, 17 November 1938; Jean Jenger (ed.) *Le Corbusier Choix de Lettres*, Basel: Berkhanser, 2002, p.122.

Moholy-Nagy[27]. However, he did give a humorous lecture, 'The Encounter with Classical Greece', in which he relayed his encounter with a Greek woman with a leg in plaster, thus undermining the seriousness of the gathering, to the delight of almost all the delegates. Schildt suggests that there is a poignancy in hindsight, as stifling post-war urbanism may be likened to the beautiful Greek bound in a cast.[28] This is not to say that Aalto foresaw this, but rather that his natural anarchism reacted against the determinism that pervaded the congress and the rather dogmatic line of leading figures. It may have been this that Aalto was likening to the plaster cast.

After the cruise back to Marseilles Aalto spent time with Le Corbusier before travelling by car to Switzerland with Moholy-Nagy and Giedion, to have more close encounters with Mandrot. From Zürich Aalto wrote home:

> We sat together in Marseilles, Le Corbusier and I, every morning. He has been incredibly friendly to me. And so have others. In Athens I was treated like the Charlie Chaplin according to Giedion. A trip like this gives a boost to one's confidence, but only when we are together can the right attitude be found – *obschon ich jetzt nur erotisch an dich denken kann* [although at the moment I have only erotic thoughts about you]. Little little little Aino. Your Alvar'.[29]

Aalto found confidence in being accepted, even if it was as the joker of the pack. He also called on Aino to bring him back down to earth to 'the right attitude'.

The Forest on the March: Paris 1937

Both Aalto and Le Corbusier attended the 1935 CIAM in Amsterdam, Aalto spending a great deal of time with Giedion. However, contact between him and Le Corbusier was renewed when Aalto spent an extended period in Paris when his Finnish Pavilion for the 1937 Paris World Fair, which he playfully called 'Le Bois est en Marche', was built. It was very well received internationally. Le Corbusier wrote, 'In the Finnish Pavilion the visitor is delighted by its deep-rooted authenticity. It has been a point of honour for the authorities to choose the right architect'.[30] Interestingly both men had disagreements with their respective commissioning authorities about their pavilions. Aalto did not attend the opening of his, and his name was not mentioned, and Le Corbusier's spiral Temps Nouveaux Pavilion opened two months after the other exhibits.[31] The two men would have met often during this time, and both participated in the fifth CIAM during the exhibition. They seem to have met again at the sixth CIAM in Zürich, in 1947. At this time the ideas that were preoccupying them were manifest in very different forms. Aalto was at the heart of the conception of the undulating Baker House (1946–9) that was to look like 'an old tweed coat' (Fig. 8.8),[32] and Le Corbusier was integrating the Modulor and *The Radiant City* into the design of the Unité in Marseille (Fig. 8.2); a marked difference of inflection to be examined in Chapter 8.

27 G. Schildt, 'Alvar Aalto's Artist Friends', in T. Hihnala and P.-M. Raippalinna, *Fratres Spirituales Alvari*, Jyväskylä: Alvar Aalto Museum, 1991, p.13.
28 Schildt, *Decisive Years*, p.102.
29 Aalto, letter to Aino from Zürich, 20 August 1933, AAF.
30 Le Corbusier, repr. in *Arkkitehti*, 9, 1937. Cited in P. McKeith and K. Smeds, *The Finland Pavilions*, Helsinki: Kustannus Oy City, 1992, p.121 and Schildt, *Decisive Years*, p.135.
31 D. Udovickl-Selb, 'Le Corbusier and the Paris Exhibition of 1937', *Journal of the Society of Architectural History*, 56, 1, 1997, pp.42–63.
32 Aalto to Robert Dean, 1947. Dean reported this to Sarah Menin in a conversation on 31 July 1985, in Boston. Dean had been a young architect with the firm of Perry Shaw and Hepburn, local architects with whom Aalto was required to work on Baker House Dormitory.

Sanity, Sensitivity and Saturation: Drinking in the 'Gap'

In the profound mental disturbance and restlessness that followed Aino's death in 1949, Aalto made many trips abroad. In Paris he met Léger, Braque, Kandinsky and Le Corbusier, who introduced him to Eugène Claudius Petit and André Bloc, who was to organise an exhibition of Aino and Alvar Aalto's work at the École des Beaux Arts in 1950. At the opening, all Aalto's Paris friends met to celebrate his work. Despite this Aalto could not clamber out of the 'gap'; no matter how successful he was, he remained dissatisfied, and full of grief and terror of death. He even missed a presentation in his honour by L'Union de Artistes Modernes, remaining obliviously drunk in a bar.[33]

After his marriage in 1952 to Elissa Mäkiniemi, a young assistant of his, Aalto began to visit Paris more frequently. He persuaded SAFA (the Association of Finnish Architects) to award Le Corbusier an honorary membership. Le Corbusier did not attend the presentation, but in turn, in 1950, offered Aalto a share in the sales of some elaborate tapestries he had designed.[34] Declining the offer, Aalto returned the photos of these in April the next year, adding that he hoped to meet him in Paris on his return from Spain.[35] Le Corbusier's diary from 1950 has an entry referring to a meeting with Aalto on 24 April.[36] He persisted with the venture, writing to friends of Giedion's and Aalto's as late as the close of 1951 seeking to sell the tapestries.[37]

In 1954 Aalto invited Le Corbusier to visit Finland to attend a 'miniature congress' of the local CIAM group, combined with a large SAFA conference, by trying to persuade him that it was only six hours by plane.[38] Le Corbusier's response was as follows:

> My dear friend Aalto,
> How amiable your letter of July 21 was, just like yourself.
>
> I should love to visit you, but cannot. I have no strength left, and yet I must bear my burden ... I know that Finland is lovely in the summer. If I could come we should not say a word about architecture. What a paradise!
>
> A week ago I built myself another kind of paradise, a shack, two by four metres (double sacred square) for my personal meditations and to write this letter. The sea is 20 metres away at the foot of the cliff. But the mistral has been blowing, and the other day it pushed me alarmingly towards the sharp rocks
>
> Aalto, my friend, *leb wohl*, my best regards to your wife, and press me hard to your heart – it will do me good. I repeat my optimistic slogan: Life is hard! Thank you, au revoir,
>
> Yours,
> [a sketch of a raven] [39]

Here Le Corbusier demonstrates the nature of the deep affection the two men felt for each other as people, not just as successful designers, although that is undoubtedly how and why they first sought each other out.

[33] Schildt, *The Mature Years*, p.141.

[34] Le Corbusier, letter to Aalto, 25 May 1950, AAF and 29 November 1950. AAF and FLC G2 1135.

[35] Aalto's secretary to Le Corbusier, 12 April 1951, AAF. Aalto's secretary informed Le Corbusier that in the current economic depression such a venture was not feasible.

[36] Le Corbusier's diary, 1950. FLC F3.9.7.

[37] Le Corbusier, letter to Denise Rene Birkerd, 21 December 1951, AAF.

[38] Aalto, letter to Le Corbusier, 21 July 1954, AAF.

[39] Le Corbusier, letter to Aalto, 5 August 1954, AAF. The shack to which he refers is the work cabin he added to his Cabanon at Cap Martin.

In the same year both Le Corbusier and Aalto were asked to be jury members for the Materazzo Prize for Architecture in Brazil, which was eventually won by Gropius. There the two were named honorary members of the Brazilian Architects Association. Aalto was in close contact with Oscar Niemeyer during this time, likening the Brazilian's house to an exquisite flower that could not be transplanted.[40] 'I think very positively of the tropical flowers of your architecture. For me it represents a gay and sweet comparison to Corbu's often repeated words: "Life is hard and so is architecture". It is very important to rail in our art on the right track.'[41]

In 1954 Aalto and Le Corbusier were also among over fifty architects to be asked to design blocks of apartments for the 1957 Interbau Exhibition. The solutions, discussed in Chapter 8, are very characteristic of their individual approaches to the problem of mass housing.

In March 1957 Le Corbusier wrote to congratulate Aalto on winning the RIBA Gold Medal.[42] Two years later Le Corbusier was among guests, such as the Gullichsens from Finland, the Giedions from Switzerland, Braque, Alexander Calder, Cocteau and Giacometti who attended a party to celebrate the completion of Aalto's Maison Carré, for the wealthy international art dealer Louis Carré, built just outside Paris.

Later Elissa Aalto recalled that Le Corbusier's 'features and facial expressions showed great sensitivity', belying the aggression of his writings, and sometimes his behaviour.[43] She recalled a lunch party at Cladius-Petit's home, when Le Corbusier strode in straight towards a painting and said 'rather rudely "Where has that come from?" Baffled, the poor host replied, "Cher maître, it is you who gave it to me". To which Le Corbusier stated that the painting was not yet ready. The whole situation was in a way funny, and yet so embarrassing at the same time'.[44]

Nevertheless, messages of warm affection passed between Aalto, his wife and Le Corbusier over the years.[45] There is evidence that the Aaltos visited Paris almost every year from 1949 onwards, sometimes passing through en route to other destinations, such as New York in 1964.[46] Knowing the closeness of their friendship, it is likely that Aalto met Le Corbusier as often as was possible. On one occasion, during their 1959 visit to Paris, Elissa sent Le Corbusier flowers, and the latter reciprocated with a flirtatious letter of thanks.[47] Aalto wrote of seeing Le Corbusier just months before he died, in a letter to Claudius Petit, who had become a good friend. 'I shall never forget our diner à trios, nor our friendship that united us ... I loved and admired Le Corbusier.'[48]

In 1965 Aalto wrote an obituary for Le Corbusier.

> This sad moment is of course not the time for a critical assessment of the works and career of my colleague. That is for the critics to provide. Collegial criticism arises in other circumstances than after one has lost an esteemed colleague.
>
> From our very first meeting in the company of our avant-garde colleagues to the very last, only a few months ago, we have been united by a personal, completely disinterested friendship.

[40] Aalto, interview with a local paper, Brazil, 1954, cited in Schildt, *The Mature Years*, p.238.

[41] Aalto, letter to Niemeyer, 1954, cited in ibid., p.239.

[42] Le Corbusier, letter to Aalto, 1 March 1957, AAF and FLC G1 11 251.

[43] E. Aalto, 'Contacts' in Hihnala and Raippalinna, *Fratres Spirituales Alvari*, p.11.

[44] Ibid.

[45] For example a telegram to Le Corbusier sent by Elissa and Alvar Aalto, 6 October 1962. 'Nos Meilleures Felicitations', AAF.

[46] Letters and telegrams to and from hotels in Paris provide evidence of these journeys. Letters referring to the trip to New York are dated 24 October 1963, 30 October 1963, 18 November 1964, AAF.

[47] Le Corbusier to E. Aalto, 6 July 1959, FLC G1 1671.

[48] Aalto, letter to Claudius Petit, summer 1965, AAF.

I wish to express my respect to a friend thus *post factum*. My respect was heightened by the fact that his spirit sprung from classical roots, deriving its strength from the distinctive Mediterranean character which formed a counterbalance to his versatile work, difficult as that work was owing to his combative position.

I therefore pay homage to his oeuvre, but especially to my friend.[49]

Aalto himself was to die in 1976.

In a recorded conversation with Schildt in 1967. Aalto said, 'The Bauhaus has never interested me; more so Jugend in its continental origins, Henri van de Velde and the others. Le Corbusier reached me indirectly as a general feeling in the air during these years. He had for the most part expressed himself in books'.[50] From archival information it is evident that the influence of Le Corbusier on Aalto was actually profound during the 1920s, to say nothing of their subsequent deep personal friendship. Aalto's wish to veil, if not to actually to deny his closeness to Le Corbusier is very interesting. Apart from the obvious initial influence of the 'five points for a new architecture' demonstrated in the Turun Sanomat, Paimio Sanatorium or Viipuri Library, Le Corbusier's placing of free-form elements to contrast with the strict rationalism in, for example, the entrance canopy of the League of Nations design, may have confirmed Aalto in his composition of a similarly free-form entrance to Paimio. However, from that building onwards Aalto's 'organic line' was not ornamental but fundamental, as will be demonstrated later. From the 1930s their relationship was warm, and any influence was more mutual, as Le Corbusier began openly to admire Aalto's work.

Conclusion

Le Corbusier, a decade older than Aalto, took a position as trail blazer (or 'dictator' as some would see it) of the modern way. Aalto meanwhile was an iconoclastic individual who encountered this trail, took a few steps along it, but then diverged from the path markedly, even during the first years of his association with the CIAM. Ironically, during this marked divergence from the dogma-laden road, Aalto deepened his personal friendship with Le Corbusier, perhaps because of the extent to which the two men thought alike on the subject of nature.

49 Aalto, *Arkkitehti*, 12, 1965 in Schildt, *Own Words*, p.248.
50 Conversation between Aalto and Schildt in G. Schildt, *Alvar Aalto Sketches*, Cambridge, MA: MIT Press, 1986, pp.170–2.

Chapter 4

Radiant Nature Writing

Having discussed the influence of nature on the upbringing and education of Le Corbusier and Aalto, it is appropriate to explore its role in their developing design philosophies. It has been seen that Le Corbusier, who referred to himself as 'a man of letters' was much more dogged in looking elsewhere for inspiration for his work than Aalto, who we know read a great deal, but worked in a way that was ostensibly more instinctive. Le Corbusier published innumerable books while Aalto wrote articles and lectures collected and published in full after his death, but did not seek to publish a complete thesis of architecture in book form. Indeed he often implied that such was anathema to architecture in his view.[1] In this chapter we will draw on both their literary and their artistic output to make a comparison of Aalto's and Le Corbusier's individual approaches to nature.

The two men were interested in blurring the boundaries between biology and planning, seeing the process of design as a natural process, and the products of this process as needing to be in harmony with nature. This is of primary importance, and our examination will include detailed assessment of some of the specific ways in which they endeavoured to blur the boundaries between buildings and environments and indeed to improve upon nature's own work. The more disturbing and 'cruel' side of nature and its relationship with their ideas will be discussed, and will be linked back into the main thesis of this book, that of their need to create an idealised view of nature to fill the 'gap'. Throughout his career Aalto associated nature with the capacity to facilitate material and psychological health. Le Corbusier too believed that by making links between man and nature in design it would be possible to promote what he called the 'psycho-physiological' health of both the individual and society.

[1] C. St-John Wilson explores this in *The 'Other' Tradition of Modern Architecture*, London: Academy Editions, 1995.

[2] Le Corbusier, *Modulor*, London: Faber, 1954, p.78.

Culturing Cells

Le Corbusier likened the act of designing to 'the work of nature which proceeds from the inside outwards, uniting, in the three dimensions, all the diversity, all the different intentions in perfect harmony'.[2] Creativity was a 'profound primordial function' animating 'even the lowest cell of organic life'.[3] For Aalto 'biology's and culture's own method of creation' was to build 'cell by cell'.[4] He, like his Swiss counterpart, associated the processes of natural and artistic creation. In the opinion of Le Corbusier the city was a 'living organism'[5] and 'urbanism' a problem of 'biological organisation'.[6] The cellular structures of the heart and the leaf[7] are offered up as examples for architects.[8] Aalto too was to observe that 'Nature, biology, has rich and luxuriant forms', believing that combinations of 'cellular organisations' could offer a procedure for architects to follow.[9]

Radiant Growth: A Symbol for a Modern Architecture

Le Corbusier believed that it was vital to return to the 'origins' to counteract 'the disturbance created by machines which has turned everything upside down and created a wholly unbalanced society'. His whole life effort focused upon his plan for making this happen.

> My task ... concerns especially re-establishing or establishing harmony between man and their environment. A live organism (man) and nature (the environment), this immense vase containing the sun, the moon, the stars, indefinable unknowns, waves, the round earth with its axis inclined on the eliptic producing the seasons, the temperature of the body, the circulation of blood, the nervous system, the respiratory system, the digestive system, the day, the night, the solar cycle of twenty-four hours, its implacable but varied and beneficent alteration, etc.[10]

In his many books and writings he developed a 'plan', his view of the cosmos, one that extended from the smallest electron to the planets (focus of his famous and often erroneously quoted statement 'the plan is the generator').

Like Aalto, Le Corbusier spent many years attempting to devise a cellular housing unit suitable for mass production, large numbers of which could then be brought together to form a community, many of which were vaulted in form.[11] For Le Corbusier it was vitally important to perfect the individual unit of housing as 'in Nature, the smallest cell determines the validity, the health of the whole'.[12] By restructuring the city, 'the cell of the social body ... the family' would be restored once more to its previous health. Whilst Le Corbusier wrote of the cell in nature he was simultaneously thinking of the monastic cell, in particular that of the monastery at Ema near Florence, which he first visited in 1907, describing it as a 'radiant vision', a 'modern city' dating 'from the fifteenth century'. 'The noblest silhouette in the landscape, an uninterrupted crown of monks' cells; each cell has a view on the plain, and opens on a lower level on an entirely closed garden. I thought that I had never seen such a happy interpretation of a dwelling.'[13]

The monastery at Ema provided the inspiration for all the housing projects that were to follow and was central to Le Corbusier's conception of the Radiant City.[14] 'I would like to live all my life in what they call their cells' he wrote.[15] Le Corbusier thus turned his energies towards creating a cell of housing that would be similarly successful – a basic building block of his housing schemes which could be brought together to create a community. For this as for many other

3 Le Corbusier, *The Decorative Art of Today*, London: Architectural Press, 1987, p.192.
4 Aalto, 'National Planning and Cultural Goals' in G. Schildt, *Alvar Aalto Sketches*, Cambridge, MA: MIT Press, 1986, p.100.
5 Le Corbusier, *Towards a New Architecture*, London: Architectural Press, 1982, p.33.
6 Le Corbusier, *The Marseilles Block*, London: Harvill, 1953, pp.13 and 17.
7 Le Corbusier, *Une Maison – un palais: A la recherche d'une unité architecturale*, Paris: Crès, 1928, p.78.
8 Ibid., p.33.
9 Aalto, 'Rationalism and Man' in G. Schildt, *Alvar Aalto in his Own Words*, New York: Rizzoli, 1997, p.93.
10 Trans. from F. Pottecher, 'Que le Fauve soit libre dans sa cage', *L'Architecture d'aujourd'hui*, 252, 1987, p. 62; Le Corbusier, *Precisions on the Present State of Architecture and City Planning*, Cambridge, MA: MIT Press, 1991, p.vii.
11 Le Corbusier, *Towards a New Architecture*, p.210.
12 Le Corbusier, *The Marseilles Block*, p.17. Such ideas developed out of Le Corbusier's work with CIAM on the development of housing.
13 Le Corbusier, *Precisions*, p.91
14 Ibid. For a critique of the role of nature in the Radiant City see 'The Return of the Repressed: Nature', Diana Agrest, *The Sex of Architecture*, New York: Harry N. Abrams, 1996, pp.58–61.
15 G. Grisleri, *Le Corbusier, il viaggio in Toscana*, 1907, exhibition catalogue, Florence, Palazzo Pitti: Cataloghi Marsilio, Venice, 1987, p.17.

problems he looked to examples in nature for inspiration, in particular the cellular homes of insects.[16] Juan Antonio Ramirez has written extensively about the influence of the apiary on Le Corbusier's housing schemes in his book *The Beehive Metaphor*.[17]

Having set out to build economically and efficiently to standard dimensions, Le Corbusier sought a way of establishing just what those dimensions should be. To this end he derived a system of proportion that was rooted in a variety of sources: day-to-day observations of the world around; measurement of cars, boats, buildings; technology and science; ancient religion and philosophy; art; and, of course, nature. In this category crystal, flowers, wasp nests, leaves and shells were all subjects of study, as his sketchbooks testify. In explaining his sources of inspiration Le Corbusier quoted the words of his friend Andreas Speiser in *Modulor 2*:

> In the spatial world the images of the numerical world are projected, first by nature itself, then by men and above all by artists. It can be said that our duty on earth and during the whole of our life consists precisely in this projection of forms issued forth from numbers, and that you, the artists, fulfil that moral law to the highest degree. Not only is it possible to appeal simultaneously to geometry and to numbers, but to do so is the true purpose of our life.[18]

For Le Corbusier, to pursue the possibilities of number was not an aesthetic game but a moral imperative and indeed an act of faith. Through it he would create 'happiness in an age of confusion'.[19]

Through the use of the Modulor Le Corbusier hoped to create a cohesive environment in harmony with nature, in other words radiant. This term, receiving its fullest expression in the book *The Radiant City*, published by Le Corbusier in 1933, warrants some exploration.[20] He wrote in *Conversations with Students* that 'in 1935 the Radiant City appeared. The word "radiant" ... has a meaning that surpasses a merely functional connotation. It has the attribute of consciousness, for in these perilous times, consciousness itself is at stake, more important than economics or technology lessons for students'.[21]

In *New World of Space*, published in 1948, Le Corbusier described the phenomenon of radiance in a chapter entitled 'Ineffable Space':

> The flower, the plant, the tree, the mountain stand forth, existing in a setting. If they one day command attention because of their satisfying and independent forms, it is because they are seen to be isolated from their context and extending influences all around them. We pause, struck by such interrelation in nature, and we gaze, moved by this harmonious orchestration of space, and we realise that we are looking at the reflection of light.[22]

For Le Corbusier the flower, like its environment, was structured according to the mathematical laws of nature. It conformed to the same rules. It was in dialogue with the rest of nature, yet it remained an independent entity. To see a flower in relationship with nature was to see the 'reflection of light'. From his

16 Le Corbusier, *Decorative Art of Today*, p.13.
17 J.-A. Ramirez, *The Beehive Metaphor: From Gaudi to Le Corbusier*, London: Reaktion, 2000.
18 Le Corbusier, *Modulor 2*, London: Faber & Faber, 1955, p.205.
19 Le Corbusier, *The City of Tomorrow*, London: Architectural Press, 1946, p. 75.
20 Le Corbusier, *La Ville Radieuse*, Paris: Éditions de l'Architecture d'Aujourd'hui, 1935.
21 Le Corbusier, *Le Corbusier Talks with Students*, New York: Orion, 1961, p.27.
22 Le Corbusier, *New World of Space*, New York: Reynal & Hitchcock, 1948, p.7.

Left: 4.1
Symbol of the twenty-four-hour day.
Entrance stone, Unité Firminy-Vert.
Le Corbusier, 1959–67.

Below right: 4.2
Union of opposites. Detail from Le
Corbusier, *Le Poème de l'angle droit*,
Paris: Éditions Connivance, 1989,
p.35.

Above right: 4.3
Lecture room ceiling, Viipuri Public
Library. Aalto, 1928–35.

reading of Provensal, Le Corbusier would be aware of the links that the theologians of the Middle Ages made between God and light; it is therefore probable that he believed that the experience of radiance would bring man closer to the divine order at the heart of things.[23]

'The perfect object is a living organism, animated by the sense of truth … The object of truth radiates power. Between one object of truth and another, astonishing relationships develop.'[24] Le Corbusier believed radiant architecture would similarly impose its influence upon the surroundings. 'Effect of a work of art (architecture, statue or painting on its surroundings: waves, outcries, turmoil (the Parthenon on the Acropolis at Athens), lines spurting, radiating out as if produced by an explosion: the surroundings, both immediate and more distant, are stirred and shaken, dominated or caressed by it.'[25] Such radiant architecture would be connected with other edifices, both old and new, built in the same spirit and with the same sensitivity to geometry.

The notion of radiance implies the presence of energy. Certainly electricity was a very important theme in Le Corbusier's work, as can be deduced from his plans for *Le Poème électronique* for the Brussels World Fair of 1958. Le Corbusier included an image of an atomic bomb within sequence 5 of *Le Poème électronique* entitled 'How time moulds civilisation'. This followed on from images of aeroplanes and of radar dishes receiving messages from space, all forms of interconnection.[26]

Like one of Le Corbusier's favourite symbols, that of the twenty-four hour day (Fig. 4.1), the electricity wave is cyclical, it represents a flow of energy from positive to negative and back again.[27] Electricity could for this reason be used as a powerful and modern way in which to represent the oppositions central to the architect's ideas. The cross and arrow symbols that occur in 'outil', the final square of *Le Poème de l'angle droit* have been linked by Daphne Becket-Chary to the sexual symbols for man and woman, but they are also evocative of the positive and negative signs in electricity.[28]

23 Henry Provensal, *L'Art de demain*,
    Paris: Perrin, 1904, p.182, in
    Fondation Le Corbusier hereafter
    referred to as FLC.
24 Le Corbusier, *Decorative Art of Today*,
    p.192.
25 Le Corbusier, *Modulor 2*, p.26.
26 Le Corbusier, *Le Poème électronique*,
    Paris: Les Cahiers Forces Vives aux
    Éditions de Minuit, 1958,
    unpaginated.
27 'Cultiver le corps et l'esprit mettre
    dans des conditions favorables
    positive ou négative'. Le Corbusier,
    Sketchbooks Volume 2, London:
    Thames & Hudson, 1981, sketch
    503.
28 D. Becket-Chary, 'Le Corbusier's
    Poem of the Right Angle,' unpub.
    MPhil thesis, Cambridge, 1990.

Le Corbusier does seem to have made some connection between electricity and love. Men and women need each other but 'contact is impossible because the voltages are too different'.[29] Le Corbusier wrote of the Radiant City that: 'This prodigious spectacle has been produced by the interplay of two elements, one male, one female: sun and water. Two contradictory elements that both need the other to exist.'[30]

The buildings of the Radiant City would be designed around this idea of the union of opposites, male and female (Fig. 4.2), the idea being that they would encourage harmonious relationships between the men and women who lived in them. Key to Le Corbusier's vision of the healthy cell, the family, is the relationship between man and woman, 'the fundamental law of nature, the act of making love'.[31]

It was the giving and receiving of love, electricity, radiance that formed the basis for his symbol of the 'open hand', built as a monument at Chandigarh in the Punjab. In the harmonious world that Le Corbusier envisaged individual cells would be connected by a kind of invisible energy. 'The wave of architecture like a wave of electricity surrounds the earth and there are antennas everywhere.'[32]

Flexible Growth: A Model for a Modern Architecture

Whilst Aalto advocated the application of modern methods of production in architecture as a means of standardisation, he was wary of lifeless uniformity. 'Nature herself is the world's best standardisation committee, but in nature standardisation is practised almost exclusively in the smallest possible units, the cells ... Architectural standardisation must take the same path.'[33] Aalto found a flexible standardisation in the cells and tissues that he saw as the building components of which human life is composed. He believed that 'The blossoms on an apple tree are standardised, and yet they are all different. That is how we, too, should learn to build'.[34] The accommodation of human life could not be dealt with 'in a different way from biology's other units'.[35] His experiments in timber, in which he extrapolated the structure of the wood into sculptural form, and then applied it to furniture and architecture, illustrate this well (Figs. 2.6 and 2.7). This is especially evident where a sketch of one such experiment is juxtaposed with the generation of a building, as with Vuoksenniska Church (1955-9, Fig. 6.8), but the technique was apparent earlier in work such as the laminated ceiling at Viipuri Library (Fig. 4.3). Indeed, Strengell highlighted

29 Le Corbusier, *When the Cathedrals were White: A Journey to the Country of the Timid People*, New York: Reynal & Hitchcock, 1947, p.152.

30 Le Corbusier, *Radiant City*, p. 78.

31 Le Corbusier, *Precisions*, p.29.

32 Ibid., p.17.

33 Aalto, 'The Influence of Construction and Materials on Modern Architecture', 1938; repr. in Schildt, *Sketches*, p.60.

34 Aalto, 'Interview for Finnish Television', July 1972; repr. in Schildt, *Own Words*, p.271.

35 Aalto, 'Rationalism and Man', 1935, in Schildt, *Sketches*, p.47.

these important techniques at the time. 'Not only has Aalto discovered a new and original technique [for making furniture], but at the same time he has logically derived from it an equally new and original architectural form.'[36] Aalto himself wrote, 'Nature, biology, offers profuse and luxuriant forms; with the same constructions, same tissues and same cellular structures it can produce millions and millions of combinations each of which is an example of a high level of form. Human life comes from the same roots.'[37] Part of the outworking of this was the enthusiasm with which Aalto led the move to standardise materials and details in the Finnish construction industry, encouraging the availability of good-quality design and construction.[38] As will be demonstrated in Chapter 8, Aalto's deep personal belief in nature-inspired flexibility was practised in Baker House Dormitory (1946-9, Fig. 8.8) and Berlin Hansa Apartments (1955-7, Fig. 8.15), and was fine-tuned in Bremen (1958–62, Fig. 8.13).

As suggested earlier, Aalto's discussions with Gropius and Moholy-Nagy in the early 1930s influenced the development of his thinking about the place of nature in architecture. By the 1940s he went all out to challenge 'the views that ignore the importance of growth and internal variation in architecture',[39] suggesting that 'variety and growth reminiscent of natural organic life are the very essence of architecture'. He had come to believe that 'nature's variability' offered the 'only true style' – one that derived from the same root as human life, and that an essence of both is a richness that comes from constant change.[40] Indeed, Aalto observed this variability in vernacular building.[41] He was convinced that 'the physiological, social and psychological problems' faced in the modern era could be met with this flexible system rooted in 'the inner nature' of architecture that is 'a fluctuation and a development suggestive of natural organic life'.[42]

Aalto made repeated references to this thinking about the application of nature's 'endless variation of organically growing forms', suggesting that 'architectural standardisation must tread the same path'.[43] He felt that this approach would guarantee the creation of 'a wealth of nuances' that were vital to mental health.[44] In this way it may be said that his interest in nature and biology literally 'in-formed' (in other words gave form to) his work, becoming an analogy through which his artistic form grew.[45] This is not to suggest that he slavishly copied nature's forms, nor that he sought to represent nature.

In the mid-1950s Aalto began to concentrate on highlighting the dangers of inhibiting 'people's natural individuality and the natural variations of their surroundings',[46] criticising the growth of 'totally rootless airborne internationalism'.[47] By now he was confident enough to state that the solution, flexible standardisation, 'actually exists'. He then adopted the term 'humane standardisation', thus giving it a moral dimension, referring to it as a 'biological democracy'. Indeed, he sought to challenge the notion that 'established forms and uniformity' were the 'only way to achieve architectural harmony'.[48]

The contrast between Aalto's speech in London in 1950,[49] and his RIBA Gold Medal speech, 'The Architectural Struggle' in 1957 demonstrates the shift between his confidence in the modern experiment and the beginnings of a sense of despair. He opened his RIBA discourse by stating that 'There are only two

36 G. Strengell in *Helsingfors Journalen*, 1934, cited in Schildt, *Alvar Aalto: The Decisive Years*, New York: Rizzoli, 1986, p.84.

37 Aalto, '*Rationalism and Man*', 1935, in Schildt, *Sketches*, pp. 47–51.

38 Aalto led the standardisation committee of SAFA in the 1940s and 1950s. He sought to continue the work of Morris and Van de Velde (with whom Aalto's mentor Frosterus had worked) for improvement in the quality and design of mass-produced goods, and thus an increase in the spiritual quality of life. Standertskjöld suggests that in all his work he sought creative form that could comprise standard elements to exploit the true nature of the materials and the function. 'Alvar Aalto and Standardisation' and 'Alvar Aalto's Standard Drawings 1929–1932', in R. Nikula, M.-R. Norri and K. Paatero (eds), *The Art of Standards*, Acanthus, Helsinki: Museum of Finnish Architecture, 1992, pp. 74-84, and pp. 89–111.

39 Aalto, 'Influence of Construction', in Schildt, *Sketches*, pp. 60–3.

40 Ibid.

41 Aalto, 'Architecture of Karelia', 1941 in ibid., pp. 81–2.

42 Aalto, 'The Influence of Structure and Materials on Modern Architecture', 1938; repr. in Schildt, *Own Words*, p.101.

43 Aalto, 'Influence of Construction', in Schildt, *Sketches*, pp.60–3.

44 Aalto, 'The Reconstruction of Europe is the Key Problem of Our Time', *Arkkitehti*, 1941, 5, pp.75-80. Repr. in *Own Words*, pp.149–57.

45 Langer's definition of an image and a model offers a useful tool here. She suggests that a model shows 'how something works' and an image represents the overall, external form, not exemplifying the construction of the object it symbolises, but 'abstract[ing]' its phenomenal character'. Applied here, this might suggest that Aalto's composition techniques can be argued to have been modelled, to some extent, on the essence of natural cell growth: the process of becoming, while also imbibing something of natural

4.4
Atrium, Villa Väino. Indian ink and paint on pasteboard (242 x 136 mm). Aalto, 1926.

phenomena. Langer suggests that 'the creative symbol represents the tensions, rhythms and activities of the unfelt substructure of life'. S. K. Langer, *Mind: An Essay in Human Feeling*, Baltimore: John Hopkins University Press, 1988, p. xiii.

[46] Aalto, 'Art and Technology', Inauguration into Finnish Academy, 1955; repr. in Schildt, *Sketches*, p.129.

[47] Ibid.

[48] Aalto, 'The Architectural Struggle', RIBA 1957; repr. in Schildt, *Sketches*, p.147.

[49] Aalto, 'Finland Wonderland', Architectural Association London, 1950; repr. in Schildt, *Own Words*, pp.185-90.

[50] Aalto, 'Architectural Struggle', in Schildt, *Sketches*, p.146.

[51] Ibid., p.147.

[52] Ibid., p.146.

[53] Ibid., p.145.

[54] Le Corbusier, *Le Poème de l'angle droit*, Paris: Éditions Connivance, 1989, Section B3, 'Mind'.

[55] Aalto, 'National Planning and Cultural Goals', in Schildt, *Sketches*, p.100.

[56] Ibid.

[57] Aalto, 'From Doorstep to Living Room', *Aitta*, 1926; repr. in Schildt, *Own Words*, pp. 49–55.

[58] Le Corbusier, *Journey to the East*, Cambridge, MA: MIT Press, 1987, p.240.

things in art – humanity or its lack'. Although polemical, Aalto seems to have wanted to stake out his defensible ground, suggesting that his nature-inspired 'elastic standardisation' could and should be used for the benefit of humankind, not just economists, because it could 'raise the spirit too' with its 'human qualities'.[50] Flexible standardisation was therefore given a role in facilitating 'harmony with the human being and [being] organically fitted to the little man in the street'.[51] He offered a veiled reference to Le Corbusier, arguing that 'The search for a module [represents] the slavery of human beings to technical futilities that in themselves do not contain one piece of real humanity'.[52] When asked by a visitor 'What is the module of this office?' he was to reply 'one millimetre or less'.[53]

Atria and Annunciation: Extending Boundaries of Garden and Room

In Le *Poème de l'angle droit* Corbusier described a space fully open to the environment:

> Whole in itself
> Coming to terms with the terrain
> Open to the four horizons
> Lends its roof
> To the company of clouds
> Of azure or the stars [54]

He and Aalto shared a desire to integrate interior and exterior, thus bringing man closer to nature. This they sought to do in a number of different ways. One way in which Aalto was to extend this theme was by suggesting that the city should 'become part of the countryside'.[55] This should be 'a gradual path of development one step at a time, building cell by cell ... It is, after all, biology's and culture's own method of creation'.[56]

Courting Relations

The two men also sought out examples of buildings from the past where the relationship between exterior and interior was blurred. The atrium garden of the Pompeiian house was a specific source of inspiration for them both. In 'From Doorstep to Living Room', written in 1926, Aalto expounded many ideas about the relationship of architecture to nature, concentrating on the virtues of the atrium house as a mechanism for uniting 'the more intimate rooms with the open air', and drawing inside and outside together.[57] He had already practised these ideas in the Villa Väinö for his brother (Fig. 4.4) and the foyer of the Workers Cooperative building from the mid-1920s. For Le Corbusier the atrium house was similarly an exemplar of good architecture. He admired it for its order and for the subtle ways in which space and light were disposed within it.[58] He wrote of the peace and tranquillity of the Roman house, 'the open sky of the atriums' and the 'courtyards that were also partly gardens'. He noted that here each family would have 'trees, its flowers, its trickling fountain'.[59]

Aalto explained that in Finnish homes 'there is almost invariably something helpless and aesthetically impure about the way in which the interiors of the building opens outward', believing that the nature of the Nordic climate has been (but need not be) a stumbling block in this regard. He illustrated this point with Fra Angelico's *Annunciation* (c.1432–3; Fig. 4.5), suggesting that it held the truth about the nature of 'entering a room' and 'the trinity of human being, room and garden'.[60] Aalto believed that the painting's profundity lay in the way that it demonstrated the prominence of the human figure in the unity of room, external wall and garden. 'The garden (or courtyard) belongs to our home just as much as any of the rooms.' He affirmed the need to see the garden and interior as 'a closely knit organism', and the need to take 'the problem of form organically'.[61] Le Corbusier too was fascinated by the paintings of the early Renaissance, admiring in particular Piero della Francesca's *Flagellation* (c.1450–60), a blurring of internal and external space similar to that in the *Annunciation*.

4.5
Fra Angelico, *The Annunciation*, c.1432–3. Central panel.

Aalto actually illustrated his essay with Le Corbusier's Esprit Nouveau Pavilion as an example (Fig. 4.6), adding the caption, 'a brilliant example of the affinity of the home interior and garden'.[62] He went on to ask, 'is it a hall open to the exterior and taking its dominating character from the trees, or is it a garden built into the house, a garden room?'[63] Here the ambiguity is transformed into a plurality of meaning.

In 'The Architecture of Karelia', dated 1941, Aalto drew attention to the ways in which the vernacular form allows the analysis of 'human life's relationship to nature and shows how human life and nature harmonise'.[64] He said later that he did not have a feeling for folklore, but felt that 'the traditions

59 Le Corbusier, *Radiant City*, p.186.
60 Aalto, 'From Doorstep to Living Room' in Schildt, *Own Words*, p.50.
61 Ibid., p.52.
62 Ibid.
63 Ibid.
64 Aalto, 'The Architecture of Karelia', 1941, *Uusi Suomi*; repr. in Schildt, *Sketches*, pp.80–3.

4.6
Terrace garden, Esprit Nouveau
Pavilion. Le Corbusier, 1925.
Photograph from Le Corbusier and
Pierre Jeanneret, *Oeuvre Complète
Volume 1, 1910–1929*, Zürich: Les
Éditions d'Architecture, 1995.

[65] Conversation between Aalto and
Schildt, 1967, in ibid., p.171.

[66] Aalto, 'Architecture of Karelia'. This
is also addressed in S. Menin,
'Fragments from the Forest: Aalto's
Requisitioning of Forest, Place and
Matter', *Journal of Architecture*, 3,
2001, pp.279–305.

[67] Le Corbusier, *Une Maison – un
palais*, p.50.

[68] Aalto. 'From Doorstep to Living
Room' in Schildt, *Own Words*.
Aalto's italics.

that bind us lie more in the climate, in the material conditions, in the nature of
the tragedies and comedies that have touched us'.[65] He suggested that such
architecture has 'an affinity to nature' which was profoundly 'logical in its beauty',
countering the notion that such settlements were 'chaotically fragmented'.[66]

Le Corbusier was similarly enthusiastic about simple vernacular
architecture. For example, a simple timber house becomes the focus of his
attention in *Une Maison – un Palais*. Here he consciously uses the language of
nature to refer to the way in which such a house is 'planted' like a fig tree.[67]

Even at an early stage of his career Aalto wrote in terms of the
psychological functions, citing the importance of having a room that differs
from others, and that '*symbolises the open air under the home roof*',[68] such as a
spacious kitchen with an open fire and a rustic floor. He seemed to be calling for
the integration of elemental fundamentals into refined architecture. Similarly it
was Le Corbusier's desire to draw attention to the simple but sacred acts of life,
such as cooking and eating. To this end he made special efforts to include the
kitchen within the main living space of his later houses, usually with a view out
onto the landscape. When conducting a radio interview in the Unité Marseilles,
Le Corbusier spoke of the kitchen as 'the fire, the hearth, that is to say something

ancestral, that eternal thing which is the very key to everything'.[69] Although the kitchen was modern, built with the minimal efficiency of a ship's cabin, it retained this essential quality in Le Corbusier's mind.

In 'From Doorstep to Living Room' Aalto also likens the potential of 'the hall as an open-air space', wanting to minimise the contrast between the 'garden interior' and the 'outside hall'.[70] His main illustration for these ideas is the Pompeian Atrium house, in which 'the ceiling is the sky'. The outworking of this can be seen in the foyers of many of Aalto's later multipurpose buildings, such as Finlandia Hall, with its flowing internal piazza. Similarly a common topos in Le Corbusier's buildings is to access the cavernous hall space by walking beneath the pilotis. It seems that Le Corbusier believed this area was a cool, cave-like space pleasant to inhabit. In *Precisions* he described the area below the pilotis of the Villa Savoye as a cave.[71] The hall itself is often almost fully glazed to minimise the contrast between exterior and interior. This blurring of space can be seen with clarity in an image of the entrance of the Pavillon Suisse (1929–33) where two men sit just outside the hall smoking pipes in armchairs beneath the pilotis, looking out at the verdant view (Fig. 4.7).[72] Le Corbusier subtitled the image with the question 'What are these pilotis for?' The area beneath the curvaceous pilotis was thus an extension of the hall, both being interior/exterior spaces. This message was reinforced in the Pavillon Suisse by the presence of a large mural facing what Le Corbusier called the 'organic' stairs showing natural organisms on a vastly blown-up scale (Fig. 4.8).[73]

In 'From Doorstep to Living Room' Aalto does seem to have drawn on the recently published ideas of Le Corbusier in *Vers une architecture*. According to R.-L. Heinonen, Aalto is simply repeating Le Corbusier word for word here with, for instance, the Finn's 'raised interior' equating with Le Corbusier's 'atelier room'.[74] Schildt seeks to resist this notion, suggesting that Aalto was already influenced by Le Corbusier in a number of visual and concrete ways, but not necessarily in any theoretical issues.[75] Both men, Schildt argued, shared a general wish to do away with the barrier between inside and outside, but there is a distinct difference in their approach to this. Certainly Le Corbusier wanted external space to be conceived as an interior, with the sky as the ceiling, his roof garden rooms being one example. Aalto, on the other hand, desired that the outside should inhabit the interior of buildings, as is demonstrated, for example, in his use of internal piazza spaces. Incidentally there is a clear climatic justification for this distinction. Schildt believes these ideas are opposite, and lead to opposite results, accusing Le Corbusier's architectural logic of producing 'sterile rows of skyscrapers in *La Ville Radieuse*', as opposed to Aalto's freely flowing interiors.[76]

4.7
'What are these piloti's for?' Swiss Pavilion. Le Corbusier, 1929–33. From Le Corbusier and Jeanneret, *Oeuvre Complète Volume 2*, p.84.

4.8
Mural, Swiss Pavilion. Le Corbusier, 1929-33. From Le Corbusier and Jeanneret, *Oeuvre Complète Volume 2*, p.85.

[69] Translated from Pottecher, 'Que le Fauve soit libre dans sa cage', p. 62.
[70] Aalto, 'From Doorstep to Living Room' in Schildt, *Own Words*, p. 53.
[71] Le Corbusier, *Precisions*, p.138.
[72] Le Corbusier and Pierre Jeanneret, *Oeuvre Complète Volume 2*, 1929–34, Zürich: Les Éditions d'Architecture, 1995, p.84.
[73] Ibid., p.85.
[74] G. Schildt, *Alvar Aalto: The Early Years*, New York: Rizzoli, 1984, p.219. R.-L Heinonen, *Funktionalism läpimurto Suomessa*, 1986, Helsinki: Museum of Finnish Architecture, 1986.

Sun, Passion and Light

Aalto demanded that the natural energy of light and air must be brought directly into buildings. In 'The Dwelling as a Problem', from 1930, he addressed the issues close to both his and Le Corbusier's hearts. 'The biological conditions for human life are, among others, air, light and sun ... Each dwelling should be constructed so that it includes a usable outdoor space which biologically is equivalent to the nature man was accustomed to before the large cities developed.'[77] He continued, 'the sun is a source of energy' that should not remain unused, and promptly practised this in Paimio Sanatorium. In 'Rationalism and Man', 1935, he pursued this theme, concluding that 'we can in other words accept the criticism that much of rational lighting is inhumane'.[78] Aalto referred to the way the end of a building could twist, like a branch, towards the sun, demonstrating this during a meeting with his clients at MIT (Fig. 8.10) and then in built form (Fig. 8.8).[79] He developed many different techniques for getting natural light into the interior of buildings, be it through circular roof lights or sculpted into his clerestory windows that float like light-filled vessels.[80] Thus caught, light is brought into the dark northern expanses and is released to lighten the air's perpetual heaviness in winter. In this way Aalto begins to draw energy into the building as light, sky and air conjoin to enliven space, seasonally adjusting the cold air, as characters in the internal landscape.

Le Corbusier was well known for his rallying cry of 'sun, space, greenery' when attempting to convert his audience to the cause of the Radiant City. Indeed, the word 'radiant' was exemplified by that perfect conjunction of sun and sea, the Mediterranean.[81] Mary McLeod has noted that for the regional syndicalists, a group with which Le Corbusier was involved, the Mediterranean sun represented 'the essence of France's classical heritage; both rational thought and spiritual joy'.[82]

As well as providing vital illumination, the sun had an important symbolic role in Le Corbusier's work. Le Corbusier defined 'male' architecture as 'strong objectivity of forms, under the intense light of a Mediterranean sun', while 'female' architecture was described in terms of 'limitless subjectivity rising against a clouded sky', in other words, it was more nebulous.[83] His architecture became a marriage of these two opposites, in alchemical terms, a highly charged and erotic interplay intended to work upon the inhabitant through what he called 'a psycho-physiology' of the feelings.[84]

Le Corbusier's interest in ancient mysticism has been cited above, but here an explanation of sun and light in his architecture finds its most 'tangible' manifestation. Orpheus was closely linked to Apollo, god of the sun. Having journeyed into the underworld he acted as an intermediary between the dark and the light. According to Denis de Rougemont, a contemporary of Le Corbusier's involved in his scheme for La Sainte Baume (1945-62), Orphism 'syncretised all the myths of Night and Day', the soul was seen as 'divine or angelic, imprisoned in created forms – in terrestrial matter, which is Night'.[85] It is possible that Le Corbusier tried to symbolise the presence of Orpheus through exactly such use of light and darkness.[86] This may be why the architect chose to devote the first

75 Schildt describes how Aalto borrowed the drawing of the Acropolis from Le Corbusier's book in a number of layouts in the 1920s. Schildt, *Early Years*, pp. 214-30. Le Corbusier, *Towards a New Architecture*, p.43.

76 Schildt, *Early Years*, p.219–20.

77 Aalto, 'The Dwelling as a Problem', *Domus*, 1930; repr. in Schildt, *Sketches*, p.32.

78 Aalto, 'Rationalism and Man', in Schildt, *Own Words*, p. 91.

79 Aalto, 'Senior Dormitory M.I.T.', *Arkkitehti*, 4, 1950, p.64.

80 This is explored by various scholars, including W. Miller, 'Thematic Analysis of Alvar Aalto's Architecture', *A&U*, October 1979, pp.15-38, and C. Pianizzola, 'Sole e Tecnologia per una Architettura della Luce', Istituto Universitario Architettura Venezia, unpub. thesis, 1996.

81 Pearson has written of the significance of the word 'radiant' in terms of sound. C. Pearson, 'Le Corbusier and the Acoustical Trope', *Journal of the Society of Architectural Historians*, 56, 2, 1997, pp.168–83.

82 M. McLeod, 'Urbanism and Utopia: Le Corbusier from Regional Syndicalism to Vichy', Dphil thesis, Princeton, 1985, p.245.

83 Le Corbusier, *Modulor*, p.224.

84 Ibid., p.113. See a discussion of G.T. Fechner's experimental work in 'psychophysics' and its influence on Le Corbusier in J. Loach, 'Le Corbusier and the Creative Use of Mathematics', *British Journal of the History of Science*, 31, 1998, p.196.

85 D. de Rougemont, *Passion and Society*, London: Faber & Faber, 1958, p.64.

86 Letter Trouin to Le Corbusier, 27 December 1960, FLC 13 01 189.

square of the iconostasis of *Le Poème de l'angle droit*, a series of lithographs and text written between 1947 and 1953 (Fig. 4.9), to a rendition of his symbol of the twenty-four hour day, an image of the line made by the sun as it tracks above and below the horizon (Fig. 4.1). A similar image occupies a full-page spread in Section A1 of *Milieu*. It is accompanied by these words:

> The sun master of our lives
> far off indifferent
> He is the visitor – an overlord
> he enters our house …
> Punctual machine turning
> since time immemorial
> engenders every instant of the
> Twenty-four hours cycle the gradation
> the nuance the imperceptible
> almost providing
> a rhythm. Yet brutally
> he breaks it twice –
> morning and evening. Continuity
> is his but he
> imposes an alternative –
> night and day – these two phases
> rule our destiny: a sun rises
> a sun sets
> a sun rises anew[87]

Although the sun could shine all the time he chooses to 'impose an alternative'. He has some reason in bringing about a state of darkness. There is a necessity for a balance of dark and light within the cosmos.

Fritz Griffiths and Marietta Millet have suggested that the *brise soleil* played an important role in Le Corbusier's architecture, not only because it controlled lighting levels but because it had a symbolic function.[88] Like the horizon line in his diagram of the twenty-four-hour day it was a place where sun met shadow. The brise soleil would thus act as a reminder to the inhabitants of the building of the need to balance such oppositions within their own lives. Le Corbusier sculpted an image of the twenty-four-hour day into the entrance stones for his Unités (Fig. 4.1) and extrapolated these into façade reliefs (Plate 27).

Mater, Matter and Materials

Aalto often demonstrated his basic premise of human dominion over nature, and his belief that culture enhanced the natural realm of being. 'Sometimes, however, we feel that we do not have enough pure nature at our disposal, and then we try to plant the beauty of the wilds at our very doors. In fact we should apply the opposite principle, starting with the environment we live in, and adding our buildings to it, to the improvement of the original landscape.'[89]

[87] Le Corbusier, *Le Poème de l'angle droit*, section A1, 'Milieu'.
[88] F. Griffin and M. Millet, 'Shadey Aesthetics', *Journal of Architectural Education*, 37/3, 4, 1984, pp.43-60.
[89] Aalto, 'Architecture in the Landscape of Central Finland', *Sisä-Suomi*, 28 June 1925 repr. in Schildt, *Own Words*, p.21.

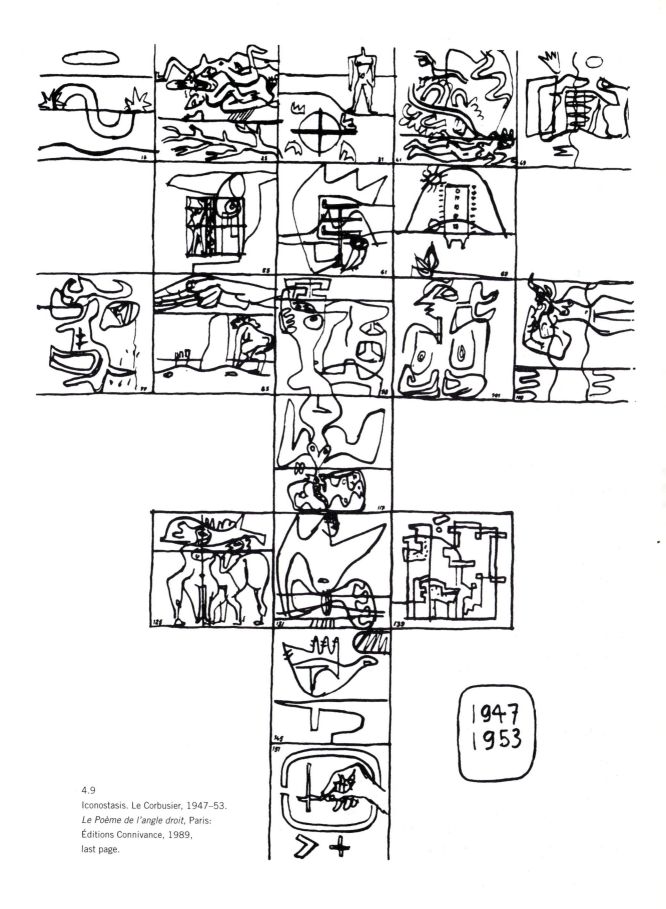

4.9
Iconostasis. Le Corbusier, 1947–53.
Le Poème de l'angle droit, Paris:
Éditions Connivance, 1989,
last page.

For both Aalto and Le Corbusier it seems there was a feeling that nature needed to be mediated by the architect in order to attain its full potential.

Mother Earth, Mind and Body

This issue of the placing of buildings was one of the first Aalto raised in his early writing.[90] Accepting that 'nature' was no longer untouched, but rather 'the combination of human efforts and the original environment',[91] he wondered what makes medieval churches 'be in total harmony with their surroundings'.[92] He suggested that this sympathy with the landscape results from the handcrafted surfaces, the purity of building materials, the simple lines that harmonise with the landscape, and the ageing process.[93] In this way, he believed, the building creates a 'mood' – it reaches out to us. Aalto felt that a degree of 'tact' was needed in dealing with any environment into which new buildings were to be placed.[94] A natural permission to age was crucial to this thinking, being manifest in the creation of prematurely ruinous elements that root his buildings in their context.

Aalto also associated the theme of *Sterben und Werden* (dying and becoming), discussed above, with the notion of the 'city as a growing organism', calling for 'an elastic system for orchestrating the city's growth in all its different forms'.[95] Such ideas suggest that he saw a continuum between human creations and other natural forms in the landscape as in his early call, to 'build naturally'.[96] In Italy, although 'not an inch of ground remains intact', there is no lack of 'scenic beauty'.[97] The problem is not a matter of 'nature conservation' or a return to the wilderness, but rather it is a matter of culture (and taste) and understanding about man's relationship to nature. Aalto believed that the essence of beauty lay in this. Often this led to him creating new landscapes with and in the building, as a sketch of the conception of Viipuri Library (Fig. 6.2) and the Main Building at Otaniemi (Fig. 4.10) demonstrate. This idea is also manifest in exaggerated form in the detailing of how buildings touch the earth or rock, as demonstrated in the basement entrance to Villa Mairea (Fig. 7.20).

A similar tension can be found in Le Corbusier's work. He too wrote in terms of 'aiding' not 'blotting out' the landscape through the subtle introduction of building, for example through the introduction of a vast circular housing scheme at La Sainte Baume in Provence.[98] It has been seen that for Le Corbusier radiant buildings would be connected with other edifices, both old and new, built in the same spirit and with the same sensitivity to geometry. Furthermore, architecture could be 'made radiant' through the use of the Modulor.[99] By introducing an edifice built according to the tenets of nature it may be that he thought he would be drawing attention to her laws.

> Only the architect can strike a balance between man and his environment (man = a psycho-physiology; his environment = the universe, nature and cosmos).
>
> The physical universe is reflected in technics. These are the conquests of man, gained by the subtlety and astuteness of man refusing to accept defeat in the midst of cosmic and natural events which are

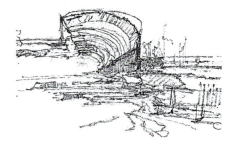

4.10
Perspective sketch of main building, Helsinki University of Technology, Otaniemi. Pencil on paper, 300 x 443 mm. Aalto, 1955-64.

90 Aalto, 'Motifs from Times Past', *Arkkitehti*, 1922; repr. in Schildt, *Sketches*, pp. 1–2.
91 Aalto, 'Architecture in the Landscape of Central Finland', in Schildt, *Own Words*, p.21.
92 Aalto, 'Motifs from Times Past'.
93 Ibid., p.1.
94 Aalto, 'Housing Construction in Existing Cities', *Byggmästaren*, 1930; repr. in Schildt, *Sketches*, p.5.
95 Ibid., p.6.
96 Aalto, 'The Temple Baths on Jyväskylä Ridge', *Keskisuomalainen*, 22 January 1925; repr. in Schildt, *Own Words*, pp. 17–19. See also Aalto, 'Architecture in the Landscape of Central Finland', in Schildt, *Own Words*, pp. 21–2.
97 Aalto, 'Architecture in the Landscape of Central Finland', in Schildt, *Own Words*, p.21.
98 Le Corbusier, *Oeuvre Complète Volume 5*, 1946–1952, Zürich: Les Éditions d'Architecture, 1995, p.36.
99 Le Corbusier, *Modulor 2*, p.306.

relentless and indifferent to his fate. The choice lies between the life of a shepherd vegetating amongst his flocks (a life which may not be devoid of greatness) and participation in a machine civilization, the function of which is to bring about a simple and all powerful harmony through action, courage, daring, invention and direct participation.[100]

In Le Corbusier's work there seems to be an uneasiness about nature in her profoundest or most wild sense. He was fully aware of 'the indifference of natural forces to man'.[101] Like the women in his paintings (Plate. 6), nature could be both uncanny and disturbing, out of control. Simultaneously he adored and was in awe of the mystical and material reality of each.

Aalto wrote repeatedly of the need to come down to earth: 'the more we occupy ourselves with these purely theoretical games … the more we forget Mother Earth, where man, after all, had his habitat and where happiness – in any case the temporal – is to be created'.[102] Le Corbusier believed it necessary to create a balance between the bodily and the spiritual. It was for this reason that he admired the sixteenth-century writer François Rabelais who symbolised 'the right angle', that which 'interests the body, the soul and the gut of man'.[103] That Le Corbusier associated nature with the body in this case seems likely. The balance between the two is one of the central themes in Le Poème de l'angle droit:

> Erect on the terrestrial plain
> Of things knowable you sign a pact of solidarity
> With nature: this is the right angle[104]

The horizontal line of the terrestrial plane forms a right angle with the line linking us to the sky.

Aalto believed that 'immediate contact with nature' enriches life and addresses the social and psychological factors facing architecture.[105] Yet he also recognised that not only mechanisation, but human actions themselves 'estrange us from nature'.[106] The architect's task is therefore one of mediation as well as creation – 'to make our life patterns more sympathetic'.[107]

Forest, Tree and Timber: The Matter of Material Culture

The work of both Aalto and Le Corbusier is full of physical or metaphysical references to trees. One difference between Aalto and Le Corbusier is evident in their treatment of trees. Le Corbusier described the tree as a 'magnificent symbol', inadvertently revealing the extent to which he dwelt upon the meaning rather than the experience of natural phenomena.[108] Mary Seckler has traced the role of the tree in Le Corbusier's early work where it appears in abstracted form, for example in the balconies of the Villa Fallet.[109] (Fig. 2.2) Le Corbusier built his architecture around trees, for example in the Esprit Nouveau Pavilion, largely it seems to make a point about the connection between his building and nature. Instructions for how to plant a tree appear in the frontispiece of The Radiant City (Fig. 4.11). The tree appears again at the front of Conversations with Students. Le Corbusier refers to the cross at Ronchamp as a tree. Both the tree and the leaf recur as important symbols in his work.

[100] Le Corbusier, Modulor, p.111.

[101] Le Corbusier, When the Cathedrals were White, p.116.

[102] Aalto, 'The Architect's Concept of Paradise', 1957; repr. in Schildt, Sketches, p. 158.

[103] Le Corbusier, Sketchbooks Volume 3, 1954–1957, Cambridge, MA: MIT Press, 1982, sketches 645-6.

[104] Le Corbusier, Le Poème de l'angle droit, section A3, 'Milieu'.

[105] Aalto, 'Building Heights as a Social Problem', Arkkitehti, 1946; repr. in Schildt, Sketches, pp. 92–3. Aalto suggested that psychological factors should be taken into consideration by planners in their siting of public buildings. 'Town Planning and Public Buildings', 1966; repr. in Schildt, Sketches, pp. 166–7.

[106] Aalto, 'Between Humanism and Materialism', 1955; repr. in Schildt, Sketches, p.131.

[107] Ibid., p.132.

[108] Le Corbusier, Le Corbusier Talks with Students, p.83.

[109] M.P. May Seckler, 'Le Corbusier, Ruskin, the Tree and the Open Hand' in R. Walden (ed.) The Open Hand, Cambridge, MA: MIT Press, 1982, pp.42–96.

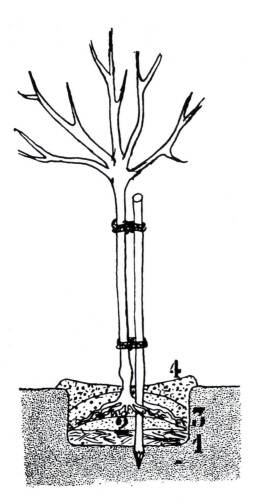

To plant a tree well: 1. good earth and basic manure
2. a covering of fine soil
3. very fine vegetable earth
4. subsoil and fertilizer

In order to pinpoint the meaning of the tree for Le Corbusier it is necessary to turn again to the writings of Teilhard de Chardin, for whom the tree symbolised the process of evolution. Teilhard saw this whole process as one which man should feel a part of, one that man should engage in, recognising what has passed and what goes on ahead, one that man should admire in an act of 'quasi-adoration'. At the heart of the process is a feeling of 'sympathy ... of each separate element for all that is most unique and incommunicable in each of the co-elements with which it converges in the unity, not only of a single act of vision but of a single living subject',[110] the idea being that here at the end of the process we will be 'divinised' through 'access to some supreme Centre of universal convergence'.[111] The fundamental issue of importance is that man, and indeed all matter, contains a fragment of the divine.

Whilst Le Corbusier was evidently aware of the pleasant shady quality of trees, their experiential or material qualities do not seem to have been foremost in his mind. The same cannot be said for Aalto, who seems to revisit the sentient experience of wood, trees and the forest in his work, as well as seeking to replicate something of ad hoc forest geometry. Wood also represents Aalto's reaction to Modernism, in that it is not steel or concrete. Simultaneously it

4.11
Drawing showing 'how to plant a tree'. Le Corbusier, *The Radiant City*, London: Faber, 1967.

[110] P. Teilhard de Chardin, *The Future of Man*, London: Collins, 1964, p.135.
[111] Ibid., p.136.

indicated a spiritual closeness to nature whilst providing haptic warmth. Wood connotes variety and flexibility, compared to the sterility and coldness of modern materials, which Aalto considered to be somehow less humane.

Indeed, Aalto was soon to lead Modernism into the forest in search of the abundant physical substance and the rich archetypal symbolism of wood (Fig. 4.2), not necessarily because he had taken on nationalist or right-wing sentiments, but because it was in that realm that he felt most at home. Although, as cited, he had initially reacted against the status quo (in other words Saarinen), Aalto's desire to encourage natural growth to literally imbibe the very conception of his designs is a return rather than a revolution.

While wary of technology, believing that what had 'originally' been 'a physical guarantee of freedom' had come to restrict humankind, Aalto believed nature to be a lasting symbol of freedom. As such, it should form a basis for architecture.[112] It was for this reason that he turned to wood, which had long 'protected' folk from the powerful forces of nature, be it wolf or biting snow,[113] using it this time to protect humankind from the progress of rational Modernism and technology. Such ideas are central to his scheme for Muuratsalo, discussed in Chapter 5.

For Aalto it appears that the importance of nature grew from its capacity to lend form to architecture, through the example of cellular growth, its material impact upon the built environment, and its capacity to maintain and even enrich life in the psychological realm. Wood was central to these ideas; its 'biological characteristics, its limited heat conductivity, its kinship with man and living nature, the pleasant sensation to the touch it gives', all suggest it as a suitable material through which to design a sympathetic world.[114] Generally he did not build wooden buildings, but utilised the semantic richness of wood to enliven his architecture. Thus wood, like his 'wave', became a trope for the individuality of his buildings and indeed his mind, as well as for their yearning for something natural amidst the new forms and materials of the modern epoch.

Aalto knew that material nature, what he called 'Mother Earth', such as the forests around Jyväskylä, could be environments of unencumbered emotional personal space that offered a realm of security and safety. This is close to Winnicott's Potential Space, a psychological place without impingements, where unprocessed feelings may be experienced.[115] It seems that Aalto instinctively knew that such nature-contact could be a substitute neo-maternal environment.[116] He even invited the exploration of a progression from the Latin *mater* (mother, maternal love or origin) to *materia* (wood, timber, matter, reason, or cause) – from mother to matter and material – in an interview with Karl Fleig in the late 1960s. He went on to explain his notion of 'materia'.

> ... it translates purely material activity into the related mental process.
>
> The principles of human civilisation are largely based on *materia* ... Matter is a link. It has the effect of making unity ... The links in *material* leave open every opportunity for harmonious synthesis ... Wood is the natural material closest to man ... readily available, not merely for constructive purposes but also for psychological and biological ones ... Wood is more a biological material than a rustic one.[117]

[112] Aalto, 'Finland as a Model for World Development' 1949; repr. in Schildt, *Own Words*, p.171.

[113] Aalto, 'The Housing Problem', 1930 in ibid., p.80.

[114] Aalto, 'Wood as a Building Material', *Arkkitehti-Arkkitekten*, 1956; in Schildt, *Sketches*, p.142.

[115] D.W. Winnicott, *Playing and Reality*, Harmondsworth: Penguin, 1971, p.108.

[116] Environmental philosophers have examined this for some time. Specific attitudes to nature amongst Finns have also been widely analysed. Amongst these are A. Reunala, 'The Forest and the Finns', in M. Engman *et al. People, Nation, State*, London: Hurst, 1989, pp. 38–56 and 'The Forest as an Archetype', in special issue of *Silva Fennica*, 'Metsä suomalaisten Elämässä', 21 April 1987, p.426.

[117] Aalto, 'The Relationship between Architecture, Painting and Sculpture', in B. Hoesli, (ed.) *Alvar Aalto, Synopsis: Painting Architecture Sculpture*, Zürich: Birkhäuser, 1980, p.25. Also in Schildt, *Own Words*, pp.265-9.

Aalto consciously associated natural materials, and the process of making, with the processes of thought that grow into a society and civilisation. By highlighting the correlation with psychology and biology Aalto also drew his ideas deeper, in a manner that seems to yoke his personal experiences to the nature of his architecture.

In the same context Aalto stated that, in his opinion, materials 'need a long testing period to become effective in human civilisation ... Modern architecture does not mean the use of immature new materials: the main thing is to refine materials in a more humane direction'.[118] To this end he rejected steel in furniture design, suggesting that such 'wrongness lies in the fact that the rationalism does not go deep enough ... steel and chromium surfaces are not satisfactory from the human point of view'.[119] This position was, in part, based on his understanding of the physical and psychological nature of comfort, and generated many of his details. 'It is from those little things that we should build a harmonious world for people,' he observed.[120]

Aalto saw wood as 'a living material, produced by growing fibres, something like the human muscular system'[121] – hence the experiments with wood from the mid-1930's described in Chapter 2, in which he discovered wood's capacity for variation and nuance that fitted with his philosophy of architecture (Fig. 2.6). 'Wood will no doubt maintain its position as the most important material for sensitive architectural details', he argued, emphasising its value 'psychologically'.[122] Again Aalto demonstrated the theme of the psycho-physical, associating nature with psychologically ameliorating phenomena. He wanted to bring the processes of architecture into line with other aspects of the natural human experience by linking these processes with other phenomena of biological life. He strongly believed that such closeness to nature reintroduced and then guaranteed the freedom that technology had offered but had failed to produce.[123] He also believed that it might give fresh inspiration in terms of both form and construction.[124]

Le Corbusier similarly used materials in a conscious attempt to create a feeling of unity with nature, even experimenting with earth building as at La Sainte Baume. Grass roofs and roof gardens would make the inhabitants of a building feel that they were living under and within the very earth itself – something both he and Aalto had experimented with in houses in the 1930s, as Chapter 7 will demonstrate . Timber played a central role in the interiors of his later buildings, as panelling or as a palimpsest leaving its imprint in the rough concrete. Concrete, for him, was a 'material of the same rank as stone, wood or baked earth'. He added that the 'experience is of importance. It seems to be really possible to consider concrete as a reconstructed stone' – in other words, as a natural material equivalent to earth.[125]

For Le Corbusier 'rusticity of materials would in no way hamper a clear plan and a modern aesthetic'.[126] He described traditional materials such as brick and timber, used extensively from 1935 in the Petit Maison de Weekend, as 'friends of man', suggesting that they would act upon him in some beneficial way (Fig. 7.12). He emphasised the fact that both concrete and whitewash had their origins in ground stone, a natural material.[127] 'I will create beauty by

[118] Aalto, 'The Relationship', in Schildt, *Own Words*, pp. 268–9.

[119] Aalto, 'The Humanising of Architecture', *Technology Review*, 1940; repr. in Schildt, *Sketches*, p.77.

[120] Aalto, 'The Architectural Struggle', in ibid., p.147.

[121] Aalto, 'The Relationship' in Schildt, *Own Words*, p.268.

[122] Aalto, 'Wood as a Building Material', in Schildt, *Sketches*, p.142.

[123] Aalto, 'National Planning', in ibid., p.101.

[124] Aalto, 'Experimental House, Muuratsalo', *Arkkitehti – Arkitekten*, 1953, in ibid., p.116.

[125] Le Corbusier, *Oeuvre Complète Volume 5*, p.190.

[126] Le Corbusier and P. Jeanneret, *Oeuvre Complète Volume 2*, p.48.

[127] 'The experience is of importance. It seems to be really possible to consider concrete as a reconstructed stone.' Le Corbusier, *Oeuvre Complète Volume 5*, p.190.

contrast, I will find the opposite element, I will establish a dialogue between the rough and the finished, between precision and accident, between the lifeless and the intense and in this way I will encourage people to observe and reflect.'[128] The detailing of the building would thus be used to create an opportunity for a lesson on the meaning and resolution of oppositions in people's own lives.

Internal Conflict and the Union of Opposites

Most of Aalto's lectures and essays move quickly to questions of taming technology in order to address the realm beyond physical problems, dwelling on the places where human psychological or physical experience generates practical problems, 'a combination of technical, physical and psychological phenomena, never one of them alone'.[129] For example, he cited his personal experience of the problem of glare as a bed-ridden patient.[130] He constantly referred to the 'struggle' for 'synthesis' – and it is no accident that he repeatedly wrote in embattled terms.

The process of imbuing architecture with the phenomena of nature seems to have provided both men with some sort of inner psychological equilibrium as their creative careers intensified and matured. Their work was increasingly orientated towards the phenomena of nature as they construed it. Aalto, for one, sought to manifest such an equilibrium between the psychological processes of creativity in design and the biological creations observed in nature – that process of 'building cell by cell'.[131] Indeed, in his obituary of Asplund, in 1940, Aalto took the chance to celebrate the association between the psychological and emotional well being of humans with experiences of nature and natural resources. He described how the Swede 'proved that the art of architecture continues to have inexhaustible resources and means which flow directly from nature and the inexplicable reactions of human emotions'.[132] Le Corbusier wrote that creativity was 'a profound primordial function' which 'animates even the lowest cell of organic life'.[133] Aalto echoed his words with his call for an architecture that would demonstrate the processes of growth and change inherent in nature, 'biology's and culture's own method of creation'.[134]

When he sought to explain his design process in 'The Trout and the Mountain Stream', Aalto addressed the perennial problem of how to attain a sense of unity in architecture, citing Italy as 'the classical source of unity'.[135] He made it clear that he was aware of how any such unity was made up of many small reconciliations. Again and again we see him making reference to the nuances and intricacies of human life. In his opinion too many small oppositions between different architectural elements 'unite to become psychological problems' or 'internal frictions'.[136] Thus he moved swiftly to his own attempts to delve into his subconscious, while designing to calm 'the quarrelling sub-problems'.[137] Indeed, the role he assigned to 'instinct' in this article may be read as his experience of his inner drive. He wrote of creative work 'based on the knowledge and the data that we have stored in our subconscious'.[138] Here Aalto was discussing the continuing human creativity to which Winnicott alludes, since although the subject is architecture, the process

[128] Ibid.

[129] Aalto, 'Humanising of Architecture', in Schildt, *Sketches*, p.78.

[130] Aalto, 'Rationalism and Man', in ibid., p.49, and 'Humanising Architecture', in ibid., p.77.

[131] Aalto, 'National Planning', in ibid., p.100.

[132] Aalto, 'E.G. Asplund in Memoriam', *Arkkitehti*, 1940, in ibid., p.67.

[133] Le Corbusier, *Decorative Art of Today*, p.192.

[134] Aalto, 'National Planning', in Schildt, *Sketches*, p.100.

[135] Aalto, 'The Trout and the Mountain Stream', *Domus*, 1947 in ibid., p.96.

[136] Ibid., p.96.

[137] Ibid., p.97.

[138] Ibid., p.97.

is creativity. As a psychological activity the process of creativity lays down traces of itself in the psyche, and therefore it is also a process of psychological growth. Aalto likened his work to the creation of abstract art, which he describes as a process of 'crystallisation' that can only be grasped 'intuitively' by the subconscious.

In 1955 Le Corbusier wrote of his own design process in the pamphlet *Textes et dessins pour Ronchamp*. On being given a design problem to solve, his first step was to store it in his 'memory' and not allow himself to make any sketches for months.

> The human brain is made in such a way that it has a certain independence: it is a box into which one can pour in bulk the elements of a problem and let them float, simmer, ferment.
>
> Then one day, a spontaneous initiative of one's inner being takes shape, something clicks; you pick up a pencil, a stick of charcoal, some colouring pencils (colour is the key to the process), and give birth onto the paper: out comes the idea.[139]

Le Corbusier described the process of making the initial design for the chapel at Ronchamp in the biological terms of 'gestation' and then 'giving birth upon the page', commandeering the language of female procreativity for his cause. It may be that in so doing he drew upon the ideas of Plato who wrote of 'poets and artists' as 'souls that are pregnant ... with wisdom and virtue'. Plato's opinion that children produced in this way would be 'fairer and more immortal [sic]' than mortal offspring may have been in Le Corbusier's mind when he wrote in this way.[140] Alternatively it could simply be that he wanted to emphasise the fact that the process of giving birth to an idea was a natural biological function.

The trauma Aalto suffered in childhood was to re-emerge, resulting in repeated bouts of hypochondriacal illness and even episodes of psychosis.[141] The themes of his work, such as the careful relation of opposites, may have evolved in response to such internal conflicts. Indeed, Schildt describes how, 'One of Aalto's most striking characteristics was his adaptability and sensitivity to the psychological climate of his surroundings',[142] perhaps rooted in his own sensitivity to the aftermath of his mother's death and the various needs of those affected within the home. Aalto seems to have turned this round to become a mechanism to ensure empathy and manifest his humanism – 'ausser sich gehen' as he put it, borrowing from Goethe's expression regarding the need to see things from another's viewpoint.[143]

Le Corbusier's conception of the relationship of opposites, already cited, was at the heart of his interest in Orphism; a key mechanism by which he contrived to address the 'gap'. Le Corbusier was, after all, not blind in his pursuit of unity. In fact he seems to have recognised the futility of the task, portraying himself as Don Quixote tilting at windmills on a quest in the name of his idealised lady, nature (courtly love exercised a particular fascination for the architect). When flying over the earth in an aeroplane he was to observe that the horizon line, an essential element of his symbolic repertoire, was not straight, as in his stylised version, but curved. He knew that there were problems with his theories, but he wanted to believe in them. Paradoxically it was the tension

[139] Le Corbusier, *Textes et dessins pour Ronchamp*, Paris: Forces Vives, 1955, unpaginated.

[140] Plato, *Symposium*, in S. Buchanan (ed.) *The Portable Plato*, Harmondsworth: Penguin, 1997, p.168.

[141] The psychiatrist Yrjö Alanen, Aalto's son in law, describes Aalto's mental state of mind in G. Schildt, *Alvar Aalto: The Mature Years*, New York: Rizzoli, 1992, p. 14.

[142] G. Schildt, *Alvar Aalto: The Decisive Years*, New York: Rizzoli, 1986, p.103.

[143] Aalto, 'Speech for the Centenary of Jyväskylä Lyceum', 1958; repr. in Schildt, *Sketches*, p.163.

between these two viewpoints, that of belief and non-belief in the cause of unity, that was central to his creativity and his cause.

Such a tension between opposing phenomena arose repeatedly in Le Corbusier's thinking. For instance, he devised a further law based on his observations of nature: the Law of the Meander (Fig. 4.12). This law, in many ways equivalent to that of the twenty-four-hour day, pertains to water, the feminine opposite to the sun in Le Corbusier's terms. Peter Carl observes that the 'parable' of the meander 'is one manifestation of his conception of the sea as the destiny of all things, and that from which new things will appear'.[144] Instead of tracking the path of the sun here Le Corbusier tracks the path of a river as it erodes looping meanders from 'left to right' through the earth, becoming increasingly sinuous. Suddenly 'at the most desperate moment' there comes a point where the curves meet – 'Miracle!'– and the water breaks through, creating a straight line once more. For Le Corbusier this was a metaphor for the way in which the solution to a problem will suddenly become apparent. 'It is a paradox,' he was to observe.[145] This description calls to mind Aalto's own explanation of his creative process: 'Great ideas arise from the small details of life; they spiral out of the earth.'[146]

4.12
Law of the meander. From Le Corbusier, *Précisions sur un état présent de l'architecture et de l'urbanisme*, Paris: Crès, 1930, p.142.

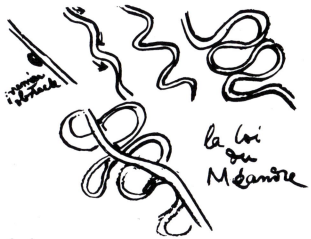

Conclusion

Not only was nature a suitable model for architecture, it was, for Aalto and Le Corbusier, a model for the very act of creativity itself, a continuing act of creation in and of themselves. In this chapter we have seen that the two men thought of their designs as products of an organic process. Drawing upon Orphic ideas, Le Corbusier turned to geometry in an attempt to reinforce this link between his creations and those of nature, to make them radiant, like the living molecules of the universe. Aalto meanwhile used nature as a model for his process of flexible standardisation, utilising nature's laws to justify his interest in variety and responsiveness. Both felt strongly the need to break down the barriers between home and the environment and to draw attention to the essential pleasures of nature through the careful manipulation of light, space and materials, using examples of ancient and vernacular architecture to justify their cause. This is a theme that will be developed in the following chapters.

[144] P. Carl, 'Ornament and Time: A Prolegomena', *AA Files*, 23, 1992, p.55.
[145] Le Corbusier, *Precisions*, pp.142–3.
[146] Aalto, 'Culture and Technology', *Suomi-Finland* – USA, 1947; repr. in Schildt, *Sketches*, p.94.

Chapter 5

The Mysticism of Nature and the Agony of Life: Cap Martin and Muuratsalo

It is important at this stage in the exploration of nature in the lives and works of Le Corbusier and Aalto to examine the personalities of the two men and the ways in which they coped during the Second World War. This was a period of great tension and professional frustration from which both were to emerge emotionally scarred. Indeed, it may be no coincidence that at around this time both men decided to build personal retreats, Le Corbusier at Cap Martin and Aalto at Muuratsalo. Ostensibly small and simple schemes, each represents, in concentrated form, the essence of their ideas about nature. A close examination of these buildings draws into the public realm aspects of their personality and motivation that would otherwise have remained veiled. At this time the two men sought to withdraw more often from society, assuaging the agony of life with regular immersions in the mysticism of nature.

All but Manic Zeal

The path from their humble beginnings to respected international creative figures is complex but important. So far we have addressed the accumulation of ideas and influences towards their creative maturity, but to this must be added important aspects of their personalities. This will assist in understanding Aalto and why Le Corbusier felt compelled to create and find architectural philosophies focusing upon nature as an agent of integration.

An Inner Force and the Question of Work

From unstable beginnings both men developed an immense motivation to prove themselves. In 'Mise au point' Le Corbusier wrote, 'Everything is a question of perseverance, of work, of courage ... There are no glorious signs in heaven. But courage is an inner force, which alone can justify or not justify existence.'[1] Working determinedly to justify himself to the end was a difficult and at times lonely mission, as can be seen by his description of painting as 'a duel between the artist and himself with the battle taking place within, inside and unknown to the outside world'.[2] He refused to let his wife Yvonne have any children because he was worried that his 'life would be very hard as an architect'. It may be that he felt that children would present too much of a responsibility and a burden, preventing him from getting on with his work.[3] Citing a similar drive, Schildt reports that Aalto was so 'obsessed with his need or desire to create that anything that might hinder his work aroused distaste'.[4] Yet in response to this all but manic zeal, Aalto often collapsed physically and mentally and was incapable of creative work.[5] In terms of his family Aalto simply did not let his children interfere, and although he enjoyed intense 'play' with them on occasions, he sought to force them into moulds which, sadly, were ill-fitting.[6]

Feelings of depression about their achievements and the lack of recognition of their greatness dogged both men. Le Corbusier seems not to have become actually ill like Aalto, although he was weighed down by the lack of recognition more regularly.[7] On occasion, during his early career, he ran from Paris to his brother when things became too difficult.[8] Later in life he wrote complaining letters, an example being one to his mother dated 1954, saying that he felt 'vile and low'.[9] He had the presence of his mother with him for much longer than Aalto, since his mother lived to be 101, dying in 1960, only five years before Le Corbusier himself. His brother, Albert outlived him. Aalto, on the other hand, who grew from childhood tragedy rather than clear on-going familial dysfunction, would embroider threads of his past into a glowing mantle. This was a successful mechanism for self-maintenance until the mantle fell, as he slipped repeatedly into depression, illness or even psychosis.

Although the extent of the adult psychopathology of each man is difficult to determine with precision, that both Aalto and Le Corbusier exhibited episodes of great drive, verging, on occasions, on manic behaviour, and then suffered from periods of great depression is generally accepted. Such driven, overactive behaviour renders a person elated, often in denial of obstacles, and suffering from illusions of grandeur that inevitably collapse.

Acceptance and the Prophecy of Love

Le Corbusier was profoundly shocked when esteemed persons failed to show him the respect and attention he felt he was due. He was, for example, surprised and annoyed by the fact that his employer Peter Behrens acted like an employer, rather than a father figure, with no inclination to offer help or bestow affection on the newest employee in his office. Le Corbusier wrote, 'he only knows how to terrorise us, and we find no concern, no affection'.[10]

When he designed a boat with which to access his retreat at Muuratsalo Aalto called it 'Nemo Propheta in Patria' – a prophet is never recognised in his own land, an opinion with which Le Corbusier would have concurred. Generally,

[1] Le Corbusier, 'Mise au Point', in I. Žaknić, *The Final Testament of Père Corbu*, New Haven: Yale University Press, 1997, p.100.

[2] Le Corbusier, *Sketchbooks Volume 4, 1957–1964*, Cambridge, MA: MIT Press, 1982, sketch 506.

[3] Quoted in C. Jencks, *Le Corbusier and the Continual Revolution in Architecture*, New York: Monacelli, 2000, p.191.

[4] G. Schildt, *Alvar Aalto: The Mature Years*, New York: Rizzoli, 1992, p.301.

[5] Schildt uses this expression to describe Aalto's work pattern. Ibid., p.220.

[6] Hanni Alanen, Aalto's daughter, has said that, for instance, when she wanted to study nursing she was forbidden by her father, who stopped speaking to her for a time. E. Tuovinen (ed.) *Technology and Nature*, New York: Phaidon Video, PHV 6050.

[7] Le Corbusier's father repeatedly worries about his son's health in his journal. H.A. Brookes, *Le Corbusier's Formative Years*, Chicago: University of Chicago Press, 1997. In a letter of December 1920 to Ritter Le Corbusier tells him that he has heard of young people who experience a period of depression following one of enthusiasm. He asks Ritter to explain this or provide a cure. Letter Le Corbusier to Ritter, December 1920, FLC; quoted in J. Lowman, 'Le Corbusier 1900–1925: The Years of Transition', unpub. PhD thesis, University of London, 1979, p.42.

[8] Loach gives examples of the closeness of the brothers, citing occasions in 1910 when Le Corbusier was in a philosophical crisis and headed straight for Dresden. J. Loach, 'Jeanneret Becoming Le Corbusier: A Portrait of the Artist as a Young Swiss', Book Review, *Journal of Architecture*, 5, 2000, pp. 229–34.

9 Letter Le Corbusier to his mother, 16 December 1954, Fondation Le Corbusier, hereafter referred to as FLC, R2 (2) 96.

10 Le Corbusier, postcard to Ritter, 14 December 1910, cited in Brookes, *Formative Years*, p.245. (Trans. by Mary Kalaugher and Meg Parques.)

11 Ibid., p.234.

12 Le Corbusier to Hugues Desalle in 'The Final Year', last recorded interview, 15 May 1965, Paris in Žaknić, *Final Testament*, p.122.

13 Le Corbusier, 'To my Brother', in Ivan Žaknić, (ed.) *Journey to the East*, Cambridge: MIT, 1994, p.4-5.

14 Le Corbusier to Henry Pessar in 1965, in Žaknić, *Final Testament*, p.67.

15 Schildt reports this in *Mature Years*, pp.306–7. Juhani Pallasmaa is at pains to deny Schildt's accusations, suggesting to S. Menin (personal communication, 1998) that there is no basis in fact for them. Roger Connar explores the nature of this antipathy towards Aalto in R. Connar, *Aaltomania*, Helsinki: Rakennustieto, 2000.

16 D.W. Winnicott, 'The Capacity to be Alone', in *Maturational Processes and the Facilitating Environment*, London: The Hogarth Press, 1965, p.34.

17 A. Storr, *The School of Genius*, London: André Deutsch, 1988, p.21.

18 This is analysed in depth in S. Menin, 'Relating the Past, Sibelius, Aalto and the Profound Logos', unpub. PhD thesis, Newcastle University, 1997.

19 Aalto, in letter to Aino, undated; repr. in Schildt, *Mature Years*, p.130.

20 Schildt reports the memories of Viola Markelius, wife of his architect friend Sven Markelius, who recalled her affair with Aalto, stating that 'She stands in this biography for the many women Aalto had met during his long life, with whom he shared his zest for life and who retained a warm memory of him'. G. Schildt, *Alvar Aalto: The Decisive Years*, New York: Rizzoli, 1986, p.52.

however, their outward public expression was of rueful humility. Whilst admitting 'a crisis of profound anxiety' in a letter to his friend William Ritter in 1910[11], Le Corbusier's main public expression to the end of his days was 'Discontented, never'.[12] Those who met Le Corbusier and Aalto clearly experienced only a part of the truth about these men, since feelings of vulnerability were often hidden behind confident faces. An instance of this is the 'top dog' manner that Aalto was determined to maintain, on the instructions of his father. Le Corbusier hinted at his own insecurity in his letter, 'To My Brother', with which he opened his book *Journey to the East*: 'I wish this piece that I am dedicating to you were better! But I have nothing else ... we have been helping each other for years. We won't stop, will we?'[13]

Late in life Le Corbusier began to sink into gloom and his guard came down, leading him to confide in a relative stranger, Henry Pessar, the fact that for most of his life he had been 'smashed down'.[14] Later the aged Aalto was also greatly depressed by what he and others, such as Schildt, perceived as a rejection of him and his achievements by radical young Constructivist Finns in the 1960s and 1970s,[15] some of whom began to champion both him and his work soon after his death.

Suffering Solitude or Society

An aspect of self that is markedly different in the characters of the two men was their attitude to and need of solitude. Undoubtedly something of a fear of being alone expressed itself in Aalto's extrovert character. He could not bear to be alone, creating working environments in which adoring young assistants worked away with manic gusto, sometimes facilitated by a bottle of red wine. In 'The Capacity to be Alone' Winnicott expressed the belief that experience of being alone in the company of another (particularly mother) is vital for development and security.[16] Clinging behaviour, which Aalto exhibited throughout life, is indicative of insecurity and the roots of dependency, and can be seen to be intertwined with manic-depressive disorders. Indeed, as Storr indicates, 'The capacity to be alone thus becomes linked with self-discovery and self-realisation; with becoming aware of one's deepest needs, feelings and impulses'.[17]

Aalto seems to have generally been socially freer than Le Corbusier, more comfortable with others. He was an extrovert whose need of the energy and confidence he could draw from such encounters meant he thrived in company. For Aalto isolation triggered a downward cycle of depression, and solitude had to be filled with activity in nature, in hard, mind-occupying work, or more commonly drink.[18] A yearning for contact and relationship may have been at the heart of his interest in mystical matters. He wrote to his wife Aino in 1932, 'Always when I thought of you in my loneliness, it was as if I had begged you to help me ... I missed you terribly and at the same time there was something painful about it'.[19]

Aalto was also renowned for his love affairs, to which Schildt refers directly and indirectly.[20] Despite his bravado, he was a deeply insecure individual. Such insecurity was the grounding, so to speak, on which Aalto built his creative process, a process, it seems, of self-maintenance that involved designing episodes of 'relating' forms or facilitating the interaction of people.[21]

In contrast Le Corbusier felt that 'It is in solitude that one can struggle with one's ego, that one punishes and encourages oneself.'[22] In childhood he sought isolation from parental pressure, and this became the model for creative endeavour: 'shelter for his meditations in a quiet and sure spot'.[23] This concern for aloneness also went to the heart of his spiritual life, and was a key to his outworking of dwelling environments for others, believing that it was necessary to create spaces for solitude and meditation in every home. This is not to suggest that he was not concerned about community, as will be demonstrated in Chapter 8, but it is a pointer to a basic aspect of his character.

Having been preoccupied with father figures in his early life, once he settled with his extrovert wife Yvonne Gallis he seems to have been less in need of the close entanglement with male mentors that characterises his youthful emotional engagements. He, like Aalto, was free with his love affairs, as the episode with Taya Zinkin demonstrates.[24] Zinkin suggested that he saw these as somehow being amoral episodes of male functionality.[25] Yet, since Le Corbusier then wanted to protect Yvonne from the reality of this form of functionalism by saying merely 'Connais pas' to any of his girlfriends who that chose to telephone him at home, remaining in his way faithful in Paris,[26] he did recognise the damaging emotional effect of his actions, even within the different moral sphere of the 1940s and 1950s. Aalto paid much less attention to the feelings of his two wives, sometimes even flirting in their presence.[27]

The degree to which their women acted as holding environments for Le Corbusier and Aalto cannot be underestimated. It is demonstrated by the magnitude of the depressive breakdowns they each suffered when their wives died. In Yvonne, Le Corbusier had found balance, devotion, humour, yet 'peace, silence and service'[28] and someone who was more instinctual than intellectual and brought him back to earth when his ideas became too fanciful.[29] In Aino, Aalto found a level-headed, protective figure who could critically share his vision and balance his fantasies with common sense. After the deaths of their wives the men were unable to be creatively productive for some time. However, this is not to suggest that the emotional support provided by their marriages was sufficient to stop the bouts of depression. On the contrary Aalto continued to fall into hypochrondriacal illness within the relationship too.

Le Corbusier and Aalto were both undeniably complex characters who exhibited a number of paradoxical traits. Both were simultaneously outgoing, capable, if driven cultural heroes, and self-doubting, collapsed and frightened individuals. It is as if the capability and the collapse were two completely different experiences that seemingly had nothing to do with each other, as if they were happening to two different people. Yet there is an important relationship between the realities of creativity and collapse that enriched the creative work of both men.

[21] S. Menin, 'Relating the Past: the Creativity of Sibelius and Aalto', *Ptah* (Alvar Aalto Foundation), 1, 2001, pp.32–44.

[22] Le Corbusier, letter to L'Eplattenier, 22 November 1908, cited in Brookes, *Formative Years*, p.153.

[23] Le Corbusier, *Precisions on the Present State of Architecture and City Planning*, Cambridge, MA: MIT Press, 1991, pp.17–18.

[24] See also M. Bacon, *Le Corbusier in America*, Cambridge, MA: MIT Press, 2001, p.121.

[25] T. Zinkin, 'No Compromise with Le Corbusier', *Guardian*, 11 September 1965.

[26] Jencks, *Continual Revolution*, p.194.

[27] Aino Aalto threw a female colleague out of the car on a trip to Norway after she and Aalto had been flirting together. Schildt, *Decisive Years*, p.64. Elissa recalled that 'In the usual sense of the word [husband] he wasn't perhaps absolutely ideal. But he was a very warm person'. Tuovinen (ed.) *Technology and Nature*, (video).

[28] Jencks, *Continual Revolution*. p.194.

[29] Letter, Trouin to Le Corbusier, 29 January 1958, FLC 13 01 143.

War and the Expedient Nature of Helplessness

While political concerns do not play an important role in the work of either Le Corbusier or Aalto, left-wing ideas would appeal to both in terms of ideas of co-operation and community. Simultaneously the strong front presented by right-wing factions, embodying a regional and Romantic idealised vision of the Homeland, would simultaneously strike a chord with each; especially to the insecure self amidst the upheavals of war.

War, Commissions and Flexing Moral Fibres

The construction of the forest home, Villa Mairea (Plate 23), was just coming to an end as Aalto returned from the opening of his Finnish Pavilion at the New York World Fair in early summer 1939 (Fig. 6.13). As political troubles in Europe spilt over into military hostilities and the Winter War began in Finland, Aalto's brother committed suicide rather than be sent to the front, and Aalto's equilibrium was shaken to the core by his terror of death. He panicked, and ran away to a Stockholm hotel, 'unable to admit his trauma'.[30] Eventually he was forced to put on a uniform, but quickly used his connections to get himself transferred to Helsinki, and then to the United States in March 1940, to a chorus of disapproval. At this point many friends witnessed, for the first time, deep contradictions in his personality.

Seeking to withdraw from danger, Aalto meanwhile arranged some lectures to publicise the attractions of Finland in America.[31] By the time he arrived (in March 1940), however, a peace treaty had been brokered, and so he reoriented his mission into a call for help in the reconstruction of Finland. Although he was appointed visiting professor at MIT in 1940, Aalto achieved little in terms of fund-raising for his homeland. Having ignored letters from friends pleading with him to return to Finland, such as one from Mairea Gullichsen, he was eventually ordered 'to return to his post' in Finland in October 1940.[32] Finding a place for himself in the Government Information Centre (basically a propaganda agency), Aalto turned his attention to the reorientation of the journal, The Human Side, in which he would bring together mentors and colleagues such as Gropius, Wright, Moholy-Nagy, Lewis Mumford and Carrel.[33] Although nothing further came of the journal, it bears witness to his attempt to reinvigorate debate at a time of Totalitarianism.

Schildt concludes that Aalto's record during the war years was a series of failures. The desperate reality of war seems to have weighed him down, hindering his ability to play and create. Commentators have described this stage of Aalto's career as a 'conservative' period.[34] As part of his propaganda work he wrote about the purity of indigenous building, and expressed organicist rhetoric similar to that of Nazi architects such as Werner March who were offering *völkisch designs*.[35] During a time when his terror was close to engulfing him, Aalto increasingly began to articulate his interest in nature and the processes of growth. This, rather than political expediency alone, may explain why he was drawn towards Nazi ideology.

[30] Schildt, *Mature Years*, p.14.

[31] Aalto also suggested that he show the housing exhibition which had closed after a week in Helsinki, and that he should be allowed to refurnish his New York World Fair Pavilion with new pro-Finnish information.

[32] Telegram to Aalto 8 October 1940. Alvar Aalto Foundation, hereafter known as AAF.

[33] Draft outlines of 'The Human Side' are in AAF.

[34] K. Jormakka, J. Gargus and D. Graf in *The Use and Abuse of Paper*, Datutop 20, Tampere: Tampere University, 1999, p.27.

[35] Jormakka, Gargus and Graf argue that this 'Karelianist' period could be said to span from the conception of Villa Mairea (1937–9) through his years as a propagandist and articles such as 'The Architecture of Karelia' (1941), the unrealised designs for houses including Villa Tvistbo of 1944, until his return to MIT, in 1945. Ibid, pp.26–8.

His interest in Ernst Neufert's standardisation programme led Aalto to invite him to Finland in 1942, while Finland was hosting Nazi troops. Aalto had discussed the relationship between mechanical standardisation and good architecture on his sojourn at MIT, only to continue the discussion in Helsinki, through his German contacts. In this way he liaised between sworn ideological enemies.

Le Corbusier, like a number of his syndicalist colleagues, had a brief and unsuccessful flirtation with the Vichy regime which was to tarnish his reputation. Auguste Perret also tried to work with Vichy, but soon after joined the Resistance, a fact that helped him to secure a number of important post-war contracts. Significantly Le Corbusier did not join the Resistance like his old colleagues Perret and Charlotte Perriand. Having had his fingers burnt by the Vichy experience, Le Corbusier spent the rest of the war years quietly working on his ideas and paintings. During this period he began to address the housing problem by toying with the idea of creating self-build houses. He was also greatly concerned with the issue of global unity at this time.

After the war, as their careers slowly took off once more, a greater blow was to strike both Le Corbusier and Aalto. Yvonne was to become increasingly stricken by chronic gastritis and was becoming crippled by osteoporosis, and Aino was to be diagnosed with inoperable cancer.

Retreating Resistance and the Higher Existence

Although both Le Corbusier and Aalto had failings politically, and lacked *realpolitik*, neither of them compromised his commitment to architecture, because this was so essential an outlet for their creativity and thus their very lifeblood. Indeed their sense of the nature of dwelling was deepened, being brought closer to the reality of subsistence existence experienced by many during war time. Perhaps one limitation in their thinking was due to the fact that neither wanted to address the tragedies of war and apply the same moral rigour to the wider situation that they applied to their art. However, both men did succeed in developing their own ideas about housing during the war years, and were thus ready at least to stimulate the discussion, if not actually succeed in winning design contracts when the war ended.

Aalto, like Le Corbusier, depended first on his public career and second on his wife. Yvonne and Aino were more forgiving than the public, which resented the god-like status that was building around these 'masters' of Modernism. The war years had seen a collapse of their architectural realms, and a great deal of manoeuvring to remain in positions of influence. The collapse of their personal realms stimulated deeper psychological manoeuvring.

Elemental Meditation or Modern Mediation:
Personal Retreats as Places of the Soul

The search that Le Corbusier and Aalto shared for ways of bringing about the cohabitation of metaphysical reality with the domestic, the communal and even the commercial worlds, as well as the purposively religious, was undoubtedly intertwined with the pressure of their driven lives. One manifestation of this search was a simultaneous need to withdraw physically and metaphysically, which climaxed when they each created places of retreat in their favourite natural settings. An analysis of their personal retreats at Cap Martin and Muuratsalo reveals something of their attitude to the concept of dwelling, and indeed to mysticism and nature at this time of personal crisis.

In both schemes there is only a small track to the buildings, but, since both are built on rock above water, boat access is possible. Otherwise the geography of central Finland provides a deep contrast with the natural realm of the Mediterranean.

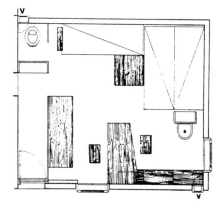

5.1
Plan of Cabanon. Le Corbusier,
1951–2. From Le Corbusier
and Jeanneret, *Oeuvre Complète*,
Volume 5.

Life and Death at Cap Martin

If for Le Corbusier the dwelling was the sacred space, none could be more so than the tiny cabin that he was to build on Mediterranean coast at Cap Martin. This, like Ronchamp, was to be a place of healing and reconciliation, a holding environment, this time on a deeply individual scale.

Le Corbusier composed his little Cabanon at Cap Martin (Figs 5.1 and 5.2) while sitting in the café L'Etoile de Mer on 30 December 1951 as a birthday gift for his wife, who was becoming gravely ill. He found her slow demise agonising, as his access to the world of laughter and entertainment was lost, and he refused to discuss her condition.[36] Yvonne died in discomfort in 1957. Le Corbusier was deeply disorientated by this death, which was followed in 1960 by that of his mother.

Yvonne's doctor, Jacques Hindermeyer, reports that 'in her last years she couldn't move ... Once arrived at Cap-Martin, she had to be delivered down the little path to the Cabanon in a wheelbarrow; that was the only solution'.[37] For Le Corbusier this loss of human dignity was inconceivable, and revealingly he said to one interviewer, 'I feel so good in my Cabanon that without a doubt I will meet my end here',[38] which he eventually did. Not only was the little house a place to retreat into nature, it was also a place to which he could withdraw before death. Le Corbusier felt that logically he should not fear death, a total and ultimate immersion in nature, and his writings, particularly 'Mise au Point', his 'Final Testament', see him oscillate between feelings that it is 'a beautiful thing' and a matter of unjust 'grotesquery'.[39]

Cap Martin enjoys a classic Mediterranean climate – warm winters and hot summers. The hillside on which the Cabanon is built is rocky and arid, and what soil there is remains dry for much of the year. Here he had found a place of peace and harmony with nature in which he could be creative, and thus recreate that which he had found in Mount Athos in 1911 and had sought to

[36] Dr Jacques Hindermeyer cited in Žaknić, *Final Testament*, p.65.
[37] Ibid.
[38] Le Corbusier, interview with Brassaï. Ibid., p.66.
[39] Ibid., p. 61.

5.2
Cabanon, Cap Martin. Le Corbusier,
1951–2. Reproduction of one
complete page from Le Corbusier,
My Work, London: Architectural
Press, 1960, p.156.

recreate for others in the Unités: 'Monks' cells ... secret gardens ... an infinity of landscape ... a tête-à-tête with oneself'. It was a place to be overwhelmed by a 'sensation of extraordinary harmony'.[40] Cap Martin may therefore offer a telescopic view into the oeuvre and the personal universe of the architect. Here he sought to undergo the 'treatment of silence and solitude'.[41]

Squaring the Sacred with the Secular

Although Le Corbusier claims to have conceived the basic idea for the simple dwelling in an instant, and to have drawn the final form in 45 minutes,[42] the details were actually contrived with the help of five colleagues (including Jean Prouvé and Charles Barberis) at his atelier over a considerable period thereafter.[43] This slight revision of history is important since it highlights Le Corbusier's wish to suggest that there was something archetypal in this specific project.

Le Corbusier negotiated the right to build 'a room' on the hillside owned by the landlord and café proprietor, Robert Rebutato, arguing that from there he would oversee the building of the Roq et Rob holiday apartment scheme he had designed for him. What transpired, in 1957, were five much simplified 'Unités de camping', which were simple extrapolations of his own Cabanon.

The Cabanon itself sits on rock some 20 metres above the sea. Originally it was to be a sleeping space for two with basic toilet facilities, a living space outside in summer, with a writing desk placed to enjoy the view of Monaco, the beach and Cap Martin.[44] After this the plan was divided into a simple dwelling space for two built in 1952 (the Cabanon), and the even simpler workplace (or 'chamber de travail') added, just 15 metres away, in 1954. This became a shrine-like hut that symbolically crept away from the already aphoristic living space, in search of even greater solitude and closer union with the elements, edging towards the cliff edge. A simple path separates the two spaces.

Modern Modesty or Monasticism?

Built of logs the scheme is ostensibly simplicity itself. Yet, despite the basic nature of the facilities, the simplicity is not rustic, rather being exquisitely fine in its conception of proportion and layout, indicating the actual significance of the design time.

In Chapter 4 it was seen that Le Corbusier saw architecture in terms of a 'marriage of lines'[45] between opposing masculine, geometric and feminine 'nebulous' elements. It is therefore curious that Le Corbusier chose to create the Cabanon in such a perfect orthogonal form. Natural organic curves are however omnipresent in the surrounding landscape with which the Cabanon itself contrasts. They are also evident in the murals, largely of the female body, with which Le Corbusier chose to adorn the internal walls and ceiling.[46]

Given the constraints of space Le Corbusier was forced to challenge the idea that separate functions should occur in discrete areas (Fig. 5.1). Conceived as a functioning whole, the Cabanon has only a few pieces of essential furniture to articulate the space. The little building was an opportunity to produce a practical functioning minimum dwelling using the principles of the Modulor,

[40] Le Corbusier, 'Unités d'habitation de grandeur conforme', Paris, 1 April 1957, FLC U3 07 176, cited in Žaknić, *Final Testament*, p.64.

[41] Le Corbusier to Prof. Renato Gambier, Venice, 16 June 1965, FLC G3 07 197, cited in Žaknić, p.63. Žaknić discusses Le Corbusier's common preference for isolation (pp.43-4), and cites Dr Jacques Hindermeyer's recollection that Yvonne's withdrawal during the last years of her illness gave Le Corbusier 'more time to immerse himself in creative work', p.61.

[42] Le Corbusier, *Modulor 2*, London: Faber, 1955, p.239.

[43] B. Chiambretto, *Le Corbusier à Cap Martin*, Marseille: Éditions Parenthèses, 1987, p.33.

[44] Ibid., p.38.

[45] Le Corbusier, *Le Livre de Ronchamp*, Paris: Les Cahiers Forces Vives, 1962, p.146.

[46] In one image of the Cabanon in the *Oeuvre Complète* Le Corbusier shows a strip of paintings, all variants on the theme of the goddess soul figure whose curves echo those in the grain of the timber above, to a degree that must have been intentional. Le Corbusier, *Oeuvre Complète Volume 5, 1946–1952*, Zürich: Les Éditions d'Architecture, 1995, p. 62.

referring to its interior dimensions of 3.6 by 3.6 metres as the *application révélatrice* (the revealing implement).[47] An example of this practicality is demonstrated in the attention Le Corbusier paid to good air circulation through the use of the ventilator (the *aérateur*).[48]

The complex hierarchy of relationships between inside and outside developed as the plan was divided into elementary surfaces and partitions. The spiralling of elements in and around the plan was a principal stratagem, crystallising one of Le Corbusier's basic ideals of referring back to Byzantine cross-plan churches, and even referring back to Pythagoras and Vitruvius, via Matila Ghyka in the 1930s. This places Le Corbusier's composition in the line of antiquity, anchoring his doctrine in the spaces of ancient times. It was intended that the structure and the details of construction should be invisible; they should not interfere with how one perceived the essence of the scheme.

It was necessary to integrate its ethereal character with its functional usage, assuring the practical human occupation of such archetypal space.[49] Chiambretto suggests that this did not result in a devaluation of the original conception but rather its verification.[50] The seriousness with which Le Corbusier took the subject of geometry can be seen from the lengths to which he went to make sure that the Cabanon was built to exactly correct proportions. Indeed in building the Cabanon in accordance with the Modulor Le Corbusier believed it would become radiant, in harmony with nature, exercising a beneficial influence on all those that who dwelt in it.

Authentically Rooted

At Cap Martin Le Corbusier sought to create a building that impacted appropriately on the natural context. Being built to Modulor proportions, a geometrical system derived largely from the ideas of the ancient Greeks, the Cabanon would also be inherently Mediterranean. Chiambretto writes that his vision was to 'combine old and new, respond to site, climate, vegetation, views and local precedent'.[51] He wanted to create a place that had access to the view on at least three sides of the building, and so composed a lightweight wooden composition that touched the earth lightly. In building in timber he was alluding to the 'primitive' hut at the roots of architecture, a theme that is repeated from time to time in his work, most notably in his design for the Maison Errazuriz.[52] Oddly the Cabanon is also reminiscent of a Swiss chalet and is arguably out of context in this environment of stone and concrete buildings.

Construing his mystical heritage through an obscure family connection with the Cathars, Le Corbusier believed Cap Martin was in some way a *pied-à-terre* which touched his ancestral roots. There, Curtis suggests, Le Corbusier could become a 'noble savage', living out his days at the heart of a Mediterranean that 'embraced both a love of the archaic and a sort of solar paganism ... the search for a mythical classical landscape to be translated into modern terms'.[53] Like the Neolithic men whose art he so admired, Le Corbusier decorated the Cabanon with that most basic and eloquent adornment, the print of his own hand. Indeed, photos show Le Corbusier naked, sitting at his altar-like desk to work,

47   Ibid.
48   The *aérateur* became part of the so-called 'undulating glass panel system' which allowed sun-control, fresh air to breathe, automatic cross-ventilation by gravity throughout the day and night, and complete protection from mosquitoes and other insects. Jean Prouvé and Charles Barberis were the real pioneers in this field within Le Corbusier's atelier.
49   A third phase of design began when Prouvé declined to be further involved. This phase marked the integration of the architecture of the Cabanon; was it to be primarily a perfect geometric space or primarily an efficiently functioning Cabanon? This involved systematic attention to detail, in millimetres, to integrate them into his original vision of the space.
50   Chiambretto, *Cap Martin*, p.38.
51   Ibid., p.14.
52   See for example Le Corbusier's sketch in which he draws a simple timber hut and then indicates how with the passage of time it is transformed into the Unité cell. Le Corbusier, *Oeuvre Complète Volume 5*, p.186.
53   W. Curtis, *Le Corbusier, Ideas and Forms*, London: Phaidon 1986, p.169.

demonstrating that the admixture of the archaic and the paganism was potent. These images are equal to the many anecdotes told of Aalto exercising naked on the terrace of his home in Munkkiniemi. Whether the building was sufficiently comfortable for Yvonne when she was crippled with illness is another matter. Nevertheless, it is essential to understand that Le Corbusier felt that the mystical richness of the setting was the greatest medicine that he could provide, believing in the essential needs of humankind for solitude, simplicity and spiritual connection with nature through, for instance, the almost ritualistic cleansing he undertook daily in the sea.[54]

Naturally Considerate Interventions

In his book My Work (from 1960) Le Corbusier indicates the 'fresh' inspiration that informed the design of the Cabanon. He precedes photographs and a small description of the Cabanon with two pages describing his architectural principles in terms of a heart and lungs, including anatomical drawings that he likened to the complexity of the roots, trunk and branches of a tree.[55] He illustrates the Cabanon itself with eight photographs, the first of which shows the architect disappearing over rocks to the beach to undertake his ritual bathe (Fig. 5.2). Then there are details of the other little building, and a shot of the splendid view of the coast. For Le Corbusier there was an 'inseparable unity' between the two little buildings: 'Architecture and planning = favourable siting, circulation, views (inside and out), ventilation (air constantly renewed and even temperature)'. The text ends with an ironic note that 'Building a home like this is forbidden by bye-laws'.[56] This illustrates Le Corbusier's wish to demonstrate the practical fundamentals of architecture in the little building, which are naturally vehicles for the deeper, life-enriching ethereal nature of the architecture. He spent increasing periods of time at the Cabanon until the time of his heart attack in the sea that he loved so much, in 1967.

Muuratsalo and the Mediation of Memory

Aalto's Experimental House project, as he first called his summer house at Muuratsalo, also grew from the potent mingling of life and death, having been conceived in 1952 when he was beginning to rebuild his life after Aino's sudden death from cancer in 1949. The testament of friends and family repeatedly indicate the extent of the level of trauma and subsequent depression that he experienced following this event.[57] Aalto was restless; he worked little, but travelled and drank a great deal. He had lost Aino's motherly encouragement and anchoring. Perhaps because it was near Jyväskylä, where he had lived from a young age, had first set up in practice and had met and married Aino, that Aalto managed to rouse himself from his creative paralysis to concentrate, lovingly, on the Säynätsalo town hall project. Significantly, at this time Aalto was searching for a new tutelary goddess, another mother figure who would guide and sustain him, and with whom he could fly creatively. It was during the town hall project that he began a relationship with a young assistant, Elissa Mäkiniemi, and was then able to pull his way out of the 'gap' of grief and loss.

[54] Le Corbusier lists his favourite hobby as swimming. Jean Petit, Le Corbusier lui-même, Paris: Forces Vives, 1970, p.18.

[55] Le Corbusier, My Work, London: Architectural Press, 1960, pp.154-7.

[56] Ibid., p. 157.

[57] Aalto's friend J.M. Richards offers one account of the time of her death: '[Aalto] was totally disorientated, lost his customary ebullience and drank until his friends despaired of his future.' J.M. Richards, Memories of an Unjust Fella, London: Weidenfeld & Nicholson, 1980, p.203.

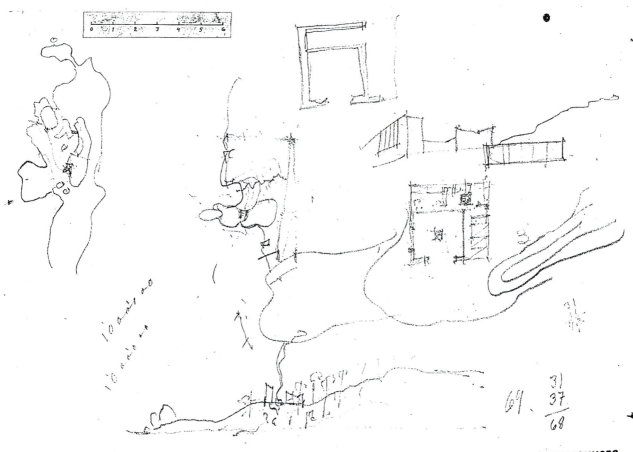

5.3
Design sketches for Summer House,
Muuratsalo. Aalto, 1952–3.
Pencil on paper.

In the person of Elissa, Aalto found hope and enough security to throw himself into the process of world-building again. Together they discovered an unusually attractive unspoilt shore site on the island of Muuratsalo, close to Säynätsalo, a large granite island rising gently from Lake Päijänne, in central Finland, covered with a mixed forest of birch and pine, with a pitted floor of boulders lushly draped with berry bushes, fungi and ferns. It was here that he embarked upon the building of his summer house.

Like Le Corbusier at Cap Martin, Aalto wanted Muuratsalo to be a relaxing, inspiring workplace in a natural setting. Composed with death still in the air, manifested in the antique aura of decay that pervades some of the details, the place is nonetheless a tactful realisation of a new beginning. Ironically, although Aalto craved personal contact as much as Le Corbusier favoured isolation, the Finnish retreat provided a degree of isolation unimaginable on the now crowded shores of the Mediterranean.

Nature Courting Culture

Aalto's Experimental House was to be a retreat, comprising simple living accommodation forming two sides of a brick-paved courtyard, enclosed on the third side by a tall but punctured brick wall (Fig. 5.3). The fourth side is largely open, although the wall returns to suggest a degree of enclosure and protection. These high external wall planes envelop the outside living space which extends beyond the cultured courtyard, across the granite boulders, down to the water where the numerous interventions, such as tiny jetties, assist humankind in both their access to and withdrawal from the elements.

The courtyard plan calls on two historical precedents: the vernacular farmstead enclosure and the Roman courtyard. Although he was a thoroughly forward-looking Finn, it has been seen that Aalto knew and loved vernacular forms and configurations, understanding the deep logic behind forest buildings, often integrating something of their logic and detail with his modern designs.

The building's square footprint, around which the living spaces seem somehow to spiral, is set back from the shore, high up on the smooth granite rock. The house is, according to the season, introverted or extroverted. Its relationship with nature is seasonally mediated by the courtyard, at the heart of which is a sunken fire-pit, signifying the oldest actions of humankind in relation to nature (Fig. 5.6). Aalto wrote: 'the whole complex of buildings is dominated by the fire that burns at the centre of the patio and that, from the point of view of practicality and comfort, serves the same purpose as the campfire, where the glow from the fire and its reflections from the surrounding snow-banks create a pleasant, almost mystical feeling of warmth.'[58]

The scheme demonstrates many of the principles that Aalto explored in his article 'From Doorstep to Living Room', cited in Chapter 4.[59] In summer the courtyard is a fully utilised outside room, satisfying the Finnish need for an 'aesthetically direct contact with the world outside' (an outward-looking summer face), and a 'winter face' which 'turns inward and is seen in the interior design' emphasising the 'warmth of our inner rooms' (an interior landscape which became so common in Aalto's work).[60] Here Aalto uses the physical sky (Fig. 5.4), rather than creating its metaphysical kin which he conceived in Viipuri and elsewhere, where he recreates the sky symbolically with ingenious systems of roof lights (Fig. 6.2). As a seasonally limited room, inhabited visually and symbolically when it is too cold to inhabit physically, the courtyard acts as a sensitive screen between inside warmth and outside cold, a place of transition, a defensible space, like the vernacular stockyard, enclosed by the huts and fence.[61] For Aalto 'the garden wall' was the 'external wall of the house' (Plate 7).[62]

The west wall of the courtyard is, in part, the outside wall of the living space, but it goes on to be a sacral element, as it becomes a white timber screen through which sky light filters, as it does through the trees beyond (Fig. 5.4). It signifies birch trees, sacred in Finnish folk-culture, and abundant on the site, becoming a symbolic interface between the simultaneous realities of the home-enclosure and forest-enclosure, and between the physical and the metaphysical realms. It may even offer something of a palimpsest of pagan ritual tree worship. The screen wall then comprises both 'decayed' brick (the void) and 'growing'

[58] Aalto, 'Experimental House, Muuratsalo, 1953'; repr. in G. Schildt, *Alvar Aalto in his Own Words*, New York: Rizzoli, 1997, p.234.

[59] Aalto, 'From Doorstep to Living Room', 1926 in ibid., p.49.

[60] Ibid.

[61] Simple huts of this kind are called 'aitta' and 'kota' in Finnish.

[62] Aalto, 'From Doorstep to Living Room', in Schildt, *Own Words*, p.49.

5.4
View of trellis and courtyard, Summer
House, Muuratsalo. Aalto, 1952–3.

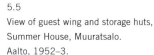

5.5
View of guest wing and storage huts,
Summer House, Muuratsalo.
Aalto, 1952–3.

wood (the trellis). The wall returns to form the fourth side of the courtyard, where the majority of it is missing, leaving nature beyond to complete the enclosure. Herein is an aura of immanence, of engagement with something in the process of happening. Fragments of column fluting or stretching room forms are in the process of transmuting towards growth or decay. Aalto was a master at objectifying the intuitive and metaphysical reality of his forms.

The main room resembles something of the traditional multipurpose 'tupa' space, with an open fire, and with the addition, in this case, of a small loft-studio nestling beneath the apex of the roof. At the meeting of the two wings is a small kitchen. The modest bedrooms and bathroom are accessed by a cloister-like corridor which faces the courtyard, being either pierced by the sun through its doors and windows, or shuttered tight against the cold.

A door leads from the back of the building into the guest accommodation, beyond which are freestanding woodsheds (Fig. 5.5). This area, of timber construction (added after the completion of the main part of the house), provides an important 'tail' to the house complex, draped up the contours of the hill, anchored to the rocks that form part of the site. Although the last of the planned living huts were not built, the transition between the court-like house and these increasingly shed-like outbuildings seems to be another representation of the transition between civilisation and nature, rooting the building physically to the floor of the forest and metaphorically to its culture.

Existence and Experiment: The Proximity of Being in Nature

The house has both a modest structure and form, built (in part) from bricks rejected from the town hall project. From beyond, it has something of the appearance of a white-painted Mediterranean monastery upon a cliff (Fig. 5.4). Aalto seems to declare the dominance of civilised man over nature, while simultaneously creating a pantheistic call to prayer of the vulnerable amidst the power of nature. From within, the courtyard has the feel of 'an old tweed coat'[63] or a worn tapestry, as some fifty brick experimental panels give off warmth and a sense of ancient rusticity, but also giving the fabric a certain sense of unsettledness or even frenzy (Plate 7).

Not only did Aalto experiment with brick types and configurations at Muuratsalo, he also tried using an ancient granite-boulder foundation system (Fig. 5.5) and even sought to heat the house in the winter with a pump using solar energy stored in the water of the lake. He wrote of the house, 'Proximity to Nature can give fresh inspiration both in terms of form and construction',[64] demonstrating his progressive interest in technology, but always wanting to test such progress against experience of human frailty.

The sauna, too, is an intriguing experiment with wood from the site (Fig. 5.6). Here Aalto borrowed the vernacular accent of round wood, but invented a new form. Although it looks like a conventional *aitta* hut construction, this small building is slightly triangular. Usually logs are shaved to a consistent diameter and the pitch is achieved through other means, but here the design's clarity arises from placing all the naturally tapering pine logs in the same direction, which results in a gentle mono-pitch roof. Standing on the shore with four simple boulders for foundations, the little building has a turf roof and a minuscule changing room in front of a genuine smoke sauna.

Death and Becoming

Aalto also articulated the idea of providing elements that are 'deliberately presented as a ruin',[65] grasping the notion of *Sterben und Werden* (death and becoming) and again acting it out in his composition of the summer house. The confrontation of culture and nature is speeded by Aalto's determination to prefigure this future moment of reconciliation in the present. Indeed, Aalto seems to suggest that architecture must accelerate ageing through the premature requisitioning of the majesty of ancient forms. He had, for instance, a goal of inviting vegetation to engulf his vestigial forms, such as stepped amphitheatres (Fig. 4.10), drawing the edifices towards history. The creation of such a visual dialogue between a formally depleted historic reference and the forces of nature that over millennia would have caused such dereliction may signify harmony between the natural and manmade

[63] Aalto, with reference to the effect he desired for the brick texture of Baker House Dormitory, MIT, in conversation with Robert Dean, of Perry Shaw and Hepburn with whom Aalto was associated while working on Baker House, MIT. Robert Dean repeated this comment to Sarah Menin in a conversation in Boston, July 1985.

[64] Aalto, 'Experimental House, Muuratsalo, 1953' in Schildt, *Own Words*, p.234.

[65] Aalto, 'From Doorstep to Living Room', in ibid., p.54.

5.6
Aalto emerging from sauna,
Muuratsalo.

environments, but also connotes dialogue between these realms. This Aalto also engineers through the formal acknowledgment of a building's need to accommodate rock, as for example when lime-washed or brick walls become granite as they meet, and step up rock at Kauttua (Plate 25) and Otaniemi (Plate 8).

In Aalto's hand these may be read either as dereliction or recolonisation, as decay of civilisation, sculptural accretion, or the growth of form. This may represent a formal translation of Aalto's scepticism and his tendency to encourage multivalent readings of architecture and life including, on occasion, the 'downright illogical'.[66] For instance the overgrown timber steps behind the main part of the house, which mirror those at Säynätsalo town hall and the university at Otaniemi (Plate 8), may represent both the simplest technique of terracing land, pushing earth back with plain boards to gain a foothold, and an overgrown remnant of a classical amphitheatre (Fig. 4.10). Coupled with such examples are the many compositional games included in the building: the oppositions of growth and decay, light and dark, as well as the classic play of palazzo and piazza.[67] Sourcing these in the realities of life close to nature, these themes intone something of an extant Pantheism, one which lightly colours life in Finland to this day (Fig. 5.7).

5.7
Aalto by fire, Muurtasalo c.1960.

Porphyrios has excavated references in Aalto's work that correlate with the eighteenth-century movement of the Picturesque, the cult of the ruin and notions of the aesthetic and ethical valorisation of nature.[68] Yet Aalto's use of such symbols is also rooted in experience of the forest ecology in which growth and decay are a continuum, a fact of which he needed to reassure himself constantly, given his own profound terror of death.[69]

The courtyard seems to signify belief in a harmonious relationship between architecture and nature, central to which is an acceptance of decay and death seemingly impenetrable to his conscious self. The imposition of a belief system in which nature's growth process forever dominates may have become vital as a way of addressing the reality of life (and death) without addressing the cavernous gap directly.

In the creative realm Aalto was at pains to associate harmony and nature. In

[66] Jormakka, Gargus and Graf, *Use and Abuse of Paper*, p.33, citing Juhani Pallasmaa without source.
[67] This composition tool is explored in depth by G. Griffiths, *The Polemical Aalto*, Datutop 19, Tampere: University of Tampere, 1997.
[68] D. Porphyrios, *Sources of Modern Eclecticism: Studies on Alvar Aalto*, London: Academy Éditions, 1982, pp.59–82.
[69] Aalto, 'Interview for Television', July 1972 in Schildt, *Own Words*, p.274.

drawing himself towards the security of classical association formally and symbolically at Muuratsalo, he also associated with the vulnerability of adopting a world-view in which the precariousness of nature's flux is accepted. Here we find part of the explanation for the adoption of the imagery of growth, to which he and others attached certain degrees of intuitive Romanticism, perhaps in his case to avoid naming the precise source of his concern for the psychological realm. Aalto rarely enunciated his sense of the mystical, but inherent to his work are elements symbolic of the processes of growth and of teleology (in other words those processes leading to a final cause). To these he also tied post-telic processes (processes of decay which take over after something has gone beyond its fruition) manifest in elements of ruin, relic or decomposition (for instance encouraging the growth and spread of ivy). In this way Aalto often consciously included vestigial, or remnant fragments of classical culture in his buildings.[70] Growth-engulfed form is not a symbol of pessimism, since it suggests perennial fecundity through detritus, and a faith in nature's regenerative cycles.

Conclusion

The ascetic Euclidean shack at Cap Martin is made rich by its very purity and poise, and what it draws from its context. Le Corbusier believed that life should comprise domestic essentials in a Platonic space, within a natural setting, and it was his deepest wish that this could be shared by those in mass housing, as Chapter 8 will show. His attempts to draw this mystical unity with nature into Modernism, demonstrated in the houses to be discussed in chapters 7 and 8, were much misunderstood at the time and later.

At Muuratsalo Aalto manifested his determination to assist modern architecture to recover 'place', but this cannot be separated from his suggestion that all architecture must reflect the nature of human experience and 'psycho-logical needs'.[71] That these two, natural place and human need, were for Aalto isomorphic is demonstrated at Muuratsalo, through the outplaying of these in his world-view, and the intricacies and nuances of the relationship between his architectural form and the natural environment. Just as he addresses fragment and entity simultaneously, so his dwellings draw from and contribute to the natural realm.

Cobb has identified a process of symbolically reforming the past of one's self through creative endeavour.[72] Whilst working upon the schemes for their two small retreats Le Corbusier and Aalto were simultaneously working and reworking their inner selves. The two small buildings act, in Winnicott's terms, as holding environments, a place of individual protection and rebirth. Just what the two architects would do when asked to create such an environment for communal spiritual renewal will be seen in the next chapter.

At Cap Martin and Muuratsalo, the two men demonstrate their common, deeply held belief in the need to relate dwelling and nature. Both were preoccupied with creating and identifying the formal and symbolic tools for such a relationship. It was, in essence, the search for metaphysical sustenance for everyday life.

70 Jormakku, Gargus and Graf suggest that Aalto's images were congruent with those favoured by some Nazi architects of the 1930s, and sit concurrently with the organic ideas of Häring and Werner March. Jormakku, Gargus and Graf, *Use and Abuse of Paper*, pp.27–8.

71 Aalto, 'Rationalism and Man', 1935, in Schildt, *Sketches*, p.50.

72 Cobb, *The Ecology of Imagination in Childhood*, Dallas: Spring Publications, 1993, p.94.

Chapter 6

Spiritual Space as a Holding Environment

Since nothing Le Corbusier or Aalto wrote fully demonstrates their attitudes and intentions towards the realms of the metaphysical and its relationship with nature, a discussion of this matter is incomplete without an analysis of buildings that specifically addressed the mystical realm. This chapter will comprise a detailed discussion of the Chapel of Notre Dame-du-Haut at Ronchamp (1955) and the Church of the Three Crosses at Vuoksenniska (1959). Drawing upon the ideas of Winnicott, we will argue that these two buildings acted as holding environments, places of refuge in which to regain contact with nature.

The ambivalence and even animosity towards the Church expressed by the two men during their youth began to wane during their latter years. Le Corbusier's mysticism was often veiled in the architectural agencies such as 'radiance', discussed above, yet that he was keenly motivated to search out and literally give form to the ineffable is without doubt. Schildt holds strongly to the opinion that Aalto, by contrast, was sceptical about all religion, putting this down to 'a Voltairean rationalism and a Goethean inclination' that pervaded his parents' home.[1] It was through these influences, Schildt argues, that Aalto chose to interpret life in terms other than that of the Church.[2] This notion defies the evidence of Aalto's writing, and fails to give weight to the sense of Aalto's words and forms that draw endlessly on the metaphysical. Schildt does however freely acknowledge that Aalto enjoyed designing the artistic elements of churches, and thus toying with the metaphysical, 'The closest the sceptical Aalto ever got to religion'.[3] It seems that Schildt is actually restricted by his own understanding of conservative Christian dogmas, rather than the more elemental spiritual experiences that are at the heart of religion and are inherent in the Latin word *religio*, meaning 'reliance' or 'connection'. This is crucial when we take into account that in such metaphysics (as both Aalto and Le Corbusier testify), psychology and spiritual concerns are actually isomorphic, often involving a need to 'relate' fully, unconditionally to another. It was this sense of

[1] G. Schildt, *Alvar Aalto: The Early Years*, New York: Rizzoli, 1984, p.184.
[2] Ibid.
[3] Ibid., p.186.

relationship that Aalto sought incessantly, it can be argued, to underpin his buildings (that 'love' for 'little man' as he put it) and vicariously his own life. He himself wrote that church building does not need art, but 'religious feeling ... It needs something else and needs it urgently. It needs pure and devout forms, whatever these forms may be.'[4] Indeed, in an article for the *Kerberos* magazine Aalto described leaving church feeling 'a complete human being ... For a moment one has received the gift of seeing the beautiful in everything.'[5] Although this comes from a light, even humorous article, it does suggest that he experienced or at least respected the witness of something metaphysical from the religious experience.

Le Corbusier gave his view of Catholicism in *Journey to the East*, written in 1911 but not published until after his death in 1965 shortly after he had revised and approved the manuscript. In his opinion:

> Protestantism as a religion lacks the necessary sensuality that fills the innermost depths of a human being, sanctuaries of which he is hardly conscious and which are part of the animal self, or perhaps the most elevated part of the subconscious. This sensuality, which intoxicates and eludes reason, is a source of latent joy and a harness of living strength.[6]

As we shall see, Le Corbusier's scheme for Ronchamp embraces that sensuality which he believed to be an intrinsic part of the Catholic Church, a sensuality that he experienced at first hand at the monastery to the Virgin at Mount Athos. Here Le Corbusier wrote of experiencing 'a fantastic vision of the sanctuary of the Virgin' where he felt in his 'limbs' the 'awe of the sacred ritual' and the 'overwhelming delirium of this moment and place',[7] an experience which he never forgot, and evidence of an architecture that was moving at both a physical and a spiritual level.

While feeling a strong attraction to what he perceived to be the sensuality of Catholicism, Le Corbusier had strong reservations about the religion and its implications. For example, when travelling across South America he wrote:

> What the ... hell did the ... *curés* come here for; we are on the violent red earth of the Indians, and these people had a soul. From my catechism I still remember this saying of Jesus Christ: 'if someone offends one of these little ones who believes in me, it were better to attach a stone to his neck and throw him into the sea.'[8]

This passage is significant, not only because Le Corbusier sides himself with ancient nature worship, but also because it gives an example of his personal experience of religion and the way in which he could turn biblical writings and religious imagery to justify his own ends, as we shall see at Ronchamp.

4 Aalto, 'Finnish Church Art', *Käsiteollisuus*, 3, 1925; repr. in Schildt (ed.) *Alvar Aalto in his Own Words*, New York: Rizzoli, 1997, pp.37–8.

5 *Kerberos* article in Schildt, *Early Years*, p.102, details not given.

6 Le Corbusier, *Journey to the East*, Cambridge, MA: MIT Press, 1987, p.162.

7 Ibid., pp.202–3.

8 Le Corbusier, *Precisions On the Present State of Architecture and City Planning*, Cambridge, MA: MIT Press, 1991, Press, p.11.

6.1
Section through the basilica of La Sainte Baume.

6.2
Design sketch of Viipuri Public Library as an imaginary mountain. Aalto, c.1929.

Ineffably Ronchamp

'The last bastion of the Vosges', the hill above Ronchamp on which the Chapel of Notre-Dame is built has always been the site of religious pilgrimage.[9] It was the site of a nineteenth-century church, struck by lightning in 1913 and rebuilt as a brick chapel which, in turn, was bombed during the autumn of 1944 by Germans attacking French troops. This left the dramatic site and a pile of rubble from which Le Corbusier's conception grew.

Caving in to Mother Earth

The essence of the chapel at Ronchamp cannot be fully understood without consideration being given to the unbuilt scheme for an 'Orphic city' of La Sainte Baume, commissioned by Édouard Trouin, the design of which stretched from around 1945 into the 1960s. The project, rejected by the Church in 1948, focused on the figure of Mary Magdalene, whose existing grotto was to be the entry into an underground basilica, the spiritual heart of the development and the culmination of a route of Orphic initiation. The central aim of the basilica at La Sainte Baume was to regenerate Christianity from its roots in the ancient mystery religions that had obvious links to still more ancient deities (Fig. 6.1).[10] Here Le

9   Le Corbusier, *Oeuvre Complète Volume 5, 1946–1952*, Zürich: Les Éditions d'Architecture, 1995, p.72.
10   E. Trouin, 'Table provisoire' for book entitled 'La Sainte Baume et Marie Madeleine', n.d., Fondation Le Corbusier hereafter referred to as FLC, 13 01 396.

Corbusier would dwell upon the role of the feminine within the church and her links with more primal feminine deities representing Mother Earth.[11] Indeed he proposed to landscape the park surrounding the grotto in an image of her body,[12] which, according to Vincent Scully, was common practice in ancient Greece.[13]

Harmony and the Psycho-physiology of Feeling

In 1950 Couturier, a Catholic priest at the heart of the *Art Sacré* movement, closely involved with the La Sainte Baume project, recommended Le Corbusier as architect for the chapel at Ronchamp. Still bitter about the Church's rejection of the earlier scheme, Le Corbusier initially refused to deal with what he called 'a dead institution'.[14] Eventually, however, he accepted, it seems because he realised that it would at last give him the opportunity to utilise so many of those complex ideas that were developed whilst working with Trouin.

This dazzling white pilgrimage chapel built on the brow of the hill and dedicated to 'Our Lady' needs little introduction (Plate 9). In form it appears like a neolithic dolmen, its vast roof, supposedly based upon a crab shell,[15] reminiscent of stone slung between three supporting towers. Its walls undulate and curve in both dimensions, simultaneously repelling and absorbing the surrounding landscape (Fig. 6.3). Its structure, a peculiar hybrid of concrete and rubble infill, is concealed in layers of thick white gunnite. Truth to materials and other such rationalistic concerns play no part in its conception. Each of its four sides is radically different, each designed in response to Le Corbusier's very particular interpretation of the Christian religion, to the surrounding landscape and to orientation. Le Corbusier wrote: 'One begins with the acoustic of the landscape, taking as a starting point the four horizons ... The design is conceived in conformity with these horizons – in acceptance of them.'[16]

For Le Corbusier the form of Ronchamp was generated in order to stir 'the psycho-physiology of the feelings' not to fulfil the requirements of religion,[17] and in this way it would become a place of initiation. Demonstrating his perpetual preoccupation with the manner in which the body would respond to architecture,[18] here he sought to engender a feeling of bodily wellbeing, which would in turn be spiritually uplifting; as Plato observed, 'rhythm and harmony find their way into the inward places of the soul' resulting in a 'true education of the inner being'.[19]

Le Corbusier believed that music and architecture were a means through which mankind could affirm 'I exist, I am a mathematician, a geometer and I am religious. That means I believe in some gigantic ideal that dominates me and I can achieve ...'[20] To this end 'an implacable mathematics' reigned over the forms of Ronchamp,[21] lending it the particular quality of radiance described in Chapter 4. 'Their agreement, their repetition, their interdependence, and the sprit of unity or family which binds them together ... is as subtle, exact and implacable as that of acoustics,' wrote Le Corbusier of its forms.[22] Le Corbusier believed the forms of Ronchamp through their geometry would bring those within the building closer to a state of Orphic harmony with the cosmos.

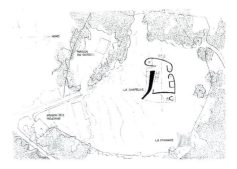

6.3
Site plan of chapel of Notre-Dame-du-Haut, Ronchamp. Le Corbusier, 1950–5 (FLC 7125).

[11] For a further discussion this scheme see F. Samuel, 'Le Corbusier, Rabelais and the Oracle of the Holy Bottle', *Word and Image: A Journal of Verbal/Visual Enquiry*, 17, 4, 2001, pp.325-38 and F. Samuel, 'The Philosophical City of Rabelais and St Teresa; Le Corbusier and Édouard Trouin's Scheme for St Baume', *Literature and Theology*, 13, 2, 1999, pp.111–26.

[12] Letter E. Trouin to Le Corbusier, 11 November 1950, FLC 13 01 45.

[13] V. Scully, *The Earth, the Temple and the Gods*, New Haven: Yale, 1962, p.11.

[14] A. Wogenscky, *Les Mains de Le Corbusier*, Paris: Éditions de Grenelle, n.d., p.18.

[15] D. Pauly, 'The Chapel of Ronchamp', *AD Profile* 55, 7/8, 1985, p.31.

[16] Le Corbusier, *Oeuvre Complète Volume 5*, p.72.

[17] Le Corbusier, *Oeuvre Complète Volume 6, 1952–1957*, Zürich: Les Éditions d'Architecture, 1995, p.52.

[18] Le Corbusier, *The Decorative Art of Today*, London: Architectural Press, 1987, p.167.

[19] Plato, *The Republic III*, in S. Buchanan (ed.) *The Portable Plato*, Harmondsworth: Penguin, 1997, p.389.

[20] Le Corbusier, *Precisions*, p.11.

[21] Le Corbusier, *Oeuvre Complète Volume 5*, p.72.

[22] Ibid.

Drought and The Water of Life

When seeking inspiration by reading through the Pilgrim's Manual for the earlier church at Ronchamp Le Corbusier underlined a reference to the fact that the chapel was built on the site of what had once been an ancient place of sun worship.[23] He saw the cult of the Virgin as building upon earlier religions allied more closely to the earth. Sitting at the top of a hill the blazing white forms of the chapel defy description, so unorthodox are they in form, the three towers connected by an enormous convex roof that covers a remarkable interior, punctured with brilliant colour (Plate 11).

Le Corbusier made connections between the building and the body of the Virgin herself by working with the Teilhardian idea of a mystical relationship between Mary and the Church, between 'virgin and mother and, since there is only one Christ, they are identified together in their maternal function'.[24] The building is an expression of Le Corbusier's ability to play with the blurred boundaries existing between Mary and the Church. He fully exploited the possibilities presented by the symbolism of 'Our Lady', to whom the chapel itself is dedicated. An example of this is his approach to the problem of the short supply of water at the top of the hill. It was suggested that Le Corbusier build a cistern into the church where rain water could be collected. Since water, Mary and the moon are symbolically linked, this requirement assisted the architect's conception of the building, enabling him to develop his interest in uterine imagery. Water cascades off the roof through a gargoyle shaped like an

6.4
Image of Mary. E3 caractères. Le Corbusier, *Le Poème de l'angle droit*, Paris: Éditions Connivance, 1989, p.129.

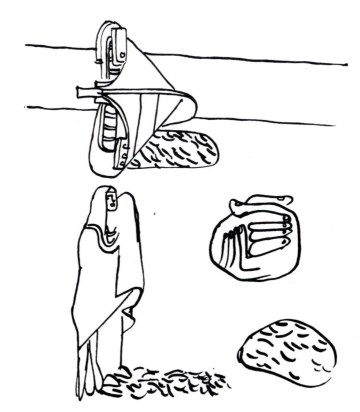

[23] M. le Chanoine Belot, Curé de Ronchamp, *Manuel du Pelerin*, 1930, p.13 in FLC.

[24] H. de Lubac, *L'Éternel Féminin: études sur un texte du Père Teilhard de Chardin*, Paris: Aubier, 1968, p.38.

abstracted pair of breasts (Plate 16) and down into a cistern, womblike in form. As if to emphasise this theme, the wall of the church curves out at this point as if in emulation of the stomach of a pregnant woman (this protrusion encloses the confessionals). Indeed Lucien Hervé, a photographer with whom Le Corbusier worked very closely, likened the rough plaster of the walls to the skin of women, continuing further the analogy of building and body.[25]

Wombs or Tombs: Figuring out the 'Gap'

Like such artists as Henri Matisse (who collaborated with Couturier and his *Art Sacré* colleagues, for example in the chapel at Vence, consecrated in 1951), Le Corbusier tried to purify and abstract the human form, but never completely beyond recognition.[26] Indeed he expressed an inability to move from representational to abstract art because he needed 'to keep contact with living beings'.[27] In Le Corbusier's opinion: 'Architecture is like a vase. It does not show off – it is from the interior that it lives. It is in the interior that the essential takes place.'[28] In form Ronchamp's towers are remarkably reminiscent of the heads of three women whose hair is shrouded by material, like that of the figure of Mary that appears on the beach in *Le Poème de l'angle droit* (Fig. 6.4),[29] and hooded women who emerge elsewhere in Le Corbusier's work.[30] The abstracted figure of Mary is thus embodied in the forms of the church, and thus reading the building symbolically, we may be said to enter her womb, to participate in the divine and be transformed.

Once inside the chapel's cool dark interior, the eye is drawn towards the conventional sculpted figure of Mary who presides in a glazed box set into the wall by the altar framed by sunlight and surrounded by a constellation of stars (Fig. 6.5). She is fixed on a pivot and can be moved to face inwards to the church or outwards to look down upon the congregation in the outdoor chapel and

6.5
Altar, Chapel of Notre-Dame-du-Haut, Ronchamp. Le Corbusier, 1950–5. From Le Corbusier and Jeanneret, *Oeuvre Complète Volume 6*, p.33.

[25] L. Hervé, *Le Corbusier The Artist/Writer*, Neuchatel: Éditions du Grifon, 1970, p.28. Le Corbusier himself referred to it as a 'skin'. Le Corbusier, *Oeuvre Complète Volume 5*, p.72.

[26] The art historian J. Coll suggests that the forms of Ronchamp may have derived from the paintings of *Icône*, the feminine deity over which Le Corbusier laboured at such length. J. Coll, 'Structure and Play in Le Corbusier's Art Works', *AA Files*, 31, summer 1996, pp.3-15.

[27] Le Corbusier, *A New World of Space*, New York: Reynal & Hitchcock, 1948, p.21.

[28] Cited in J. Alford, 'Creativity and Intelligibility in Le Corbusier's Chapel at Ronchamp', *The Journal of Aesthetics and Art History*, 16, 3, 1958, pp.293-305.

[29] Krustrup has traced this image back to its origins, a mural of Mary in S. Maria Antiqua in Rome. M. Krustrup, *Porte Email*, Copenhagen: Arkitektens Forlag, 1991, p.143.

[30] While in Ozon during the war, Le Corbusier began a series of works based on images of Yvonne cast as a Pyrennean peasant woman in a hooded robe.

[31] Le Corbusier, *Oeuvre Complète Volume 5*, p.27.

[32] B. Colomina, 'Le Corbusier and Photography', *Assemblage*, 4, 1987, pp.12–13.

[33] Le Corbusier, *Oeuvre Complète Volume 6*, p.18.

[34] E. Renan, *The Life of Jesus*, London: Watts, 1947, p.215. Le Corbusier's annotated copy is in the FLC, E. Renan, *La Vie de Jesus*, Paris: Calmann-Levy, 1906.

beyond. It seems very likely that Le Corbusier had something symbolic in mind when he made this slightly perverse arrangement. He was referring to a Mary with two very different readings.

A discussion of the Virgin Mary at Ronchamp is incomplete without bearing in mind Le Corbusier's treatment of the figure of the 'prostitute saint', Mary Magdalene, of La Sainte Baume, and his conception of Mary as a composite figure combining various paradoxical aspects of feminine deity. Indeed, in his *Oeuvre Complète* he refers to the 'Marys' in plural arriving from France on a boat from Palestine,[31] and he would not have been the first to merge the different Marys of the Bible into a composite figure. He was known to adulterate and orchestrate the photos that were taken of his works, and in the *Oeuvre Complète* the Virgin Mary of Ronchamp is depicted, very deliberately, half in light and half in shadow, half perfect and half less so, our attention drawn to her by the obtrusive spike of an umbrella (Fig. 6.6).[32]

Le Corbusier found the design of the main altar of the chapel of Ronchamp highly problematic.[33] On close inspection it seems to be strangely imbalanced, drawing the eye away from the altar, to one side where 'the Tree' or crucifix, the figure of Mary and, ultimately, the east door preside beneath the ceiling's zenith, where the vast vertical fenestration allows dazzling shafts of light to penetrate into the body of the church. Thus the imagery is drawn from Christ back to Mary and the feminine principle, and highlights the primary importance of the area to the right of the altar – reinforced by the flow of lines in the floor, the arrangement of the eccentric seating, and the angle from which Le Corbusier chose to portray the altar in his *Oeuvre Complète*.

Rolling Stones and Access to the Divine

The door to which one's eye is led is formed of concrete, a strangely impractical choice of material, and is etched with lines suggesting the coursing of stone (Fig. 6.7). In short, it is highly evocative of the stone that was rolled away from the tomb at the time of Jesus' resurrection, referring to the moment when Mary Magdalene discovered the empty tomb and wandered, inconsolable, in the gardens of Gethsemane.

In *The Life of Jesus*, a book favoured by Le Corbusier, Ernest Renan ascribed a very particular role to Mary Magdalene. 'Possessed by love' through her 'strong imagination' she 'gave to the world a resuscitated God'.[34] It was she who was witness to the resurrection; through her we have access to Christ and to the knowledge that was created by their love. It may be for this reason that the bronze handle of the east door takes the abstract form of a woman's body. As our hand encloses her waist we symbolically open the door to knowledge, and are initiated. Le Corbusier may have engaged with the Teilhardian idea that revelation, unity with the Earth, is aided by the experience of love, and only then can one pass out through the door into another reality where the sun/son rises. That the handle of the door is in some way symbolic of the Magdalene may be corroborated by the presence of the cockle shell, embedded in the concrete next to it, which, as well as being symbolic of pilgrimage, represents Venus with

6.6
Exterior chapel, Ronchamp. Le Corbusier and Jeanneret, *Oeuvre Complète Volume 6*, p.26.

6.7
Detail of east door of chapel. Le Corbusier, *The Chapel at Ronchamp*, London: Architectural Press, 1957, p.117.

whom the Magdalene is associated.

The priests who carry the cross out through the door to be positioned on the exterior chapel re-enact in a small way another more famous journey. Orientated with the rising of the sun, the east door may symbolise the death and resurrection of Jesus. By entering through the door we participate in the realm of Christ, acting out on a human scale a greater cosmic drama.

Mary, Mother and Love: Mysticism and the Paradoxical Mary

The chapel at Ronchamp represents the embodiment of a paradoxical Mary, at once mother, virgin and lover, expressing simultaneously three sides of the eternal feminine. In accordance with the tendency in the *Art Sacré* movement to make connections between biblical figures and contemporary people (seeing them as re-enacting the same ancient stories), when Le Corbusier wrote the words 'je vous salue Marie' upon the glass of the painted windows in the south wall he seems to have offered a correlation between Notre Dame and Marie his mother, for whom he had such deep respect.

According to Robin Evans, the three towers of Ronchamp were given personal associations by Le Corbusier, who named them after the Virgin Mary, his mother Marie to whom he was devoted, and Yvonne, his wife (Plate 13).[35] Indeed, Le Corbusier had been known to sketch his mother as a divinity, a giant sphinx flanked by the sun and the moon, confirming the possibility of such a link.[36] Given the considerations described here, it seems very likely that her tower, painted white on the inside, represents the mother side of the feminine, while Yvonne's, painted red, represents the sexual. Together they are subsumed within the shadow of the large white tower representing the Virgin herself.

It seems that Le Corbusier identified with archetypal truths in the life of Jesus which, for him, were symbolised by his own relationship with his wife and mother. He had experienced Mary as a reality in the women he held most dear. In the plaster by the figure of the Virgin Mary can be seen the imprint of Le Corbusier's own fingers.[37] For him her presence was very real. He had touched her, he had felt her skin. Here Le Corbusier revealed the fecundity of depth psychology in the process of creativity, as he left palimpsests of the fathomless 'gap' in the very fabric of his creativity. His experience of mother and then of women is extrapolated into form.

It has been seen that Le Corbusier consciously played games with light and shadow.[38] The chapel at Ronchamp acts as a calendar, almost a sundial marking time, the rhythms of nature. Indeed Peter Carl has drawn attention to the very deliberate way in which light penetrates the chapel at the commencement of the service celebrating the Feast of the Assumption of the Virgin, causing a shadow of the cross to extend from the altar rail.[39]

Le Corbusier sought to blur the lines between the Modulor as a form of measure and the Modulor as a form of experience. By challenging us to find the presence of the Modulor at Ronchamp, he is challenging us to open ourselves to the experience of ineffable space – the very experience of natural harmony. Le Corbusier quoted a passage from his book *L'Espace Indicible* (1945) in his book

[35] R. Evans, The Projective Cast, Cambridge, MA, MIT Press, 1995, p.284.

[36] Krustrup, *Porte Email*, p.149.

[37] J. Labasant, 'Le Corbusier's Notre Dame du Haut at Ronchamp', *Architectural Record*, 118, 4, 1955, p.170.

[38] Le Corbusier, *The Chapel at Ronchamp*, London: Architectural Press, 1957, p.46.

[39] P. Carl, 'Ornament and Time: A Prolegomena', *AA Files*, 23, 1992, p.56.

The Modulor: 'I have not experienced the miracle of faith, but I have often known the miracle of inexpressible space, the apotheosis of plastic emotion',[40] citing it again in *Modulor 2* to emphasise its importance. In the context of a discussion on the Cubist concept of the fourth dimension in art he wrote:

> For a finished and successful work holds within it a vast amount of intention, a veritable world, which reveals itself to those who have a right to it: that is to say, to those who deserve it.
>
> Then a fathomless depth gapes open, all walls are broken down, every other presence is put to flight, and the miracle of inexpressible space is achieved.[41]

He was describing a moment of mystical revelation, a state of harmony with nature, achieved through the use of mathematics – the 'key' to the 'door of miracles'.[42] Le Corbusier's notions of the mystical, of harmony and of nature are inseparable, and his buildings are an attempt to attain this yearned-for state.

By creating a building that was a celebration of the divine feminine Le Corbusier would provide the means for each individual pilgrim to gain contact with nature. In alluding to the most ancient forms of construction, the cave and the dolmen, he displayed a profound nostalgia for a time when man lived fully within nature. It seems likely that Le Corbusier felt it necessary to celebrate the role of the feminine with a masculinised Catholic church, because he believed that a balance between masculine and feminine was a law of nature and was central to the pursuit of harmony.[43]

Three in One: Between Interiority and Spirituality

Aalto designed more than twenty churches in his life, nine of which were built. From the Italianate beginnings at Muurame (1926, Fig. 2.4), which follows a basilica formula, he moved increasingly towards 'free-form' compositions in these designs, the most famous of which is that for the small village on the edge of Imatra called Vuoksenniska, begun in 1955 and completed in 1959 (Fig. 6.10). This church draws on the wedge-shaped profile of his 1929 Vallila church competition design, but moves forward to the formal freedom of Ronchamp. Unlike Ronchamp, Aalto reins in the free-form, yoking it back to Euclid's realm in a way that is characteristic of many of his buildings, connecting it with an attitude towards the 'organic' that is very significant, one that is never unbridled.

Form in Forested Frontiers

In 1947 Aalto undertook a commission from the Enso-Gutzeit company for a general plan for Imatra, after they needed to relocate within Finland's next eastern border having lost the bulk of their wood-processing plants to Stalin after the Second World War. Vuoksenniska church is located in a forested residential area which itself was part of a plan made by Aalto for the integration of urban, industrial, agrarian and natural areas around Imatra.

40 Le Corbusier, *Modulor*, London: Faber, 1954, p.32.
41 Ibid., p.27.
42 Ibid., p.71.
43 There is a pamphlet in Le Corbusier's collection in which it states that equality of males and females is a natural law. A. Mesclon, *Le Femenisme et l'Homme*, Paris: A. Mesclon, 1931 in FLC.

Aalto's call for 'tact' in the positioning and the impact of new forms in the landscape was discussed in Chapter 4.[44] In Vuoksenniska he tactfully countered the connotation and form of the many industrial chimneys in the area by placing a modest 34-metre-high tower next to the church (Fig. 6.8). It both announces the human foothold in the natural landscape and heralds the spiritual realm in the frontier zone and in the forest itself (which in pagan terms was nothing new, but in the sanitised forest industry has been completely lost). This campanile refers to two of Aalto's deep loves – the Italian *architettura minore* and Finnish vernacular churches of the late seventeenth and early eighteenth centuries.

6.8
Sketch plan, section and elevation of Vuoksenniska. Aalto, *c*.1956.

Trinitarian Tones and Tensions

In his church designs Aalto often created a 'triangularity of motifs' representing the symbol of the trinity (Fig. 6.8).[45] The trinity of doctrinal symbols for the Lutheran faith – the altar, the pulpit and the organ loft – formed the basis of Aalto's design of Vuoksenniska's worship space (Plate 10). Of the 'Church of the Three Crosses', as it is called, he wrote:

> The Church altar has been placed in a symbolic axial position, and pulpit and the organ have been installed asymmetrically. This had the automatic result that a single, asymmetric form of room was obtained, both in plan and in cross-sectional projections. The wall and ceiling surfaces have been shaped so that they reinforce the reflected sound-waves from the altar and organ ... The triad recurs inside the vault which covers the three halls. The motif converges at the altar in three unpretentious crosses.[46]

6.9
Northerly elevation of Church of the Three Crosses, Vuoksenniska. Aalto, 1955-8.

Aalto employed the imagery of the trinity at different formal levels, including the flipping between plan, section and detail,[47] as a gesture towards wholeness. This is evinced where the walls and ceiling reflect the tripartite nature of the plan, as the vaulting grows out of large pillars and the points where the massive concrete partitions are absorbed into the walls (Plate 12).[48]

He also described how he sought 'to achieve a form which is fully that of a church, but nevertheless so that the social activity is uncompromisingly provided for'.[49] The consequent overall form comprises three consecutive spaces – the sanctuary proper, and two social spaces for funeral wakes, church celebrations or volley-ball games. The north-eastern side projects an organic form towards the forest, as the three cells of space are expressed externally as massive sculpted undulations of the white washed wall, while the south-western façade is vertical and geometric. From without these three spaces appear as a heaving trinity (Fig. 6.9), but within they can be united to form one large worship space that fans out as if from the altar, cell upon cell. The spaces are

[44] Aalto, 'Architecture in the Landscape of Central Finland', *Sisä-Suomi*, 26 June 1925; repr. in Schildt, *Own Words*, pp. 21–2.

[45] Aalto, 'Riola Church', *Domus*, February 1967, p.447.

[46] Aalto, 'Vuoksenniska Church', *Arkkitehti*, 12/1959, p.201 and in a leaflet available in the church.

[47] P. Reed, 'Alvar Aalto and the New Humanism of the Postwar Era', in Reed (ed.) *Between Humanism and Materialism*, New York: Museum of Modern Art, 1998, pp.110–11.

[48] The partitions comprise approximately 400mm thick concrete walls that weigh 30 tons, providing complete acoustic insulation. K. Fleig (ed.) *Alvar Aalto Vol.1*. 1922–62, Zürich:, Verlag für Architecktur Artemis, 1990, p.220.

[49] Aalto, 'Vuoksenniskan Kirkko', *Arkkitehti-Arkitekten*, 12, 1959, p.201.

united by the mechanical removal of huge concrete partitions that slide into the curving, expanded exterior walls as needs demand, seating between 290 and 800 people. The six entrances offer different faces by which to access the different spaces without disturbing other groups using adjoining spaces.

Growing Mass from Forest Matter

Writing in 1924, of Mantegna's frescoes of hill towns, Aalto declared 'that curving, living, unpredictable line which runs in dimensions unknown to the mathematicians, is for me the incarnation of everything that forms a contrast between brutal mechanicalness and religious beauty in life'.[50] Vuoksenniska church is a manifestation of this 'religion' of his. What Aalto called the 'crust of the earth' is created here by using the building both as if it were geological massing that can be landscaped,[51] and at the level of detail through the various species of tree-like mullions enlivened by natural light (Fig. 6.10), just as the geology of the interior landscape is designed to work with the nature of sound. Indeed, a design sketch shows the emergence of this crust, which he developed from his wood experiments (Fig. 6.11), and therefore further extrapolates the 'little sister of the column', as he affectionately called the chair leg. The relationship between the church, the chair leg and the forest matter of a twig is detailed in the juxtaposition of two drawings, Figures 6.10 and 6.11; a line of argument assisted by the wood experiment placed next to a bit of branch (Fig. 2.6). Here the path from the structure of wood and the formal flexibility therein to architectural form is established.

Indeed, unlike Finland's medieval churches, the massive walls at Vuoksenniska form manipulated space, an 'in-between' that is also found between ceiling and roof (Fig. 6.11). Having benefited from the compositional freedom gained by the architects of the modern movement, Aalto utilised and expanded both the functional and the symbolic meaning of the elements of floor, wall and roof. Leonardo Mosso suggests that these therefore have little real content.[52] Addressing a similar point regarding structure and surface Randall Ott recalls Porphyrios' notion that Aalto rejected the cornerstone of Modernism – 'the distinction between structural and non-structural members'[53] – describing how 'surface and structure increasingly came to interact in his later buildings ... with these kinds of exotic interactions – of skin freely intermingling with bone – he moved even further from the tectonic rigors of Modernism'.[54]

At Vuoksenniska the massive copper roof extrapolates the forms of the interior vaulting. The drama of the transition continues to live and be effective in the transmission of light, dampening of noise, and control of the thermal environment, through the extraordinary double-glazed windows (Fig. 6.10). The expansive gesture occurs on the easterly façade in the clerestory windows, wherein the interior mullions, with their symbolic references to silviculture, are loosely mirrored by the external ones. Indeed, the windows are virtually all unique. In this way Aalto may be said to imitate the a-geometric form of the trees in order to recall the form and quality of light penetrating deep forests from above. This was prefigured in his 1937 Finnish Pavilion for the Paris World Fair (Fig. 6.13). At Vuoksenniska light becomes material like wood and rock, and is thus given purposive form.

[50] Aalto, 'The Hill Top Town', 1924 in Schildt, Own Words, p.49.

[51] Aalto referred to 'the brilliant analysis of the earth's crust' in 'The Hill Top Town', in Schildt, Own Words, p.49. See also K. Jormakka, J. Gargus and D. Graf, in The Use and Abuse of Paper, Datutop 20, Tampere: Tampere University, 1999, p.133.

[52] L. Mosso, Alvar Aalto. Catalogue 1918–1967, Helsinki: Otava, 1967, p.129.

[53] D. Porphyrios, Sources of Modern Eclecticism, London: Academy Editions, 1982, pp.4-5.

[54] R. Ott, 'Surface and Structure', in M. Quantrill and B. Webb (eds) The Culture of Silence: Architecture's Fifth Dimension, Texas: A & M University Press, 1998, p.98.

6.10
Detail of clerestory windows, Church of the Three Crosses, Vuoksenniska. Aalto, 1956–9.

6.11
Sketch of chancel section of Church of the Three Crosses, Vuoksenniska as 'little sister of the column'. Aalto, *c.*1956.

6.12
Sketch of wood experiment and chair leg ('little sister of the column'), with design of Church of the Three Crosses, Vuoksenniska. Aalto, *c.*1956.

6.13
Finnish Pavilion, New York World
Fair, 1939 (demolished). Aalto,
1938–9. Ezra Stoller

Mowing a Way through the Forest of the Mind

The building is somehow insulated from immersion in the forest by the mown grass around the church (Fig. 6.9), as if both the nature and the spirit of the forest is held back from encroaching on this spiritual refuge by the neatness of the lawns. In this way the mown grass might be said to detract from the church's external impact, but may also be seen as a sign of purification in a place that might otherwise speak of pagan times (of backwoods forest wisdom), allowing the forest to signify what it has generally represented, namely the shadow of civilisation and the holder of dark secrets. Therefore the mowing creates a sense of determination to make a human impact on the backwoods, to imprint civilisation and culture upon the wilderness and the personal Christian salvation on the indifferent pagan powers of the forest. The grass also represents the literal provision of physical protection for the soul-seeking undertaken therein.

The building thus has two main faces: one roundly turning from the forest, the other facing straight towards the enclosure offered by the minister's house and the collection of outbuildings. In this way the building complex does what many other forest settlements, like the trope of Niemelä, do in creating protection and enclosure (Fig. 7.16).

Yet in addition to this role in enriching and perhaps manipulating meaning in its cultural context and physical 'geographical' landscape, the building also has an active, symbolic role in the inner 'psycho-spiritual' realm. The building envelope is able to manipulate the inner space, as a process of turning inwards is continued in the fabric of the building in preparation for its sensitive and precious function of personal disclosure to others and to the divine. Indeed, to a greater degree than Aalto's early neoclassical churches, the design secludes and protects its interior. It has something of an introverted composition, and is not easily read from the outside.

Lighting 'In-between'

Further manipulation of the light occurs with the deep sky-light vault above the altar which casts a particularly impressive light on the interior, which then dematerialises the already amorphous form of the chancel area (Plate 15). To this end Aalto fully manipulated both the inside and outside edges of the building, using the interior space to unify disparate external forms and the external envelope as an elastic skin that enfolds the plastic interiors. In this way the 'in-between' synthesises disparate spatial elements, and allows a rich quality of light to penetrate this mediated space. Indeed, Juha Leiviska has offered the analogy of architecture being 'played' by light,[55] the rich diversity of light's spectrum throughout the year ensuring variety. The great height of the windows adds to the sense of being within a protected interior, presenting a sloping face within as mullions lean, dynamically, into the spaces.

After studying Aalto's design methodology, Gunnar Birkerts has expanded on the subject of the 'in-between', suggesting that, 'Since both shells perform different functions, they have been shaped differently. The exterior shell is there to enclose, protect and to transmit light. The interior shell is there to correct

55 Juha Leiviska, in interview with S. Menin, 6 September 1988, Helsinki.

acoustical form to the space, but also to enclose and to transmit light'.[56] This concurs with Robert Venturi's comment regarding what he called 'detached linings', in other words 'the detachment of inner and outer window openings' which modifies the light and space, not just recalling the Baroque churches[57] but in many ways surpassing them.

Freeing Form, Fleeing Euclid

Aalto's explanation in 'The Trout and the Stream' of how he dwelt on functional and practical problems (including symbols as part of the psycho-social functioning of a building) and reflected on a buildings historical role, before 'playing' with form like a child,[58] is helpful in unpacking the different dimensions of this design. The additive nature of form in Aalto's buildings seems to be a combination of geometry and the growth of natural form – although these are not mutually exclusive, as Gaudi demonstrates. Indeed, despite its amorphous massing, geometry may well have played a part in the composition of Vuoksenniska church. After all, Aalto spent a lot of time drawing façades and studying scale and proportion during his student years.

Aalto's 'playing' is manifested in the section of the church that is derived from the 'little sister of the column' chair leg he had developed earlier (Fig. 6.11). He pushes the fan form, which was to become such a staple element in his work, to fruition in both the section and the plan (Plate 12). The way the three basic church spaces grow is controlled, as if it were a geometric progression or an organism with a strong genetic code (Fig. 6.9). Indeed, many commentators have suggested that the building seems as lively as a sketch, finding form in concrete, brick, wood, glass, cooper and white marble, simple interior finishes in keeping with the dogma and aesthetics of the Lutheran faith. Reima Pietilä wrote, 'Aalto has moved his hand over and over the paper. The lines are fumbling but fully sensitive. A cloudy, total shape. "Gestalt" ... has emerged. This hand sketch is very suggestive to the looking eye: I believe there is already within it a comprehensive idea for the building because Aalto always tried to achieve an architectural approximation or synthesis.'[59] Curtis joins Pietilä, observing that, 'the vitality of the sketch seemed to be translated directly into the finished form',[60] perhaps due to the strength of the basic idea – in this case the trinity. Somehow this Christian symbol seems to represent nature-as-cosmos – Aalto's yearning for 'synthesis' which, almost pathologically, seeks to pull three into one precarious harmony into which all man's gestures (be they personal or formal) must contribute.

Curtis further suggests that 'Aalto's hymn to the forest landscape' was enacted through his 'working with biomorphic abstraction to evoke a generalised reference to the "flow" of water, to sinuous boundaries of lakes, and (possibly) to the "female" aspect of natural forces'.[61] Elsewhere, however, Curtis joins the voices of those who on the one hand accept the *raison d'être* of Aalto's church, but on the other hand describe how 'Aalto felt less and less need for a rational order',[62] and in this way undermine the view of expanded rationality that Aalto had articulated since 1935.[63] Introduced in Chapter 4, this subject will receive further attention in Chapter 8.

56 G. Birkerts, 'Aalto's Design Methodology', *Architecture and Urbanism*, May 1983, Extra Edition, p.12.

57 R. Venturi, *Complexity and Contradiction in Architecture*, London: Architectural Press, 1983, p.80. See also Reed, 'Alvar Aalto and the New Humanism of the Postwar Era' in P. Reed (ed.) *Alvar Aalto Between Humanism and Materialism*, pp.94-115.

58 Jormakka *et al.* point out that Paul Marie Letarouilly's *Edifices de Rome Moderne* was a standard text in Finland when Aalto was a student, and it is known that he spent countless hours drawing façades and studying proportion. In avant-garde circles texts on geometry emerged, being of interest for symbolic as well as theosophic reasons. Le Corbusier's *Modulor* 'is a late entry in the genre, and a work which relied greatly on its predecessors'. Jormakka, Gargus and Graf, *Use and Abuse of Paper*, p.135.

59 R. Pietilä, 'A "Gestalt" Building', *Architecture and Urbanism*, May 1983, Extra Edition, 12. Cited by Kristiina Paatero, 'Vuoksenniska Church', in T. Tuomi, K. Paatero and E. Rauske (eds) *Alvar Aalto in Seven Buildings*, Helsinki: Museum of Finnish Architecture, 1999, p.113.

60 W. Curtis, *Modern Architecture Since 1900*, London: Phaidon, 1996, p.459.

61 W. Curtis, 'Modernism, Nature, Tradition: Aalto's Mythical Landscape', in Tuomi, Paatero and Rauske (eds), *Alvar Aalto in Seven Buildings*, p.135.

62 W. Curtis, *Modern Architecture Since 1900*, p.459.

63 Aalto, 'Rationalism and Man', 1935 in Schildt, *Own Words*, p.91.

Sculpting Insight or Caving in to places of the Soul?

Entering Vouksenniska church one is struck by the drama of the space. Generally the entrance perpendicular to the chancel is used. One therefore enters perpendicular to the thrust of the main axis of the long cave-like form. In this way one seems to fall upon a process that is in full swing, in the action around the crosses in the chancel to the left. This is the opposite sensation to that offered by the more conventional basilica form that Aalto used in other churches, such as Muramme and Seinäjoki churches, where the drama unfolds ahead of oneself, and somehow tumbling towards the altar.

Entering side-on in this way, one finds the drama of the three pulsating volumes a surprise after the experience of walking through the main entrance façade, with its cool hints towards Euclidean form. Here Aalto moves from geometric order to a natural order, 'fleeing Euclid',[64] and seems to find a certain freedom (philosophical or even spiritual) in doing so, as exemplified in many of his oil paintings (Plate 14). Despite its extensive fenestration, this building presents a closed visage, hinting of its voluminous interior in its black curved roof while the side that nestles close to the forest not only adopts a different geometry but expresses something of the nature of the interior.

Richard Weston suggests that the sense of containment offers a space that 'can be read as being in continuous motion towards the altar', but which disappears precipitously behind the three crosses, leaving them in indeterminate space – 'an abstraction of Golgotha'.[65] Yet, arriving side-on to the thrust of the church's axis, one comes immediately upon this process of 'abstraction', as if an unwitting witness at Golgotha. The experience is immediate and shockingly material almost before one is conscious of it, since the crosses, not greatly elevated, are very immediate and within reach.

Indeed, as the visitor approaches the building for services such as funerals, set against the dark forest the church reaches out with a low, covered colonnade leading to the dark doorway, apparent as a void between two areas of white wall. In this way the more private entrance is not demonstrative, failing to herald an arrival, but rather offering a grave welcome. Expectation is concentrated by the haptic experience of the low, dark vestibule (common in Aalto's buildings). This demands a physical adjustment to the sense of dark interiority, as one symbolically sheds protective outside clothes. This is a physiological set-up, since, turning through ninety degrees to open the church door into the brilliantly lit sanctuary, one is immediately struck by the bleeding red of the stained-glass window opposite representing the crown of thorns (Plate 15). It is as if the building manifests a credo drawn from experiences of life, yet offering a way of processing those experiences.

Schildt suggests that Aalto's church architecture explicates a belief in 'a harmonious order common to nature, man and cultural forms, a belief in a divine element within existence'.[66] This is manifest more clearly here than elsewhere. Aalto wrote of man's tendency to err, and the way ancient religions and Christianity have at their centre the 'human factor', what he believed to be 'a childish variant of the tragedy of the whole human race'.[67] It is as if Aalto has prepared both the body and the soul for the shock of the light, of the divine,

[64] The expression is used in R. Connar, *Aaltomania*, Helsinki: Rakennustieto, 2000, p.108.

[65] R. Weston, *Alvar Aalto*, London: Phaidon, 1995, p.206.

[66] Schildt, *Early Years*, p.193.

[67] Aalto, 'The Human Factor', n.d., in Schildt, *Own Words*, pp.280–1.

and the insight of a central aspect of Christian life, that through the darkness of broken humanity comes the light – the blood-stained red glass signifying Christ's raw sacrifice. It is also significant that, if the curved form of the easterly wall represents nature and the forest, so the straight westerly wall hosts the image of human suffering. It is not unreasonable to suggest that Aalto may have felt that part of the psycho-spiritual function of the building was such a process of withdrawal and expurgation.

Phenomenally speaking, like Ronchamp, the building interior is simultaneously cave, tomb and womb. As so often Aalto created a topographic profile where the site does not offer a form of this kind,[68] so he extrapolated one from within a simple forest clearing. The process of being 'in-between' shared reality and these soul-holding realms is enacted as one moves through the extended walls, from one realm of being to another. As Aalto's writing acknowledges the metaphysical realms, so his architecture often gently accommodates human vulnerability. However in his church architecture he intended not to make us comfortable with gentle humanism, but rather to manifest a process of meeting divinity. He created a holding environment in which the human soul may fall open before God. The process of entering the building (through the 'in-between' wall) may prepare the visitor in some way for entering the 'gap'.

Conclusion

Winnicott describes how the commencement of the creative process instigates a Transitional Phenomenon to take 'the strain of relating inner and outer reality'.[69] The resulting Potential Space comprises fragments of undifferentiated experiences, drawing on the bank of perceptions, sensations and feelings from the earliest years. Through creativity these may be brought to consciousness; they may be differentiated. Cobb suggests that among children a similar differentiation of the earliest unmet human needs often takes place in nature-experience, where these needs are reconciled to a greater or lesser extent.[70] This does not heal the 'gaps' but offers a temporary salvation to the child. Artistic creativity may also address these 'gaps', especially when the creativity is in a social sphere, such as architecture, in which human needs must be addressed. In the cases of Le Corbusier and Aalto childhood dependence on nature as a stimulating safe haven seems to have meant that their most profound architectural solutions are derived from that same realm.

There is in Le Livre de Ronchamp an image of people sitting around an open fire in front of the exterior altar. The figure of Mary looks over the scene, like a pagan goddess presiding over some ancient rite (Fig. 6.14). The image provides graphic evidence of Le Corbusier's desire to create, in Ronchamp, a communal place of solace and reconciliation both with man and with nature. Its central theme is the importance of love in every sense of the word. By evoking the organic form of a woman's body and, simultaneously, rounded caves carved out through the action of water he hoped to bring us back into a state of inner

[68] M. Treib discusses this in 'Aalto's Nature', in Reed, *Alvar Aalto Between Humanism and Materialism*, p.57. Treib suggests Aalto aggregates the elements of the building programme to reinforce the morphology of the existing sites.

[69] D.W. Winnicott, 'Transitional Objects and Transitional Phenomena', in *Collected Papers*, London: Tavistock, 1958, p.240.

[70] E. Cobb, *The Ecology of Imagination in Childhood*, Dallas: Spring Publications, 1993.

harmony. Just as at Vuoksenniska, the mysticism Le Corbusier facilitated in
Ronchamp is palpable, and has been widely acknowledged as such. Abbé Bolle-
Reddat, who took charge of the chapel after it was built, repeatedly commented
that visitors, whatever their background, were profoundly moved by the
experience of it.[71] Le Corbusier relied heavily upon the use of symbolism and
geometry and his own secret agenda for architecture to bring a sense of nature
into the scheme.

At Vuoksenniska Aalto ostensibly seems to express nature in a far more
direct way, by creating the feeling of being subsumed in pseudo-natural form,
with the symbolic resonances of a natural setting such as light penetrating
through trees all around. The one symbol through which he calls on Christian
religious metaphor is the trinity. Here Aalto was consciously designing with
the 'organic line' in mind,[72] emphasising it through contrast with its Euclidean
nemesis. The 'organic line' on the eastern side of the building, with its forested
mullions and its association with pagan mysticism, represents a state of mind,
and contrasts with the largely straight western wall. It might be said that at

[71] See extracts from his diary in Le
Corbusier, *Le Livre de Ronchamp*,
Paris: Les Cahiers Forces Vives,
1962, p.100.
[72] Aalto, letter to Gropius, autumn
1930, AAF, in G. Schildt, *Alvar Aalto:
The Decisive Years*, New York:
Rizzoli, 1986, p.66.

Vuoksenniska Aalto made a soul place for others, re-creating undulating, embracing, voluminous, feminine forms through the building's mass itself. As if it is somehow vulnerable, this soul-realm is heavily protected, as it is at Ronchamp, even disguised by the extrapolating roof – the outward projection of a façade that disguises its interior. It is as if with this building Aalto manipulated the 'in-between' as a symbol of the reconciliation of inner and outer reality which was so vital in his own life. He has offered concrete ways to separate the deepest personal moments of mourning from those of social celebration by way of the massive movable walls – but sometimes these boundaries are completely opened. In this there is a fair description of Aalto the man; one in whom the social face and the deeply personal are generally quite seperate, but may through his architecture be united. This reading of which in no way diminishes his creation of Vuoksenniska church, but one which, on the contrary, unfolds the secret of its rich humanity.

Schildt suggests that Aalto held optimistic ideas of free, natural man, liberated from the tyranny of conventions (including perhaps those of personal morality) 'according to Rousseau's recipe'.[73] The same might be said of Le Corbusier. There is, however, a deeper realm of being which explains these preoccupations and drives, and which describes something of the 'gap' through the forms their mysticism took in architecture.

If the complexities of the two men's relationships with their mothers might be said to have contributed to their manifestation of a sense of detachment or engagement with nature, so too may it have stimulated an urge to explore the feminine in form, architecture and life. This was certainly made manifest, for example, in the curved forms of their buildings and, more subtly, it may have contributed to their articulation of the importance of the poetic and of 'synthesis' in their design processes. It is no accident that when they addressed a spatial invitation to the divine, the curve appears prominent, demonstrating this intense inclination towards the 'feminine', and a deep proclivity towards an embrace.

[73] Ibid., p.165.

Top: 17
View of exterior of Villa Savoye. Le Corbusier,
1929–31.

Bottom: 18
View of entrance of Villa Mairea. Aalto, 1937–9.

Top: 19
Blue bathroom Villa Savoye. Le Corbusier,
1929–31.

Bottom: 20
Entrance hall, stair and tupa, Villa Mairea.
Aalto, 1937–9.

Top: 21
Table in hanging garden, Villa Savoye.
Le Corbusier, 1929–31.

Bottom: 22
View of forest from living room, Villa Mairea.
Aalto, 1937–9.

Opposite above: 23
Gate between garden and forest, Villa Mairea.
Aalto, 1937–9.

Opposite below: 24
Roofscape of Unité d'Habitation, Marseille.
Le Corbusier, 1945-52.

Above: 25
Housing development, Kauttua.
Aalto, 1937–40.

Below: 26
Façade of Unité d'Habitation, Marseille.
Le Corbusier, 1945-52.

Opposite: 27
Relief on façade of Unité d'Habitation,
Firminy. Le Corbusier, 1959–67.

SOLEIL

ESPACE

VERDURE

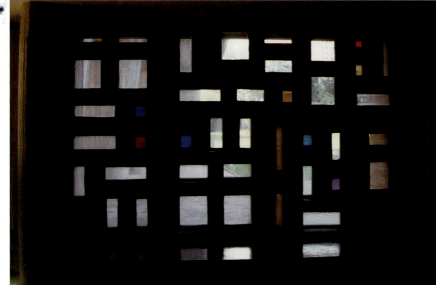

Above: 28
Oil painting, 44 x 53.5 cm.
Aalto, 1946.

Below: 29
Stained glass in entrance foyer,
Unité d'Habitation, Marseille.
Le Corbusier, 1945-52.

Opposite: 30
View towards duplex Apartment,
Unité d'habitation, Marseille.
Le Corbusier, 1945-52.

Chapter 7

World building: Nature, Biology and Luxuriant Forms

Having discussed the view taken by Aalto and Le Corbusier on the role of nature in the creation of mystical space, we will now move towards their conception of the role of nature in the dwelling. In *Mise au Point* Le Corbusier wrote that he had, for the last fifty years, felt compelled 'to introduce into the home a sense of the sacred; to make the home the temple of the family'.[1] He approached both his religious and domestic schemes with a similar aim in mind, that of bringing man into harmony with nature, an essentially sacred role. Earlier Le Corbusier had written that 'when nature integrates' itself in architecture it is then that one approaches unity. He then affirmed, 'I believe that unity is that stage to which the unceasing and penetrating work of the mind leads'[2], an aim with which it seems Aalto would have fully concurred.

In 1930 Aalto articulated his belief that dwellings must offer protection and that emotional and psychological 'problems' must be taken into consideration, creating an organic totality.[3] In his opinion patterns of dwelling had changed but the architectural solutions had not. He suggested it was important to return to the fundamental needs for protection, but also for air, light and sun. For Aalto it was vital to relate the dwelling to outside space – 'which biologically is equivalent to the nature man was accustomed to before large cities developed'.[4] Aalto knew intuitively that it was necessary to the health of individuals, and of children in particular, to have a sense of connection with nature. For him it was not a matter of choice, but an essential aspect of the proper functioning of human dwelling.

To recap, Cobb suggested that children may engage in 'world-building' in attempts to structure their life in analogy with an external system when their home environment is unstable.[5] In her opinion:

> If we consider mental development as a personal evolution from biological levels through cultural means, the intuitive but latent perceptual discovery made by the child in this exodus into nature as a deepening, evolving world image, is that his knowledge of the real world is organised

[1] Le Corbusier, 'Mise au Point' in Ivan Žaknić, *The Final Testament of Père Corbu*, New Haven: Yale University Press, 1997, p.91.

[2] Le Corbusier, *Precisions on the Present State of Architecture and City Planning*, Cambridge, MA: MIT Press, 1991, p.245.

[3] Aalto, 'The Dwelling as a Problem', 1930; repr. in G. Schildt, *Alvar Aalto Sketches*, Cambridge, MA: MIT Press, 1985, p.30.

[4] Ibid., p.32.

[5] E. Cobb, *The Ecology of Imagination in Childhood*, Dallas: Spring Publications, 1993, pp.17 and 53.

around his own perception and that he and nature are involved in some common formative purpose.[6]

The requisitioning of such Otherness in nature, both its order and the unconditional nature of its embrace, seems to have been vital in the early lives of Le Corbusier and Aalto, as was seen in Chapter 1. However, Cobb went on to cite Teilhard de Chardin's reference to 'a knowing through the merging of the self with nature and human nature on the way to God'.[7] She believed that 'the truly creative adult contrives to raise primary, less highly organised but deeply intuitive, aspects of awareness closer to consciousness with all the respect of the artist for the beauty and simplicity of his own primary materials'. This she described as 'the reverse of intellectual abstraction'.[8] In this case these materials were the very matter of building and the very nature of space. It was not, in Cobb's opinion, therefore less important for being intuitive, 'for it necessarily involves participation in nature's ongoing activities; it is relation-seeking effort'.[9] The same, it will be argued, can be said of Aalto and Le Corbusier's approach to the dwelling.

Dwelling as a Sacred Space

Taking their cue from the acute housing shortage at the time, both Le Corbusier and Aalto championed the cause of mass housing; they therefore had to justify themselves when accepting exclusive commissions for single family homes. Both maintained that such buildings offered the opportunity to try out new ideas. They were for Aalto a 'kind of experimental laboratory, where one can realise that which is not possible for the present mass production, but out of these experimental cases gradually spread ... to become an objective available to everyone'.[10] To this end, one of Le Corbusier's most individual and iconic homes, the Villa Savoye, was actually conceived as a building type suitable for possible mass production. An illustration in the *Oeuvre Complète* shows that Le Corbusier hoped to reuse this house type repeatedly for a scheme to be built in Buenos Aires.[11]

When Le Corbusier came to design individual houses he used mass-produced elements to standardised dimensions such as the vaulted roof unit. It was his hope in doing so to make connections with other 'radiant' houses built in a similar way. In the following discussion of three of Le Corbusier's individual dwellings (the Villa Savoye from the early airy white period, the penthouse at 24 Rue Nungesser et Coli built at a transitional stage in his career, and the more rooted architecture of the Petite Maison de Weekend) it will be seen that certain consistent themes are present in his domestic work, themes that relate to his desire to bring the inhabitants of his buildings into an intimate relationship with nature.

An Elemental House: Villa Savoye

The Villa Savoye at Poissy (1929–31, Plate 17) is perhaps the best known of Le Corbusier's houses. He described it as 'an object placed on the soil in the middle of the countryside'.[12] The house, 'a box in the air',[13] originally sat in isolation in the middle of a rural site, having all the characteristic elements of his domino frame and his

[6] Ibid, p.83.
[7] Ibid. pp.90–1.
[8] Ibid, p.94.
[9] Ibid.
[10] Aino and Alvar Aalto, Introduction to *Villa Mairea*, Jyväskylä: Alvar Aalto Museum, 1982, p.2. Originally published in *Arkkitehti*, 9, 1939.
[11] Le Corbusier and Pierre Jeanneret, *Oeuvre Complète Volume 2, 1929–34*, Zürich: Les Éditions d'Architecture, 1995, p.28.
[12] Ibid., p.31.
[13] Le Corbusier, *Precisions*, p.136

'five points' for a new architecture: free plan, free façade, horizontal windows, pilotis and roof garden (Plate 21). Le Corbusier wrote disarmingly in the *Oeuvre Complète* that 'The idea is simple'. It derived from the fact that the clients had a 'magnificent' site surrounded by forest some 30 km away from Paris which they accessed by car. Indeed, the size of the villa was determined by the turning circle of a large car that would drive in an arc beneath the pilotis and deposit its contents at the door.

'The other thing: the view is very beautiful,' wrote Le Corbusier, 'the grass is a beautiful thing, the forest as well: one must touch them as little as possible'.[14] 'The house is positioned in the middle of the grass without spoiling anything.' His justification for making a *jardin suspendu* ('hanging garden') on the first floor was that it would be drier and would allow the occupants to have a better view of the landscape (Plate 21). This space, simultaneously internal and external, was to act as a 'distributor of light'.[15] The photographs in the *Oeuvre Complète* are focused upon the way in which the building relates to the surrounding landscape and the garden within. Le Corbusier's description largely concentrates upon the garden, everything else is secondary, except perhaps the ramped route up to the solarium on the roof of the house.

Sitting proudly in splendid isolation, the villa is evidently built in homage to the Parthenon which received such adulation from Le Corbusier in *Vers une Architecture*; both are built using 'regulating lines' which link the building to nature. Simultaneously many details of the villa derive from the efficient ocean liners Le Corbusier so admired. When he wrote in *Vers une Architecture* of the house as 'a machine for living', he was describing how, like products of natural selection, it would work as efficiently as possible, both in practical and poetic terms.

In *Journey to the East* Le Corbusier noted the way in which the owners of the whitewashed houses in Greece painted their houses each year as a sign of renewal.[16] It seems likely that he was alluding to this practice when he created such ostentatiously white buildings as the Villa Savoye. Le Corbusier wrote again of the way in which whitewash was used in folk culture in a chapter entitled 'A Coat of Whitewash: The Law of Ripolin' in *The Decorative Art of Today*. 'Whitewash exists wherever peoples have preserved intact the balanced structure of a harmonious culture.'[17] Further, 'Whitewash has been associated with human habitation since the birth of mankind. Stones are burnt, crushed and thinned with water – and the walls take on the purest white, an extraordinary and beautiful white'. It seems therefore that for Le Corbusier whitewash was an intensely natural finish to be used to indicate a kinship with nature.[18]

Early in his career Le Corbusier had experimented with the ways in which architectural elements could be used to frame certain key Parisian landmarks when seen in the distance from the interior. This can be seen, for example, in the famous image of the roof garden of the Beistegui apartment (1932) in the *Oeuvre Complète*, in which an optical illusion caused the Arc de Triomphe to appear almost like an ornament on a mantelpiece (Fig. 7.1).[19] Le Corbusier continued thereafter to be interested in the possibilities presented by drawing a landscape into a house through the careful framing of views. This can be seen in the hanging garden of the Villa Savoye where a window with table inflects the eye out towards the view (Plate 21). Further, the villa is largely by enwrapped by

7.1
Roof garden, de Bestegui apartment. Le Corbusier, 1932. From Le Corbusier and Jeanneret, *Oeuvre Complète*, p.54.

[14] Le Corbusier, *Oeuvre Complète Volume 2*, p.24.
[15] Le Corbusier, *Precisions*, p.136.
[16] Le Corbusier, *Journey to the East*, Cambridge, MA: MIT Press, 1987, p.62.
[17] Le Corbusier, *Decorative Art of Today*, London: Architectural Press, 1987, p.190.
[18] Ibid., p.89.
[19] Le Corbusier, *Oeuvre Complète Volume 2*, p.54.

7.2
Plans of penthouse 24 Rue
Nungesser et Coli. Le Corbusier,
1933-5. Image from Le Corbusier
and Jeanneret, *Oeuvre Complète
Volume 2*, p.148.

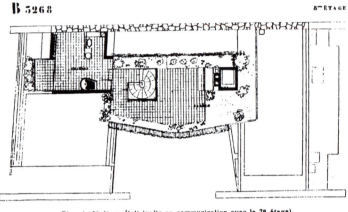

B 5268   8ᵐᵉ ÉTAGE

Plan du 8e étage (toit-jardin en communication avec le 7e étage)
Solarium et chambre d'amis

Above right: 7.3
Stair to roof, penthouse 24 Rue
Nungesser et Coli. Le Corbusier,
1933-5. Image from Le Corbusier
and Jeanneret, *Oeuvre Complète
Volume 2*, p.151.

Below right: 7.4
Fireplace, penthouse 24 Rue
Nungesser et Coli. Le Corbusier,
1933-5. Image from Le Corbusier
and Jeanneret, *Oeuvre Complète
Volume 2*, p.150.

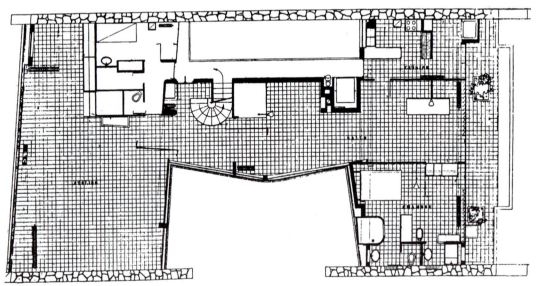

B 3267   7ᵐᵉ ÉTAGE

Plan du 7e étage. Ces deux plans soumis à l'étrange réglementation des gabarits ont nécessité une ingéniosité inlassable pour trouver les
points d'appui nécessaires et les surfaces habitables. Les gabarits avaient une raison d'être lorsqu'on construisait en charpente de bois.
Ils sont un résidu inadmissible à l'époque de la construction de l'acier et du ciment armé

20 Le Corbusier, *Journey to the East*,
    p.240.
21 On the frontispiece of Le Corbusier's
    edition of Rabelais' *Gargantua and
    Pantagruel*, in the Fondation Le
    Corbusier, hereafter referred to as
    FLC, in a note dated 1915, he
    recorded, as if for posterity, that his
    brother Albert introduced him to the
    concept of the four alchemical
    metals in 1905. He repeats the
    message inside on p. 52.
22 John Winter, 'Le Corbusier's
    Technological Dilemma' in R. Walden
    (ed.), *The Open Hand*, Cambridge,
    MA: MIT Press, 1982, p.334.
23 See F. Samuel,'Le Corbusier, Women,
    Nature and Culture', *Issues in Art
    and Architecture* 5, 2 1998, pp. 4-
    20 for a development of this theme.
24 'Reportage sur un toit-jardin', Le
    Corbusier, *Oeuvre Complète Volume
    4, 1938–1946*, Zürich: Les Éditions
    d'Architecture, 1995, p.140.
25 Le Corbusier, *A New World of Space*,
    New York: Reynal & Hitchcock,
    1948, p.116.

'une fenêtre en longueur' which draws 'the four horizons', a favourite Corbusian theme, into the house.

A sketch drawn during Le Corbusier's *Journey to the East* of a 'water temple' built into the side wall of a house indicates an early interest in how sacred water might be brought into a domestic setting.[20] Certainly the four elements receive varying degrees of emphasis at the Villa Savoye. The earth is left intact. As in many of his houses water is brought in at ground level in the form of a prominent washbasin by the front door, evoking the ritual of taking Holy Water on entrance to a Catholic church. It is further celebrated in the blue bathroom on the first floor (Plate 19). Fire is introduced in the freestanding red-brick fireplace that dominates the living room. Air is framed by the architecture of the hanging garden. Le Corbusier was already familiar with certain more arcane aspects of alchemy[21] and it is very possible that he introduced the four elements in this way on purpose, possibly even to invoke a beneficent form of magic.

Sky, Light and Concrete Life in a Parisian Garret: 24 Rue Nungesser et Coli

Le Corbusier's architecture went through a radical change during the early 1930s at around the same time as he married Yvonne, a transformation occurred in his paintings. These ceased to be an arid Purist landscape of bottles and books and began to contain certain natural objects, more overtly symbolic elements as well as women and animals. His own home, the penthouse at 24 Rue Nungesser et Coli, built in 1933, provides a good example of his architecture as it too underwent a period of transition. Once built, Le Corbusier was to change it further over time from what John Winter describes an 'open hard-edged interior' to 'the enclosed chunky-wood apartment of 1953'.[22]

Built in line with the tenets of the Radiant City and expressive of Le Corbusier's intense preoccupation with nature, the penthouse is sited in the Auteil area of Paris (Fig. 7.2). The floors themselves are supported on a line of columns that starts from a central position on the front and rear elevations, but which forms a distinctly unorthodox curve en route through the centre of the building. The coming together of oppositions is the central message of the building's iconography. At ground-floor level a circular column blocks the entry into the orthogonal building and sets the tone for what is to come.[23]

Upon entering the apartment the bulging wall opposite the door immediately deflects the eye away from the private studio towards the curved staircase (Fig. 7.3). The treads wind in circular form from the darkness of the hall past a niche containing carefully chosen objects, through a square aperture and up to the dazzling light of the roof garden above. The visitor travels up the organic curved stair to the garden and to the light. For Le Corbusier the roof garden was a space with enormous symbolic potential, the destination of the spiritual *promenade architecturale*, a place to commune with nature. Indeed Le Corbusier was delighted when his roof garden became overgrown and wild, softening the hard lines of his architecture.[24] 'The wind and sun control the composition, half man, half nature.'[25]

7.5
Dining space, penthouse 24 Rue
Nungesser et Coli. Le Corbusier,
1933-5. Image from Le Corbusier
and Jeanneret, *Oeuvre Complète
Volume 2*, p.150.

Right above: 7.6
Main bedroom, penthouse 24 Rue
Nungesser et Coli. Le Corbusier,
1933-5. Image from Le Corbusier
and Jeanneret, *Oeuvre Complète
Volume 2*, p.152.

Right below: 7.7
Vanity unit, penthouse 24 Rue
Nungesser et Coli. Le Corbusier,
1933-5. Image from Le Corbusier
and Jeanneret, *Oeuvre Complète
Volume 2*, p.152.

Right main: 7.8
Le Corbusier in his bedroom in front
of a painting by Bauchant.

Le Corbusier's studio is accessed off the hall. Here the white concrete of the vaulted roof structure contrasts with the party wall, its rich clay bricks evoking the earth. To use outdoor materials in an interior space such as this is an effective way of blurring interior and exterior. This blurring is augmented by the extensive use of glass throughout the apartment.

From the hall the visitor is drawn towards the living space with its simple fireplace above which is set a niche for displaying items from his 'particular collection': the head of an ancient Greek goddess, a bone, a pot, a handcrafted figurine (Fig. 7.4). Le Corbusier referred to them as 'objects that evoked a poetic reaction ... the vast panoply of spokesmen who speak the language of nature'. In his opinion they were 'worthy of a place in our homes'.[26] – 'evocative companions' by means of which 'friendly contact between nature and ourselves is woven'.[27] Placed in a niche above the fireplace they appear worthy of veneration like the *lares and penates* – the household gods that Le Corbusier commented upon when visiting houses in Pompeii.[28] Altar-like niches set into walls became a characteristic of Le Corbusier's subsequent domestic architecture, for example in the balconies of the Unité.

As if in homage to his friend, Le Corbusier placed one of Aalto's Savoy glass vases in a prominent place on the rectangular dining table which occupies a simple vaulted space beyond the fireplace (Fig. 7.5).[29] Adjoining it is Le Corbusier's own bedroom. Although white in finish like many of his early buildings, it evokes other precedents at once ancient and within nature. Attached to the vast pivoting door is a wide wardrobe. In order to close the door it is necessary to swing the heavy wardrobe across the opening. The rumbling noise that is made in the process and the physical effort involved is evocative of rolling a large stone across the door. The feeling within the room when it is shut is of extreme seclusion and protection.

Prominently displayed within the room is one of Le Corbusier's highly anthropomorphic vases, their bulging form reminiscent of early fertility symbols (Fig. 7.6). In *Journey to the East* Le Corbusier was to describe such a vase in the

26 Le Corbusier, *Le Corbusier Talks with
    Students*, New York: Orion, 1961,
    p.70.
27 Ibid., p.71.
28 Le Corbusier referred to 'Un toit!
    Autres dieux lares' in Le Corbusier,
    Vers une Architecture, Paris: Éditions
    Vincent, 1958, p.6.
29 Aalto entitled this vase 'The Eskimo
    Woman's Leather Breeches' –
    otherwise known as the Savoy Vase,
    from 1937.

most erotic terms, consciously blurring the boundaries between the container and the curved body of a woman.[30] The ensuite shower is itself housed in a uterine space lit dramatically from above by a single rooflight. The conjunction of a uterine form with water was to become a repetitive feature in his architecture, most literally at Ronchamp.

A vanity unit is housed in a niche accessed off the room, its entrance curved in form like the woman who would use it. The mirror within it reflects the sky, bringing nature directly into the body of the apartment (Fig. 7.7).

In a 1959 photograph of Le Corbusier in his bedroom a painting by the naïve painter André Bauchant can be seen above his marital bed (Fig. 7.8).[31] It appears to be a version of the standard Roman Catholic image of Christ crowning the Virgin Mary. Above the heads of the two figures looms a God crowned with two horns in the form of two tiny angels. Around them, in a Bacchic celebration, frolic angels. Whilst it ostensibly depicts a Christian scene, the Orphic elements (for example the horns and the grapes) indicate that it can be read in another way. It is possible to interpret the painting as an image of the union of opposites, the androgynous unity described in Plato's Symposium, with which both Le Corbusier and many of his circle were so preoccupied. To place such a painting above his own bed was a sign of his personal commitment to a God at once Christian and Dionysiac and his belief in the parallels between his own relationship with his wife and that of Mary (Virgin or Magdalene) and Jesus.[32] The painting makes his bed into an altar, the site of his union with Yvonne, with woman (in Teilhard's terms), with the earth. From the bed the couple share a panorama of the sky, sun and water: paramount constituents of Le Corbusier's radiant world.

The penthouse was for Le Corbusier a place of retreat and renewal, and a place to regain contact with nature through Yvonne, his wife, 'guardian angel' and 'foyer' (hearth) of his home.[33] Its architecture both framed and emulated her body. Le Corbusier dedicated a small pinboard to images of his wife and mother (Fig. 7.9), illustrating their importance to him. Indeed the entire apartment may

[30] 'You recognise these joys: to feel the generous belly of a vase, to caress its slender neck, and then to explore the subleties of its contours'. Le Corbusier, *Journey to the East*, p.14.

[31] Le Corbusier was Bauchant's first great supporter. Le Corbusier and De Fayet, 'Bauchant,' *Esprit Nouveau*, 17 (1922).

[32] A. Rüegg (ed.) *Le Corbusier Photographs by René Burri: Moments in the Life of a Great Architect*, Basel: Birkhäuser, 1999, p.18.

[33] J. Petit, *Le Corbusier Lui-Même*, Paris: Forces Vives, 1970, p. 120.

be seen as a shrine to the feminine, to her role in man's life, an attempt to fill with architecture the gap created so many years ago with the absence of his mother's love.

Yvonne herself complained bitterly of the amount of glass in the apartment: 'all this light is killing me!'[34] – a damning indictment in Le Corbusier's terms of an architecture where light and dark, spirit and body, masculine and feminine should exist in a balance. On a similar note Eileen Grey was highly critical of the lack of sensuality expressed in Le Corbusier's work of this period,[35] again revealing a great deficiency in an architecture that should have been conducive to intimacy.

Enveloping Modernism: Petite Maison de Weekend

The Petite Maison de Weekend in La Celle Sainte Cloud near Paris was built in 1935. One of a series of vaulted dwellings designed by Le Corbusier beginning with the Maisons Monol from 1919, and including the Maisons Jaoul (1955) and the Villa Sarabhai (1956), it marks a culminating point in the quiet transformation of Le Corbusier's work over this period. Sitting firmly on the earth, 'The principal design consideration for this little house situated under a curtain of trees, was to be as little visible as possible'. So begins Le Corbusier's description of the weekend house in the *Oeuvre Complète*.[36] It was a house designed to be enveloped within nature. Indeed the concrete cellular vaults that form its roof were covered in earth and grass, suggesting that he thought of the building as being in some way underground (Fig. 7.10).

7.9
Pinboard in Le Corbusier's apartment.

7.10
Exterior of Petite Maison de Weekend. Image from Le Corbusier and Jeanneret, *Oeuvre Complète Volume 3*.

[34] C. Jencks, *Le Corbusier and the Tragic View of Architecture*, London: Allen Lane, 1973, p.100.
[35] C. Constant, 'The Nonheroic Modernism of Eileen Gray', *Journal Society of Architectural Historians* 53, 1994, p. 275.
[36] Le Corbusier and P. Jeanneret, *Oeuvre Complète Volume 3*, 1934–38, Zürich: Les Éditions d'Architecture, 1995, p.125.

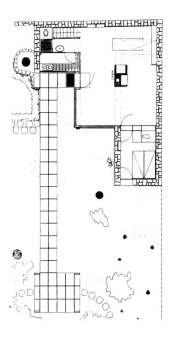

Upon arrival at the house the visitor would walk up the path, passing on the left a tree that is enveloped and embraced by wall that curves down from the house. It is reminiscent of the tree captured within concrete in the Esprit Nouveau Pavilion, a symbol that acts as an immediate and potent reminder of the importance of nature.

Protected by two rubble walls at right angles to one another the house is orientated towards the garden. It is formed out of six approximately square vaulted cells that form its structural grid. A further cell is set in the garden at some distance from the house itself (Fig. 7.11). By placing one cell in the garden Le Corbusier draws attention to the fact that the house itself is built out of individual cellular units, almost like a product of biology. He observed that the 'kiosk in the garden and the house are tied together in a very precise relationship' – a hint that some geometrical game may well have been at work.[37] This individual cell was to form a protective gazebo to shelter those eating outside on a hot day, as can be seen from a drawing entitled 'situation of the house in the land'.[38] On rainy days the roof of the little 'kiosk' was to drain into a shallow pool via a concrete gargoyle in a celebration of water. The preparation of food and drink were important events in the life of the house; according to Le Corbusier they needed to be perpetuated and indeed enhanced. The family meal was a 'solemn' occasion, which he believed was 'too often neglected'. In his opinion this 'ancient family tradition must live again'.[39] The kiosk frames the act of eating like a small temple, emphasising its sacred nature.

From a photograph in the *Oeuvre Complète* it can be seen that the dining space within the weekend house looks out onto the exterior dining space and vice versa (Fig. 7.12). The dining table within is set against a backdrop of timber panelling like the exterior dining area which is framed within trees (Fig. 7.13). Above the dining-room table, on the wall, strongly lit from a roof-light above is a large photograph of the head of a statue of a Greek goddess, seemingly Demeter.

7.11
Plan of Petite Maison de Weekend. Image from Le Corbusier and Jeanneret, *Oeuvre Complète Volume 3*.

7.12
View out to garden, Petite Maison de Weekend. Image from Le Corbusier and Jeanneret, *Oeuvre Complète Volume 3*.

[37] Ibid.
[38] Ibid., p.125.
[39] Le Corbusier, *The Marseilles Block*, London: Harvill, 1953, p.20.

7.13
Dining space, Petite Maison de
Weekend. Image from Le Corbusier
and Jeanneret, *Oeuvre Complète
Volume 3*.

Below her plants and simple pots are displayed on a long horizontal shelf. Bathed in light in this simple vaulted space she acts as a reminder of the classical past and of nature.

Le Corbusier wrote in the *Oeuvre Complète* that the 'choice of materials' for the Petite Maison de Weekend was 'very traditional', when in reality he achieved a very new synthesis of materials. The raw masonry walls were left unadorned, contrasting with panels of glass block and the white industrial tiles on the floor. It was Le Corbusier's intention to use simple detailing and natural materials to encourage those who lived in them to meditate upon what was important in life.[40] Through planning and detailing of the weekend house he hoped to encourage those who lived within it to lead an ascetic existence, in harmony both with nature and with one another.

[40] Le Corbusier, *Oeuvre Complète Volume 5*, 1946–52, Zürich: Les Éditions d'Architecture, 1995, p.190.

Main image: 7.14
Plan of Aalto's own house and studio, Munkinniemi. Aalto, 1934-6.

Below: 7.15
Plan of Niemelä Farmstead, moved from Konginkangas to Seurasaari Folk Museum, Helsinki.

Bottom: 7.16
Plan of Villa Mairea. Aalto, 1937–9.

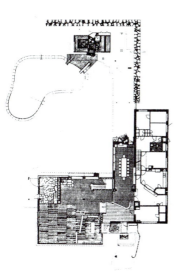

[41] Aalto, 'The Dwelling as a Problem', 1930; repr. in G. Schildt (ed.) *Alvar Aalto Sketches*, Cambridge, MA: MIT Press, 1985, p.29–33.

[42] Aalto, cited in *Alvar Aalto's Own House and Studio*, originally printed in *Arkkitehti* 8, 1937, Jyväskylä: Alvar Aalto Museum, 1999, unpaginated.

[43] Aalto, ibid.

Re-enacting Settlement

In an article entitled 'The Problem of the Dwelling', of 1930, Aalto expanded on the ideas expressed in 'From Doorstep to Living Room', in 1926. Herein he described what he saw as the issues that must be addressed in housing – by both architects and inhabitants. Key amongst these was their intimate relationship with nature within and beyond the dwelling. He wrote of the sun as 'a source of energy', 'the bio-dynamic functions' that he saw as a point of departure, and a guarantee that 'Together this milieu and the man in it form a typical totality of organic work'.[41] The bond between inside and outside had, he believed, to be established at a deep level, one that was congruent with his own struggle to relate his interior and exterior lives. Aalto's attempts to fulfil this agenda will be examined in the description that follows of his own house and studio in Munkkiniemi (1934-6) and of Villa Mairea (1937–9).

A Modern Niemelä Farmstead: Aalto's Own House and Studio

As early as 1925 Aalto wrote, 'The only proper goal of architecture is: build naturally. Don't overdo it. Don't do anything without good reason. Everything superfluous turns ugly with time'.[42] Aalto's experiments began in his own modest house and studio on Riihitie in Munkkiniemi, a suburb of Helsinki (1934-6, Fig. 7.14). This building was to be as 'universally applicable and as suitable for ordinary living as possible'.[43] In it he amalgamated the historical precedent of Roman atrium typology, while simultaneously subverting Gropius' Master House

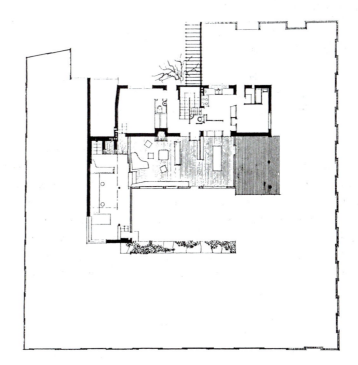

7.17
Side of Aalto's own house and studio.
Aalto, 1934-6.

7.18
Aalto examining a leaf at his own
house, c.1940.

form that he had earlier borrowed for his Paimio doctors' housing. He also introduced the vernacular in a manner akin to Hugo Häring's *Leistungsform*.[44] He incorporated nuances of farmstead textures and details with a growing sense of the archetypal needs for dwelling close to nature (Figs. 7.17 and 7.18). Indeed, the description offered by his close friend and mentor Strengell, suggests that the building was to be something of 'a modern Niemelä farmstead', rooted in its site and culture (Fig. 7.15).[45] It was a description in which Aalto delighted.

Built on a large rock overlooking Saarinen's Jugendstil cadet school, the simple L-shaped form belies the complexity of the accommodation provided. Aalto divided the building seamlessly into three. One wing is occupied by the atrium-like double-height studio, one side of which is largely glazed. This space leads, through a sliding wall, out of the main part of the house, the living space or 'tupa'. The studio also has direct access to both the garden and the roof terrace. The third part comprises a small private living room, bedrooms and balcony space on the first floor, leaving the ground-floor 'tupa' space for living and dining and eating *al fresco* on the patio.

The building structure is complex, comprising load-bearing brick and steel columns, reinforced concrete floors and timber walls. The Aaltos explained that it was designed in this way from a desire to maximise natural light and to provide shelter from prevailing winds and carefully insulated walls to protect from the severe winter climate.[46] The brick of the building is lime-washed, offering a rich, un-uniform texture. The wall of the studio wing is further softened on its terrace face with a sapling trellis, over which ivy was encouraged to grow with vigour. This is accompanied by the deep-grooved timber slats which cover the first-floor walls – a full-size detail of which was published.[47] In this modest house, as elsewhere, Aalto used wood extensively, sheathing other materials and structures, as if apologising for their tectonic matter (and even their modernity). The significance of timber in Aalto's work has been discussed in Chapter 4.

The glazed areas of the building are also adorned with simple sapling trellises that prefigure those at Villa Mairea, and internally the walls receive a variety of natural-fabric wall finishes. The garden was designed to have a ruinous feel, with fragments of stone placed in an ad hoc manner with grass between, and wide low stone walls, recalling those around medieval churches in Finland. The site is defined by timber fencing reminiscent of vernacular pole fencing, but used in a modern configuration. Such an installation of vernacular inspiration heralds a shift from Paimio's basic Functionalist agenda to something more Romantic, but nonetheless functional, without being Functionalist. Ivy engulfed the building, defying a clear reading of the distinction between architecture and nature.

Bygones, Icons and Natural Inheritance: Villa Mairea

Villa Mairea was designed for Maire Gullichsen, heir to the Ahlström Company. Maire and her husband were progressives who wanted to make a modern statement about art and society through the various commissions they offered Aalto, such as the Sunila and Kauttua housing projects. Villa Mairea (1937–9) was their own house on the Ahlström estate in Noormarkku, near Pori. The house is isolated on a coniferous wooded hill; it forms a courtyard, enclosing a

[44] The application of Häring's notion of *Leistungsform* (content-derived form) to this context is examined in S. Menin, 'Aalto, Sibelius and Fragments of Forest Culture', *Sibelius Forum, Third International Jean Sibelius Symposium*, Helsinki: Sibelius Academy, 2002.

[45] This episode is explored in S. Menin, 'Soap Bubbles Floating in the Air', in *Sibelius Forum, Second International Jean Sibelius Conference* 1995, Helsinki: Sibelius Academy, 1998, pp.8–14.

[46] Aalto, Alvar *Aalto's Own House and Studio*, p.3.

[47] K. Fleig, *Alvar Aalto, Volume 1*, Zürich: Les Éditions d'Architecture Artemis Zürich, 1963, p.65.

garden around a pool (Fig. 7.16). The main living space of the house is a large, open tupa space, central to which is an open fire (Plate 20). This opens, perpendicularly onto the dining space, beyond which is the kitchen and other service spaces. Bedroom accommodation and Maire's studio are upstairs. The sauna is beyond the house, beneath an earth-covered walkway, a vocabulary of vernacular form the accent of which becomes stronger the further one moves from the house (Fig. 7.19). This hints at the composite nature of the building: with a structure that is part steel, part concrete, part perforated brick, and with finishes in brick, stone, render, glazed tiles and most prominently wood (Plate 22).

As the vernacular exemplar grew in importance for Aalto, offering formal as well as textural nuance with which to accent his designs, so the romance may be seen to overwhelm the Functionalism. Yet there is still something of a synthesis in Villa Mairea between nature and culture, between something natural

7.19
Detail of pillars near sauna, Villa Mairea. Aalto, 1937–9.

and something manmade, something that evolves and something that is composed, something that connotes the past and something looking to the future (Plate 23). After all, Aalto was fully cognisant of the fact that there was no wilderness nature left, even in Finland – just 'a combination of human efforts and the original environment'.[48] Indeed, his belief, mentioned earlier, that the 'original landscape' could be improved, its character at the same time enhanced and suppressed within and around a superimposed form, demonstrated his orientation towards the simple beginnings of architecture – a process of adjustments of landscape from rock to cave, and from tree to column. Ironically, considering the wealth behind its commission, Villa Mairea thus re-enacts something of the fundamentals of subsistence settlements that, in 1938, were only recently fully redundant in Finland.

The Petite Maison de Weekend was completed just two years before Aalto began to design Villa Mairea. Le Corbusier's modest low-lying house prefigures numerous ideas Aalto was also to explore, including the central fireplace, the sod roof. There is a primitive hut-like gazebo in the Petite Maison and a sauna in Mairea, each resting beyond water. The very rusticity of the whole seems, in both cases, to grow from the ground. Aalto, however, seems to have been relating back more specifically to the Finnish vernacular (such as Niemelä farmstead), rather than to an archetypal hut evocative of an ancient megaron.

Indeed the Niemelä farmstead and all that it represents is of increased significance, not just in terms of texture and detail, but in offering a palimpsest of accretional processes with which Aalto could then make a compositional suggestion of form and detail. It provided an example of 'harmony' and could be 'sympathetic', as he put it, between the user and the landscape, be it natural or synthetic.[49] This accretional process draws on, amongst other things, the pattern of use and the historical allusions. Indeed, such reference to the vernacular is not merely the re-creation of an aboriginal form, but itself re-enacts some growth process.[50] Indeed, it rehearses the settlement of the first building – which in the Finnish vernacular was the sauna. Aalto, typical of Finns, saw the sauna rituals of cleansing and bathing as a vital part of human habitation (Fig. 5.7), and at Villa Mairea the pool area was the first to be built (Fig. 7.19).

Gradually the accretional 'process' that Aalto adopts begins to overwhelm the sense or reading of the building's form, since he infers that the process of dwelling is activated equally by nature around, as it is by human nature within the building. This results in an overall composition that, like the complexity of the natural environment beyond, is at best complex and inspiring, and at worst inconsistent and lacking in an overarching organisation. Yet, this 'process' (i.e., human life in close proximity to nature) may be said to be exactly that organisation, in the same way that ecological cycles are isomorphic with the process of living and moving within them.

Aalto the 'intrepid experimentalist', as Schildt describes him,[51] did not know what would result from his exploratory design of 'the most exclusive millionaire's villa in Finland', but he and his clients felt there was no contradiction between this and their work to forward a social utopia. Indeed, compositionally the building draws again on experimental modern dwellings, but these

48 Aalto, 'Architecture in the Landscape of Finland', 1925; repr. in G. Schildt, *Alvar Aalto in his Own Words*, New York: Rizzoli, 1997, p.21.

49 Aalto, in 'Villa Mairea', *Arkkitehti*, 9, 1939, reprinted in *Villa Mairea*, Jyväskylä: Alvar Aalto Museum, 1981, unpaginated.

50 See S. Menin, 'Fragments from the Forest: Aalto's Requisitioning of Forest, Place and Matter' *Journal of Architecture*, 6, 3, 2001, pp.279–305 for further explanation of this theme.

51 G. Schildt, *Alvar Aalto: The Decisive Years*, New York, Rizzoli, 1986, p.154.

references are subverted in the manner of their use. The piloti of Villa Savoye, the balconies of Frank Lloyd Wright's Falling Water, the glazed wall of Gropius' Masters' Houses all appeared repeatedly in the design sketches, yet when fragments are requisitioned their meaning is sabotaged by the nature of their use. In the eventual building, however, references to white concrete piloti are translated variously into raw tree trunks, twig-clad steel or ivy-crept concrete, and are even made diagonally playful in some instances (Fig. 7.19, Plate 20). By this time the balconies are timber-clad, with metal and timber-pole railings. The extensive glass is made shy, shrouded with vast wooden blinds both internally and externally (Plate 22), and the trellised white walls are overgrown (Fig. 7.20). Here we see Aalto being inspired by colleagues, but rarely borrowing directly, both because of the strength of his own creative imagination and because he was determined to hide his influences.[52]

Aalto seems to have set out to audit the mass of different forms and features he uses within the building with the aim of bringing forth some natural 'sympathy' in every detail, from the forest stair to the personal signature of a sculpted 'wave' above the huge open fireplace and the entrance canopy (Plate 18). Indeed, the piloti speak of their place as poetic agents in the space, not just of their functional strength and simplicity. The building spaces have modern as well as archetypal human functions to fulfil. For instance, Harry Gullichsen needed to talk business, and asked for the movable library partitions to be made permanent and sound-proofed, the upstairs family space has wall bars for young and old alike to maintain their physical fitness, and Maire wanted a quiet studio space. These functions are sometimes softened by precedent, such as the way the studio is presented as a simple shed-like appendage but has a timelessness that somehow draws it 'far beyond the Finnish vernacular'.[53] The sauna is accessed from beneath a ship-like balcony with a sod roof, past steel and then timber poles set on a stone. The house becomes increasingly rustic as it moves towards this housing of the most Finnish (and yet so fundamental) of activities. The sauna is given something of a vernacular accent (both Finnish and Japanese), and may explain the common use of the term 'universal' in descriptions of Aalto's work (Fig. 7.19). Indeed, many writers have picked up on Aalto's interest in Japan,[54] and inevitably the Japanese conception of nature was part of the allure that Eastern culture held for Aalto.[55] He wrote, 'Japanese culture, which with its limited range of forms has implanted in people a virtuosity in producing variety and, almost daily, new combinations … Their contact with nature and the ever-enjoyable variation it produces is a way of life that makes them reluctant to dwell too long on formalistic concepts'.[56]

We know that Aalto heard the call by those in the art world in Finland and abroad, through the likes of Mendelssohn, for a new synthesis in art. Even Hitler was articulating this theme.[57] Aalto had also come close to the ideas of Bergson through Yrjö Hirn and Carrell, and therefore heard the call for the unity of intuition and intellect – expressing something close to what Cobb described as 'the reverse of intellectual abstraction' cited above.[58] In Villa Mairea Aalto's notion of synthesis seems to draw disparate themes together rather than to pare their selection down to anything close to Le Corbusier's vestigial sense of

[52] Aalto claimed that 'As far as Wright was concerned I knew nothing about him until I came to USA in 1939'. 'Conversation', in Schildt, *Sketches*, p.171.

[53] K. Jormakka, J. Gargus and D. Graf in *The Use and Abuse of Paper*, Datutop 20, Tampere: Tampere University, 1999, p.21.

[54] Schildt, *Decisive Years*, pp.107–14; R Weston, *Alvar Aalto*, London: Phaidon, 1995, pp, 69, 90 and 110–11.

[55] Aalto himself referred to Japanese culture in 'Rationalism and Man', 1935, Schildt, *Sketches*, pp.47–51.

[56] Aalto, 'Rationalism and Man', 1935, Schildt, *Own Words*, p.93.

[57] In the Nazi circle minds sought to take aspects of technological progress and resist others, anchoring them back to the rustic past. B. Hinz, 'Die Malerei im deutschen Faschismus', *Kunst und Konterrolution*, München: Carl Hanser Verlag, 1974, pp.131, 166 and 185. See also Jormakka, Gargus and Graf, *Use and Abuse of Paper*, p.25.

[58] Cobb, *Ecology of Imagination*, p.94.

7.20
Detail of basement entrance, Villa
Mairea. Aalto, 1937–9.

59 Aalto, 'Interview for Finnish
    Television', 1972 in Schildt, *Own
    Words*, p.273.
60 For full explanation of this thesis see
    S. Menin, 'Relating the Past:
    Sibelius, Aalto and the Profound
    Logos', unpub. PhD thesis, University
    of Newcastle, 1997.

purity. Aalto responds to and celebrates the multiplicity of human experiences of
dwelling. Indeed, late in life he explained, 'I don't think there's so much
difference between reason and intuition. Intuition can sometimes be extremely
rational.'[59] This may have hit home particularly strongly because of his
psychological need to relate the disparate.[60] This is relevant to his open
acceptance of the multivalent nature of Villa Mairea. He did seek to anchor its
architecture back beyond what he saw as the tectonic linear logic of his

contemporaries to something less 'artificial'.[61] He also strongly favoured designs that did not use 'ordinary systems' as their starting point, but instead created one from the notion of 'man the unknown'.[62] His inspiration here may, with much justification and some irony, be said to be aspects of his own known self, 'with all the innumerable nuances of his emotional life and nature'.[63] Indeed, Pietilä suggests that Aalto's modernist approach was 'biological intuition, filling in gaps in the pattern of the Known and Unknown'.[64] Thus Aalto had come to believe that the mainstays of Modernism, technology and economy, 'must be combined with, or even be placed at the service of, life-enriching charm'.[65]

It is important to identify just how Villa Mairea remains an entity, rather than dissolving into a complex of compositional contradiction. As elsewhere, Aalto plays one form or idea off against another as if to exploit and justify his search for this 'synthesis'. It has been suggested that 'the volatile alliance between differences can be stabilised by conceptualising it in terms of oppositional pairs, such as thick/thin, simple/complex' and others.[66] In his exhaustive analysis of the building Pallasmaa identifies this theme as the play of exteriority (with monumentality, approach and authority) and interiority (arrival, protection and homeliness),[67] and believes that, rather than any sense of muddle, such a 'harmony of contradiction and opposition' provides a therapeutic ambiance.[68] Many such oppositions echo within the Villa Mairea.

At a latent level this 'equipoise between unequal partners'[69] can be seen as a synthesis between masculine and feminine elements, if like Le Corbusier we associate the masculine with cerebral architecture in orthogonal forms and feminine architecture with bodily, sensual, curvilinear forms. Anna Hall, curator at Villa Mairea for over ten years, suggests that the building is so sensual that its feminine character seems to outweigh its masculine tone. She perceives the building as a poem of love that has become somehow prostituted by the critical surveillance it has received.[70] Indeed, many have suggested it was an *opus con amore*.[71] The feminine aspects of the scheme are formal (in the numerous curvaceous forms), they are determined (in the resistance of rationalism in structural terms), and they are thorough, being both planar and sectional, formal and detailed; they are in 'process', not static. This is clear in the entrance hall, which boasts a splinter of Aalto's New York Pavilion (designed in 1938) in the undulating wall (Fig. 6.13). The masculine nature is not so dominant, existing in structure but being repeatedly compromised. Elements of rectilinearity are challenged by the inclination towards the wave, and by details that counter such moments of modernity with historical and textual nuances towards texture – a procedure Aalto began in the Viipuri ceiling (Fig. 4.2).

61 Aalto, in 'Villa Mairea', *Arkkitehti*, 9, 1939, reprinted in *Villa Mairea*.
62 Aalto, 'Erik Gunnar Asplund – In Memoriam', 1940 in Schildt, *Own Words*, pp.242–43.
63 Ibid.
64 Riema Pietilä, 'A Gestalt Building', *Architecture and Urbanism*, May 1983, Extra Edition, pp.12–13.
65 Aalto, 'Muuratsalo', 1953, in Schildt, *Own Words*, pp. 234-5.
66 Jormakka, Gargus and Graf, *Use and Abuse of Paper*, p.41.
67 J. Pallasmaa, 'Image and Meaning', in *Villa Mairea*, Helsinki: Alvar Aalto Foundation, 1998, p.85. Connar suggests that such writing is an example of the exaggerative 'over-writing' of Aalto's work. R. Connar, *Aaltomania*, Helsinki: Rakennustieto, 2000.
68 Pallasmaa, 'Image and Meaning', p.93.
69 Jormakka, Gargus and Graf, *Use and Abuse of Paper*, p.41.
70 Anna Hall, interview with Sarah Menin, Noormarkku, August 2001.
71 For example M. Lahti, *Alvar Aalto Houses: Timeless Expressions*, Tokyo: Architecture and Urbanism, 1998, p.11.

Conclusion

Le Corbusier wrote in the *Modulor* that 'The great thing is to move men, move them through the effect of a thousand incidences which illuminate the soul, surprise it, fill it to the brim, irritate it, rouse it'.[72] In this chapter we have seen that his dwellings are full of subtle details that would act as a reminder to their inhabitants of the importance of leading a simple life in harmony with nature. Le Corbusier's architectural promenade is meditative and even ritualistic, but usually designed to take the individual beyond the self in some way. In the Villa Savoye nature is introduced in a more cerebral way, through games and allusions. In his later building a more sensual response is encouraged through close contact with greenery and more natural materials.

Aalto also provided a multitude of ways in which the interior elements tactfully make reference to the natural world. His architectural promenade is not necessarily meditative, but rather encourages and enriches movement that circumstances require, drawing to the fore the process of our use (including the psychological use) of the building and its interaction with and mediation of nature. Aalto's buildings appear to be active themselves, offering repeated visual invitations to communion or activity, be it the filigree timber details which often draw attention to apertures into nature, or the growing masses of Vuoksenniska or Wolfsburg Cultural Centre.

Aalto's dislike of solitude has already been touched upon. Any dwelling he conceived may be said, therefore, to manifest a drive to facilitate the potential engagement with an Other, whether through casual encounters in expanded corridors, or in amphitheatres or large open-planned living spaces. Such a continual materialising of a longing for engagement embodies a call to relate which in the personal realm would be on the verge of an embarrassing flirtation. In architectural form it also suggests the perennial, veiled threat of nature's readiness to engulf both the dwelling and civilisation – something that is palpable in forested settings in Finland. In this sense there is an aura of immanence, of participation in the time-limited process of human living, but within a broader natural context. Indeed, in his single family dwellings he practised what he was sure should be central to all housing: a 'sympathy' which catered for the individual in relation to the group, and in relation to nature, which he believed should be enhanced by the tactful placing of dwellings.

[72] Le Corbusier, *Modulor 2*, London: Faber, 1955, p. 302.

Chapter 8

Building Natural Attachment

While attempting to create a state of harmonious natural order in their own lives, Aalto and Le Corbusier also sought to improve the lot of others, most notably through their experiments in the field of mass housing. In 1935 Aalto was clear that 'In addition to technical and general physiological properties, we must rationally study the detailed needs of individual health, to the verge of psychology and even beyond.'[1] His experience of the importance of personal contact with nature in avoiding those 'psychological slums'[2] was now used to bring some essence of nature's growth process into that of standardisation. Both men invested their insights and creations with a universal tone, something which Curtis refers to, in Le Corbusier's case, as 'a naïve environmental determinism, as if the right architecture could on its own generate human betterment'.[3]

What follows is a discussion of the role of nature in the ideas which led to the concept of the designs for Le Corbusier's Unité, as manifest in the Marseilles block (1945-52) and in Aalto's Baker House Dormitory building at the Massachusetts Institute of Technology (1946–9). The chapter will conclude with an examination of both men's contributions to the Berlin Interbau Exhibition 1957 where, since they were working to the same brief, the similarities and differences between the work of the two men can be seen more clearly.

Nature and Standardisation

United and Radiant

In Chapter 2 we saw that Le Corbusier developed an interest in town planning whilst working with L'Eplattenier. Strongly influenced by the English Garden City movement, Le Corbusier spent many years attempting to devise a cellular housing unit that was suitable for mass production which could then be brought

[1] Aalto, 'Rationalism and Man', 1935; repr. in G. Schildt (ed.) *Alvar Aalto in his Own Words*, New York: Rizzoli, 1997, p. 92.
[2] Aalto, 'Reconstruction of Europe', 1941 in Schildt, *Own Words*, p.152.
[3] W. Curtis, *Le Corbusier, Ideas and Forms*, London: Phaidon, 1986, p.12.

together in large numbers to form a community. He introduced the chapter 'Mass Production Houses' in *Towards a New Architecture* with the words:

> We must create the mass-production spirit.
> The spirit of constructing mass-production houses.
> The spirit of living in mass-production houses.
> The spirit of conceiving mass-production houses.[4]

These houses represented a new way of thinking about the world. Those who wanted to create mass-produced houses would be working for the common good. Those who were happy to live in mass-produced houses would not aspire to anything more ostentatious or more individual; they would be happy to live as equals with their neighbours. Such houses would be built with great economy and would be totally appropriate for their purpose.[5] They would change the ways in which people chose to live their lives. As Le Corbusier wrote of the vaulted Monol housing projects of 1919: 'A village well set out and constructed in series gives an impression of calm, of order, of propriety. It will inevitably impose its discipline on the inhabitants.'[6]

During the war Le Corbusier developed these ideas into the Maisons Murondins, self-build log and mud houses, which in turn influenced the design of the community of earth houses to be built at La Sainte Baume, a cellular structure closely linked to that of the Unité in Marseilles, one of a series of prototypes developed out of his Radiant City ideal.[7] There he set in concrete the same rustic marks of the formwork, as if to naturalise modernity.

Le Corbusier's plan for Antwerp, dated 1933, was designed as a 'practical instrument for international co-operation in every field.'[8] His concern for global unity was to receive expression in a number of projects including his 1947 scheme for the United Nations in New York and the Basilica of Peace and Pardon at La Sainte Baume. In his opinion it was necessary to create a 'world-wide fusion of needs and means, of economic programmes and of spiritual and intellectual points of view' in order to bring about peace.[9] In Le Corbusier's idealised vision the Modulor, his tool for standardisation, would play a central role in this process, rendering all things radiant, interconnected and harmonious with nature.

Elastic Standards

At the heart of Aalto's philosophy was the notion of 'flexible standardisation' drawn from his observation of nature's way of growing mass; 'permitting variation in spite, or rather because of the fact that the building components are mass produced' (Fig. 8.5).[10] At this time he began working on the problem of the half a million homeless Finns. He pursued the authorities at MIT to fund a research programme into housing construction, utilising these ideas, which could then be tested out in his home country.

In lectures in Switzerland in 1941 Aalto addressed the subject of the reconstruction of Europe, illustrating his talks with images of 'peasant' women cooking on a stone stove in an otherwise ruined home. He argued that buildings

4 Le Corbusier, *Towards a New Architecture*, London: Architectural Press, 1982, p.210.

5 Ibid., p.222.

6 Le Corbusier and P. Jeanneret, *Oeuvre Complète Volume 1, 1910–1929*, Zürich: Les Éditions d'Architecture, 1995, p.30.

7 F. Samuel, 'Orphism in the Work of Le Corbusier with Particular Reference to his scheme for La Sainte Baume', unpublished PhD thesis, Cardiff University, 2000.

8 Le Corbusier, *The Radiant City*, London: Faber, 1967, p.285.

9 Le Corbusier, *Sketchbooks Volume 2*, London: Thames & Hudson, 1981, sketch 662.

10 Aalto, 'An American Town in Finland', 1940 in Schildt, *Own Words*, pp.122–31.

should once again grow from the site, the locale and the needs of the individual. He also contended that 'The purpose of a building is to act as an instrument that collects all the positive influences in nature for man's benefit'.[11] In his belief 'nature' was 'the most remarkable standardisation institute of all'. Using as an example the way in which plants take energy from the sun by splaying their leaves, he argued for 'flexible standardisation' and a 'growing house'.[12] Responding to such a call, Maire Gullichsen had encouraged the Ahlström Company to mass-produce Aalto's pre-war-type houses at their Varkaus factory. The results were however disappointing, their scale and placing rendering these houses oppressive. The fact that these basic dwellings lacked any variation and adaptation to the site sickened Aalto.[13]

8.1
'What is a Unité d'Habitation?'
Image from Le Corbusier,
The Marseilles Block.

Community Building?

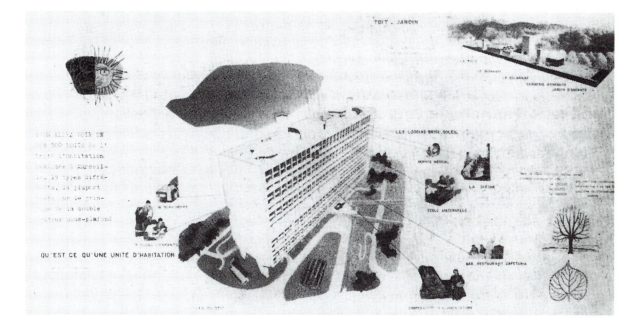

QU'EST CE QU'UNE UNITÉ D'HABITATION

[11] Aalto, 'The Reconstruction of Europe', 1941 in ibid., p.154. Aalto's lecture tour to Switzerland in 1941 was hosted by S. Giedion and A. Roth.

[12] Ibid.

[13] G. Schildt, *Alvar Aalto: The Decisive Years*, New York: Rizzoli, 1986, p.54.

[14] Notes made in the summer of 1955. Le Corbusier, *Sketchbooks Volume 3 1954-1957*, Cambridge, MA: MIT Press, 1982, sketch 520.

Le Corbusier described the Unité d'Habitation, built on an open site on the Boulevard Michelet in Marseilles (Fig. 8.1), as the fruit of twenty-five years of study that began with his study of the monastic architecture of the Middle Ages.[14] In 1945 Raoul Dautry, the first minister of reconstruction and urbanism, gave Le Corbusier permission to build the Unité at Marseilles as an experimental project funded by the government. In doing so Le Corbusier was given special dispensation to bypass building regulations and to exceed the usual budget ascribed to such projects. For Le Corbusier the Unité in Marseilles was a 'prototype', a solution to a universal problem, marking a new beginning in architecture and capable of infinite replication (a number of other Unités were constructed) (Plate 27). Its foundation stone was eventually laid on 14 October 1947 after a long struggle with the authorities.

COMMUNITY BUILDING?   145

8.2
'Une cellule normalisée et standardisée: le feu, le foyer'. Image from Le Corbusier and Jeanneret, *Oeuvre Complète Volume 5*.

Unité, Fraternité, Égalité

Built according to the tenets of the Radiant City, Le Corbusier's design for the Unité needs little introduction, having been hugely influential on the post-war generation of architects. Moulded out of deeply textured concrete the vast horizontal housing block is supported on rough cast pilotis (Plate 26). Interlocking units (some single apartments, some duplex) are set within its cellular frame (Fig. 8.2) The duplex apartments have a generous double-height balcony, and all have a built-in table evocative of an altar, allowing spectacular views of the mountains and sea beyond. A key feature of many of Le Corbusier's later works is the double-height 'hanging garden', used to great effect in the Unité schemes (Plate 30). Through the use of large folding doors the interior space could be opened out to encompass the balcony area, forming one cohesive living unit, at once interior and exterior. Communal facilities are housed at the base of the block, including the landscaped area that forms its site, and within internal streets that run through it, and on the roof where the nursery, gymnasium and theatre space form part of a spectacular, sculpted roofscape (Fig. 8.3 and Plate 24).

As discussed in Chapter 4, Le Corbusier was interested in the issues of both physical and mental health and the ways it could be affected by the surroundings.[15] Life in this 'vertical garden city', built to Modulor proportions,

8.3
Roofscape, Unité d'Habitation, Marseilles. Le Corbusier, 1945-52. Image from Le Corbusier and Jeanneret, *Oeuvre Complète Volume 5*.

[15] Le Corbusier, *Modulor*, London: Faber and Faber, 1954, p.111.

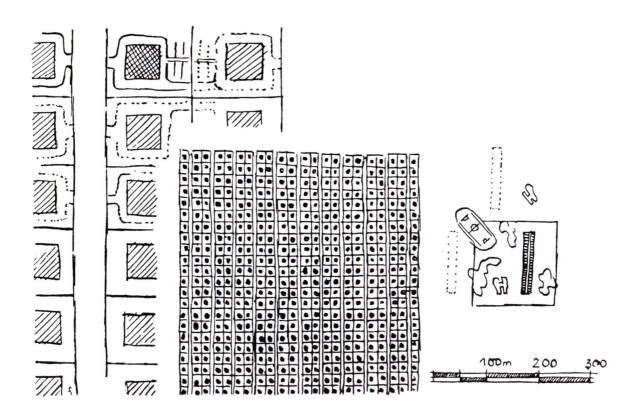

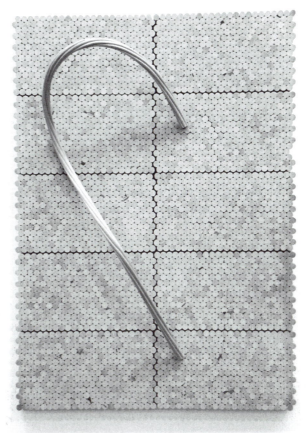

8.4
Cellular structure of city. Image from
Le Corbusier, *Oeuvre Complète
Volume 6*.

8.5
Wood experiment. Aalto, *c.*1940.

would bring its inhabitants back into contact with nature and one another.[16] Simultaneously its cellular structure would bring into relief the connection between mass housing and the organisms of biology. He wrote 'the key = the cell = the men = happiness ... the cell rules' (Fig. 8.4).[17] The juxtaposition of Le Corbusier's sketch of this cellular structure and Aalto's wood experiment offers an interesting dichotomy, representing something of the distinction between their individual readings of the nature of cellular growth (Fig. 8.5).

Within the Unité families could dwell in modest independent apartments whilst, at the same time, being able to participate in the collective life of the building. Le Corbusier's ambition was to create a building that would foster a sense of harmonious unity amongst its inhabitants. He took great care over the design of the individual units in order to give the optimum in both flexibility (through the use of pivoting walls) and privacy (for example through the use of soundproofing). He thought of the building as 'a state of equilibrium' in which conditions needed to be 'favourable to the group, while at the same time allowing sufficient freedom to its members'.[18] It was therefore vital to provide each individual with a space in which they were free to live their lives undisturbed.[19]

It is necessary to return to the theories of Teilhard in an attempt to understand why Le Corbusier placed such an emphasis upon creating a building that would satisfy the needs of both the individual and the collective. The Jesuit envisaged a society in which humanity would begin to work together more closely as it developed in consciousness.[20] Teilhard urged us to rise up above the 'uncertainties' of the world and look down upon it in order to see the phenomenon as a whole. He put himself in a position where he could see the consequence of that 'major cosmic process' which 'for want of a better name' he called 'human planetisation'.[21] Only then would it be possible to grasp the situation. His words echo uncannily those of Le Corbusier who, with similar preoccupations, entitled the second chapter of his book The Marseilles Block, 'Let's Take the Broad View.'[22]

In the opinion of the priest, as people became ever more inward looking or reflective and knowledgeable they would, paradoxically, become better attuned to one another. They would start to understand the importance of living collectively. In doing so they would be advancing the cause of evolution. In this way they would be drawn together through a mutual sympathy without any accompanying loss of personality.[23] Love, 'spiritual energy', would have the power to bind mankind and matter, together into one solid and interconnected mass.[24]

For the Dominicans of Just L'Art Sacré the Unité was evidently a building of some religious importance as they included a number of images of it in their journal devoted to sacred art. It is important to note the way that it is depicted in L'Homme et L'Architecture, a publication over which Le Corbusier had much influence.[25] In one image the vast pilotis that support the structure of the block frame images of mysterious gods in a darkened underground world. Le Corbusier referred to the space beneath the pilotis as the 'main hall' and the 'place of honour', indicating that it was very special for him.[26] Indeed it is conceivable that he thought of the route from the dark space beneath the pilotis and up to the spectacular sun-drenched roof terrace as analogous with one of initiation,

16 Le Corbusier, *Radiant City*, p.83.
17 Le Corbusier wrote of the work of the entymologist Jean-Henri Fabré who had made a number of observations about the social relationships between ants. 'We realised that natural phenomena have an organisation, and we opened our eyes. 1900. An outpouring. Truly, a fine moment!' Le Corbusier, *The Decorative Art of Today*, London: Architectural Press, 1987, p.13.
18 Le Corbusier, *The Marseilles Block*, London: Harville Press, 1953, p.17.
19 Le Corbusier, *Radiant City*, p.113.
20 P. Teilhard de Chardin, *The Future of Man*, London: Collins, 1964, p.125.
21 Ibid.
22 Le Corbusier, *Marseilles Block*, p.13.
23 Le Corbusier, *Radiant City*, p.160.
24 P. Teilhard de Chardin, *L'Énergie Humaine*, Paris: Éditions du Seuil, 1962, p. 147.
25 Le Corbusier, *L'Homme et l'architecture*, 12–13, 1947, p.5.
26 Le Corbusier, *Modulor*, p.140.

like the route through the Basilica at La Sainte Baume.[27] The architecture of the building, its tactile cavelike surfaces and forms, its harmonious colours, its coloured glass (Plate 29), its dramatic lighting and its proportions, would effect a transformation in the visitor in a number of subtle ways.[28]

Le Corbusier placed a large block of stone like an altarpiece at the entrance to the Unités at the level of the pilotis (Fig. 4.1). Cut to Modulor proportions, they were designed to help the visitor to understand the central issues at stake in the buildings. 'Symbolically the entire construction rests upon it,' he wrote of the stone at the Unité.[29] On one side of it is carved an image of the Modulor man, on the other his symbol of the twenty-four-hour day, the intention being to draw attention to the rhythms of nature. 'If, in the course of the mutation of machine civilisation, I have been able to contribute something ... it will be this sign,' he wrote.[30] The entrance block combines two oppositions, the darkness of night with the light of day, the two sides of life, and like electricity it forms a cyclical wave. It held within it the key to what Le Corbusier called 'savoir habiter': 'knowing how to live! How to use the blessings of God: the sun and the spirit that he has given to men to enable them to achieve the joy of living on earth and to find again the Lost Paradise.'[31]

Ostensibly a utilitarian housing block, the Unité, the Radiant City, embodies a complex spiritual programme, its name Unité, 'united', an expression of Le Corbusier's desire to achieve a state of harmony with nature, not just between inhabitants. 'Drawn in the nature of God, under the sky and facing the sun' the Unité would be 'a majestic work of architecture' wrote Le Corbusier.[32] It became a prototype imitated throughout the world, but rarely copied with its essence intact.

Nature, Housing and the Search for Nuance

After completing his workers' housing for the Paimio Sanatorium, Aalto was commissioned by the Ahlström Company to design a series of house types at their Sunila Pulp Plant in 1935, work that he continued through into the 1950s. There were to be houses for workers, engineers and managers, the size and comfort of which reflects a sense of hierarchy, despite what Schildt reports as being a principle of classlessness.[33]

Splaying Life Towards the Sun

At Sunila Aalto demonstrated how he sought to counter what he sensed was the psychological alienation generated by many German mass-housing schemes. He used the idea of flexible standardisation to provide individuals with a sense of privacy and an experience of the natural environment. The splayed layout of the engineers' housing block prefigures the fan motif to be used later in other schemes (Fig. 8.6).

Aalto described his starting point for the overall plan at Sunila as being the rocky topography. 'Only the south slopes of the hills are for dwellings, the valleys are traffic ways and gardens. On the north slopes the pine forest shall remain undisturbed.'[34] The description of the scheme in Aalto's *Complete Works*,

[27] F. Samuel, 'Le Corbusier, Rabelais and the Oracle of the Holy Bottle', *Word and Image*, 17, 4, 2001, p.336.

[28] Le Corbusier, 'Température', preface to the third edition of Le Corbusier, *Vers une Architecture*, Paris: Éditions Vincent: 1958, p.xi.

[29] Le Corbusier, *Modulor*, p.140.

[30] Le Corbusier, *When the Cathedrals were White: A Journey to the Country of the Timid People*, New York: Reynal & Hitchcock, 1947, p.xviii.

[31] Ibid.

[32] Le Corbusier, *L'Homme et l'architecture*, p.6.

[33] Schildt, *Decisive Years*, p.150. Schildt points out that the fact that different income groups were located in the same suburb was revolutionary, although each housing group is physically separate.

[34] Aalto in K. Fleig (ed.) Alvar Aalto, *Volume 1, 1922–62*, Zürich: Verlag für Architektur Artemis, 1990, p.96.

B²

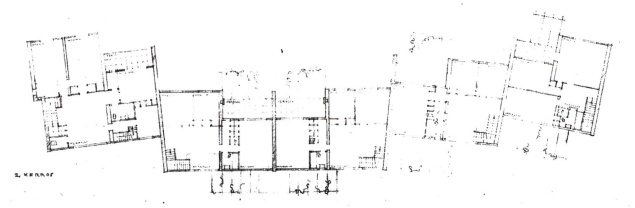

2. KERROS

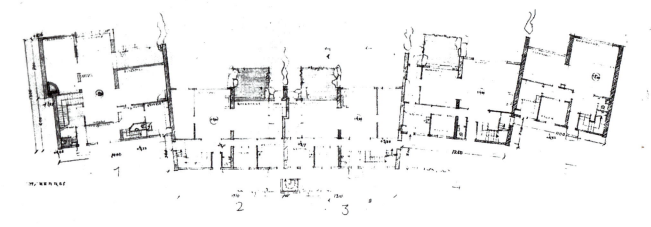

H. KERROS

1 2 3

edited by Karl Fleig and carefully overseen by Aalto himself, is telling, with an emphatic statement that 'Schematic centralisation has been absolutely avoided' and each group 'has its own architecture, formally independent of others'.[35] The first group (the workers' row houses), were two storeys with no balcony, but each with direct access to the landscape. The second were three storeys with tiny, 'practically worthless' balconies that recall those of Gropius' Bauhaus accommodation.[36] Reconfiguring the genesis of the third group, Aalto exploited the sloping terrain, with stepped terrace houses offering usable outside balcony space, and allowing all families 'direct access to nature'(Fig. 8.7). The next group of row houses for engineers were to have the best of both worlds, with direct access to nature, balconies and a flexing, staggered plan which shifted the main aspect away from neighbours, thus enhancing privacy (Fig. 8.6). The aesthetic of the staggered white-box terrace is further mediated by simple, sapling trellises that speak of vestigial vernacular occupation of such forested places.

Aalto was to shed the Modernist tokenism of the tiny 'useless' balcony and grow his ideas towards the complete flexing of the scheme in section and then in plan in order to provide direct access to the natural environment, the fresh air and greenery Le Corbusier was also calling for at this time, but with his own, quite different vision of its manifestation.

Direct Contact with the Forest

In the description of the dwellings at Kauttua (1937–40) that appears in Fleig's survey of Aalto's work there is a long introduction about the topography and pattern of habitation of southern Finland, before he then focused in on the nature of Kauttua itself. 'The region was marked by high glacial moraines and pine woods.'[37] This sparsely populated area does not immediately seem a likely site for an experiment in town planning, but Aalto believed that 'The topography of the region made it possible to select the biologically advantageous sites for residential development'.[38] Here he sought to further develop the stepped, south-facing terraced housing solution tried in Sunila, 'so that every dwelling received a direct contact with the forest' (Plate 25). The Kauttua housing is virtually free of staircases, with lateral access to the dwelling and use of half the lower roof as a terrace, ensuring complete privacy for each of the four dwelling levels. The pergolas upon the terraces are made of unstripped saplings, which contrast richly with the whitewashed walls of the dwellings. The description goes on to sound like Le Corbusier's exaltation of the vertical city – 'The only effective solution would be to adopt a vertical principle of city planning … so that man … does not have to live in the midst of the harmful gases of today's traffic'.[39] From the Kauttua housing the dirt road is virtually invisible through the trees.

Aalto, like Le Corbusier, forever developed and revisited ideas and motifs. For instance the trellises and the manipulation of lower ground entrances used in Kauttua are used in Villa Mairea too, and reappear elsewhere in his mass housing. However, in terms of his development of spatial configuration he takes much from his own house and studio, with its recomposition of the ancient and vernacular courtyard idea. Again, these are developed later, being imbued

35 Ibid.
36 Ibid.
37 Ibid., pp.105–6.
38 Ibid.
39 Ibid.

into the heart of his apartment schemes at Neue Vahr (1958–62, Fig. 8.12) and Lucerne (1965-8).

At the time of the outbreak of war in Finland, in October 1939, the Helsinki housing exhibition, organised at Aalto's instigation to demonstrate 'socially orientated housing construction on the basis of type plans', had been open only four days when a general mobilisation forced it to close. The exhibition demonstrated Aalto's desire to study the problems of type-houses and the opportunities and limitations of standardisation. At the same time he was also determined to offer every man the key opportunity to access nature with ease and to promote an awareness of the fecundity of the 'magic power' of nature,[40] that 'forest geometry' identified by critics such as Pallasmaa.[41]

8.8
Plan of Baker House dormitory, MIT
Aalto, 1946–9.

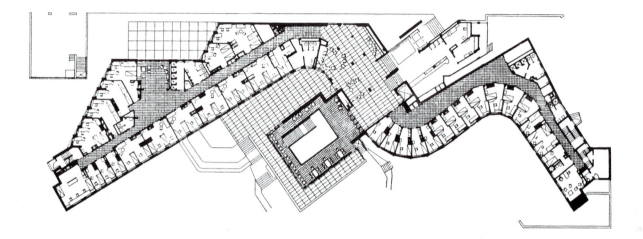

Undulating the Plan and Subverting the Context

Aalto often referred to the need for design to accommodate the nuances of emotional life.[42] From 1930 he had expressed the notion of 'elastic systems' of growth in design.[43] Simultaneously he began to write of 'organisms',[44] and 'organic architecture'.[45] Thereafter he wrote frequently about 'nature's biological organisation'.[46] Taking forward ideas about the importance of inhabitants' access to nature, within and from their dwellings, and developing the ideas about the need for privacy and a sense of the individuality of each dwelling, at the Baker House Dormitory, MIT, Aalto was pushed, during a complex and long drawn-out design process, to achieve a planning efficiency that offered back to him a design method which was to become central to many of his subsequent projects (Fig. 8.8).

After exploring many other layouts Aalto settled on the undulating plan. In part this was generated by the desire for all rooms to have views up and down the Charles River (rather than directly across),[47] to benefit from a southerly aspect, and to be up in the branches of the trees to be grown in the bays (Fig. 8.9).[48] Among the many derivations of the undulating form is the idea that it extrapolates the bow windows of Boston's Back Bay town houses. It may also be symbolic of water in opposition to the straight forms of the north side that

[40] Aalto, 'Architecture in the Landscape of Finland' in Schildt, *Own Words*, p.21.

[41] J. Pallasmaa, 'The Art of Wood', in *The Language of Wood*, Helsinki: Museum of Finnish Architecture, 1989, p.16.

[42] For example, Aalto, 'Senior Dormitory, M.I.T.', *Arkkitehti*, 1950, p.64.

[43] Aalto, 'Housing Construction in Existing Cities', 1930 in G. Schildt, *Alvar Aalto Sketches*, Cambridge, MA: MIT Press, 1985, pp.3-6.

[44] Aalto, 'The Dwelling as a Problem', 1930 in ibid., pp.29–33.

[45] Aalto, 'Letter from Finland', 1931 in ibid., pp.34-5.

[46] Aalto, 'The Geography of the Housing Question', 1932 in ibid., pp.40–6.

[47] Aalto, 'Senior Dormitory M.I.T.', and Aalto in Fleig, *Alvar Aalto vol. 1*, p.134.

[48] Ibid.

may denote functionality. If it had been Le Corbusier's scheme, this union of opposites might have signified masculine and feminine, rational thought versus intuition. Certainly in the union of opposites Aalto does relate these phenomena, but he always gives a functional reason for the forms, allowing the

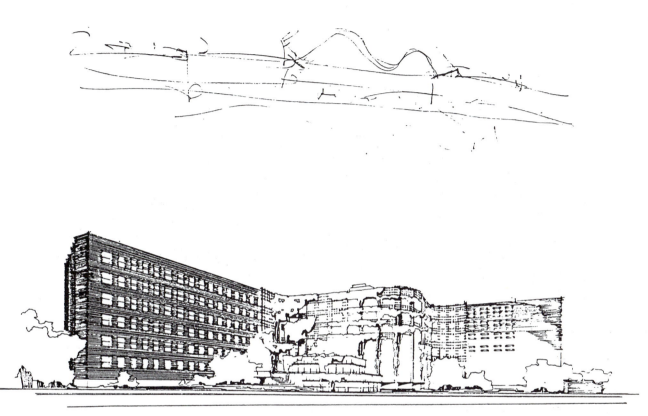

symbolic significance to live ineffably. Aalto is famous for saying that the truth about building is in building, not talk. Jormakka, Gargus and Graf suggest that the building recoils 'away from its location'.[49] This does seem to be the case, as the serpentine form withdraws from the traffic-laden Memorial Drive that separates the site from the river. Whatever the symbolism, the undulation creates a formal dichotomy, yoked back, as it is, to a functional rectilinear entrance façade.

Here Aalto created a single loaded corridor, expanding on the north side to provide glazed social spaces that are designed to facilitate casual encounters, and opening onto the great bulk of the bifurcating stair. Service rooms were also to be located on the straight, north side. Aalto designed a huge metal trellis to train ivy to engulf the undulating brick mass. Yet this, like the metal cladding for the cantilevered stair, was dropped by the authorities as a cost-cutting measure. Between the undulating element and the 'straight back, the plane of analysis and the play of fantasy', St. John Wilson suggests that a primary opposition in Aalto's work is demonstrated here.[50]

[49] K. Jormakka, J. Gargus and D. Graf in *The Use and Abuse of Paper*, Datutop 20, Tampere: Tampere University, 1999, p.76.
[50] C. St. John Wilson, *Architectural Reflection*, London: Butterworth, 1992, p.92.

Alvar Aalto
Pear NN1 1947

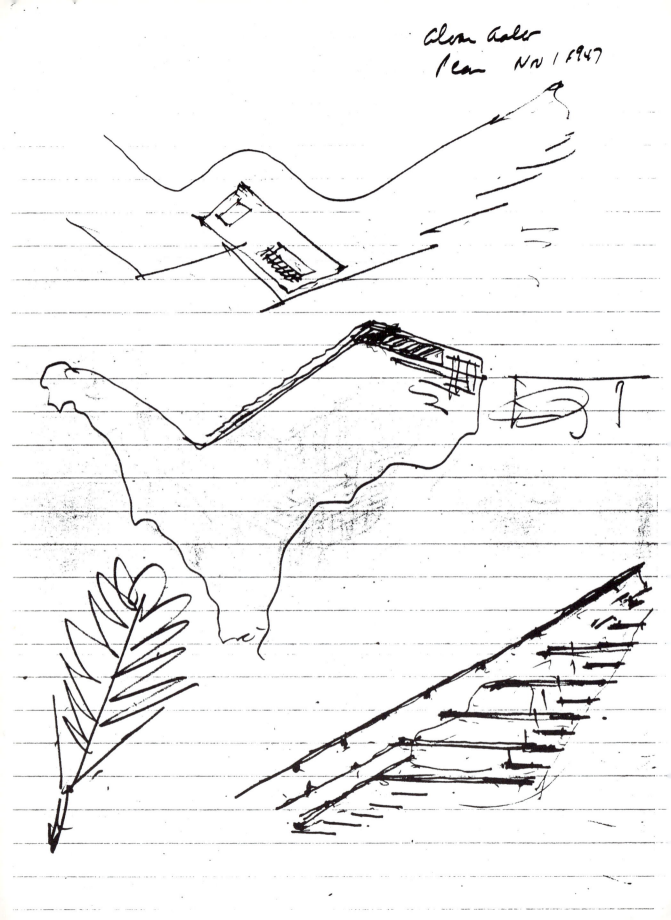

8.10
Sketch of solution to the end of
Baker House Dormitory, dated 1
November, 1947, MIT Aalto, 1947.

8.11
Rowan branch.

Although pushed by the MIT authorities to include more rooms, Aalto's bottom line was that there were to be 'no dark halls',[51] which led to the ingenious twisting of the ends of the building to include more accommodation. A sketch by Aalto from a meeting at MIT in 1947, showing the splayed opening of a branch towards the light, demonstrates the genesis of this idea (Fig. 8.10). Later he described how at the east and west ends of the building the mass grows like 'the branch of a pine tree, where the needles and smaller branches group more closely at the ends of the branches. As an element of the sun absorption the building can be compared to this general system appearing in nature.'[52] Overall, the rooms were to be as varied in plan form as possible. Aalto designed items of furniture, produced by Artek, which could be positioned within them in a number of ways, as the students wished.

Typical of his compositional technique, the building simultaneously unites and juxtaposes precedents from very different sources: the vernacular stone fireplace; the classical sunken courtyard in the dining pavilion; and the organic disposition of cell-like study rooms that are orientated towards the sun and the view wherever possible. In 1938 he had written that 'Every formal straightjacket ... prevents architecture from playing its full part in the human struggle for existence' and 'lessens its significance and effectiveness'.[53] He exorcised this tendency towards overformality through a recognition that 'architecture's inner nature is a fluctuation and a development suggestive of natural organic life'.[54] The informality of the irregular twisted bricks on the façade add a tectonic testament to individuality and a challenge to any overriding sense of a norm, of what he saw as 'powerful and inhuman monotony'.[55]

Going Vertical Against The Grain

In the fan form of Neue Vahr apartment block in Bremen (1958–62, Fig. 8.12), which also arises in many of his abstract oil paintings of the time (Fig. 8.13), Aalto claims to have sought to counter the 'depressing, closed-in feeling' of

[51] Letter from William Wurster to Aalto, 15 July 1947. MIT Archives, and Alvar Aalto Foundation hereafter known as AAF.
[52] Aalto, 'Senior Dormitory M.I.T.'.
[53] Aalto, 'The Influence of Construction and Materials on Modern Architecture', 1938 in Schildt, *Sketches*, p.61.
[54] Ibid. p.63.
[55] Aalto, 'Senior Dormitory M.I.T.'.

many small rectilinear apartments.[56] Having articulated his dislike of high-rise blocks, he nevertheless accepted such a commission on the understanding that the twenty-two-storey block was to be specifically designed for single people or childless couples, being opposed to family occupation of tower blocks.

In this scheme Aalto borrowed from Baker House the feature of rooms widening towards the window wall, thus offering 'a feeling of release',[57] towards the west-facing balcony space. In common with his earlier housing, this outside room is withdrawn from neighbours' view. Venturi recognised that here, as in Baker House, Aalto yielded to 'the inner needs for light and space toward the south, like the growth of a flower towards the sun'.[58] Finding here a distortion of Le Corbusier's rectilinear Unité plan, Venturi suggested that a diagonal force was at work.[59] Yet, in light of Aalto's sketch of the *raison d'être* of Baker House (Fig. 8.14), it seems likely that the force was indeed natural rather than purely geometric, yearning towards the light and view, and individuality.[60]

In an article addressing building heights in 1946, Aalto described the ideal of family houses being at ground level with open access to nature. However he equally recognised that often this ideal was not attainable, and that well-designed high-rise buildings, having a 'harmonious integration with nature and the community around' them, with 'flawless orientation with respect to sun and view, and many other purely qualitative improvements' were sometimes needed.[61] Aalto was aware that high-rise solutions had a drawback – 'This relates to the mystical link between home and nature'.[62] In Bremen his solution to this problem was to take the rectilinear order that Le Corbusier had established in the Domino House and amalgamated into the Unité, and distort it. Aalto once sketched something of this difference, representing his approach to flexible standardisation next to a standardised, orthogonal tower block (Fig. 8.14). It may not be Le Corbusier's concept of mass living to which he is referring, although Aalto might have flippantly suggested that it was.

Below: 8.12
Plan of Neue Vahr apartment block, Bremen. Aalto, 1958–62.

Below left: 8.13
Oil painting, 27 x 32.5cm. Aalto, c.1949.

Above right: 8.14
Sketch of comparison of towers with orthogonal and splayed plan forms. Aalto, undated.

Below right: 8.15
Plan of Hansa apartment block, Berlin. Aalto, 1955-7.

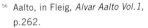

[56] Aalto, in Fleig, *Alvar Aalto Vol.1*, p.262.

[57] Ibid.

[58] R. Venturi, *Complexity and Contradiction in Architecture*, New York: Museum of Modern Art, 1977, p.82.

[59] Ibid, p.50.

[60] Griffiths suggests that the classical theatre typology is also at work – as if it is a tool with which to reinvigorate Modernism. G. Griffiths, *The Polemical Aalto*, Datutop 19, Tampere: University of Tampere, 1997, p.85.

[61] Aalto, 'Building Height as a Social Issue', 1946 in Schildt, *Own Words*, p.208.

[62] Ibid.

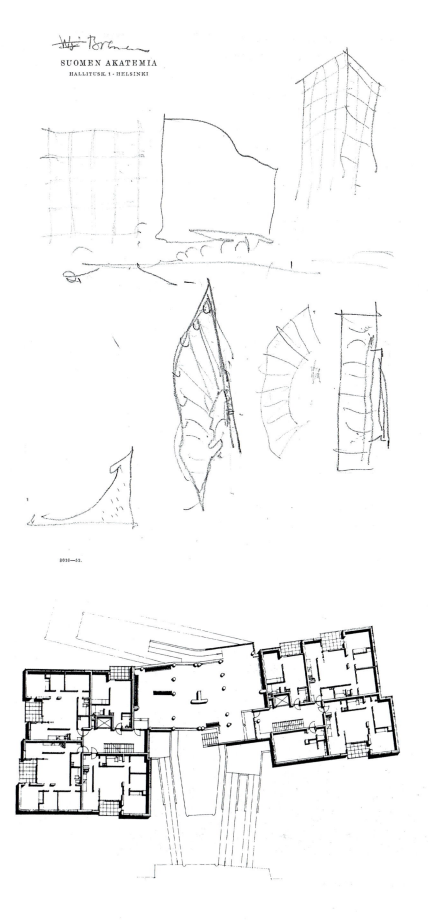

World Rebuilding: Interbau, Berlin 1957

In 1954 Le Corbusier and Aalto, along with a number of other internationally renowned architects, were approached to design apartment blocks for the 1957 Berlin Interbau Exhibition. Although the resultant buildings are not the best examples of this typology, they nevertheless represent their respective approaches to the problem of mass living.

Aalto's Hansaviertel block (1955-7, Fig. 8.15) demonstrates his principles of a minimal apartment, flexible standardisation, and the outside room or balcony. The eight-storey apartment block is divided into two slightly flexing wings. The scheme houses seventy-eight dwellings and is constructed in prefabricated concrete units. Each apartment is oriented around a central living space and dominating balconies. Aalto conceived these as an 'open atrium', a means of accessing nature and the history of architecture, via his own Villa Väinö back to those of Pompeii. 'This ingenious design', Frampton suggests, 'comprised one of the most significant apartment types to have been invented since the Second World War.'[63] He describes its primary virtue being its manner of providing 'the attributes of the single-family house within the confines of a small flat'. Here 'a generous atrium terrace is flanked by the living and dining rooms, while the whole is surrounded on two sides by private rooms'.[64] The apartments cluster about naturally lit stair-halls, the spatial inflection of which ensures that they avoid a sense of monotony and fulfil his lifelong determination to meet both the physical and the psychological needs of the individual. Here again Aalto demonstrated his 'methodical accommodation of circumstance'.[65] In 1972 he summarised his notion of elastic standardisation. 'The goal is a kind of standardisation that does not force life into a mould, but actually enhances its variety.'[66]

Le Corbusier's contribution to the Interbau in Berlin was not the best example of his Unité, yet still it was intended to restore architectural dignity to simple dwellings. At Le Corbusier's request the Unité was to be positioned outside the Interbau site, on the Olympic Hill. Without his knowledge the contractor built the lower half of the building with the post-war German UNI system of standardisation rather than the Modulor.[67] Not only did the system lack the dynamic nature of the Modulor standardisation, correlated as it was to the human body, but it meant that the ceiling heights were raised by up to a metre. Overall the result was a Unité of exaggerated girth, and gone was the 'asymmetrical and off-beat pattern of windows with typical ribbon windows'.[68] On visiting the site, Le Corbusier's horror was instantly channelled into a sketch of a colourful 'camouflage' (now gone)[69] and a determined insistence that the remaining part of the scheme be built to Modulor dimensions. Le Corbusier disowned the final building, which also lacked the social functions that he believed were crucial to the healthy life of the inhabitants. It comprises a sharp formal contradiction – inelegant bulk beneath a carefully proportioned mass imbued, Le Corbusier would argue, with an inherent aerial invitation to live life more fully. Indeed, the 'vertical garden city' offered a renewal of life in contact, Le Corbusier believed, with nature and one another.[70]

63 K. Frampton, *Modern Architecture a Critical History*, London: Thames & Hudson, 1997, p.201.

64 Ibid, p.202.

65 Aalto, 'Karelian Architecture', 1941 in Schildt, *Own Words*, p.118. See also S. Menin, 'Fragments from the Forest: Aalto's Requisitioning of Forest Place and Matter', *Journal of Architecture*, 6, 3, 2001, pp.279–305, and S. Anderson, 'Aalto and Methodical Accommodation to Circumstance', in T. Tuomi, K. Paatero, E. Rauske (eds), *Alvar Aalto in Seven Buildings*, Helsinki: Museum of Finnish Architecture, 1998, p.143.

66 Aalto, 'Interview for Television', 1972 in Schildt, *Own Words*, p.271.

67 L. Benevolo, *History of Modern Architecture 2*, Cambridge, MA: MIT, 1971, p.738.

68 P. Blake, *No Place like Utopia*, New York: Norton, 1996, p.225.

69 Ibid. Blake witnessed Le Corbusier sketch this recovery plan, and describes how controlled he was. He also comments about the change in him since Yvonne's death. Ibid., p.226.

70 Le Corbusier, *Radiant City*, p.83.

Conclusion

Both Le Corbusier and Aalto were critical of what they perceived to be inhuman and soul-destroying mass housing driven by considerations of minimal spatial requirements. They wanted to create something intrinsically more humane, 'to the human scale' as Le Corbusier put it, encouraging reverie in fresh air, the sun and the greenery. This involved them both in contorting the articulated rules of Modernism that Le Corbusier had enunciated earlier, but that architects of less skill and imagination had allowed to become dogmatic.

Christian Norberg-Schulz suggests that both men had what Wright called a 'hunger for reality'.[71] However, as earlier chapters demonstrate, he is misguided in suggesting that Aalto had experienced a more 'natural' way of life than Le Corbusier, meaning that it took longer for the latter to achieve buildings of the 'presence and character' of the Unité.[72] In Chapter 1 we demonstrated that both men grew up steeped in the natural world, and hungered for the opportunity to imbibe their creations with such natural attachment. The heterotopic ordering of Aalto's work is widely accepted to have countered Modern Rationalism and the 'homogenous grid'.[73] Yet we have sought to demonstrate that within Le Corbusier's work too there was a counter-insurgence of nature-inspiration, if not actually a drive which could be identified as iconoclastic in the modern realm of his own making which became more clearly manifest from the mid-1930s. Le Corbusier's drive for spartan forms and interiors is characterised by many as a failure to provide humane architecture, although, as we have shown, few architects sought more determinedly to address the whole reality of modern man. Le Corbusier began, with increasing bitterness, to recall his vision of L'Esprit Nouveau:

> Town Planning expresses the life of an era.
> Architecture reveals its spirit.

'Some men have original ideas and are kicked in the ass for their pains,' he was to observe.[74]

[71] C. Norberg-Schulz, *Genius Loci: Towards a Phenomenology of Architecture*, New York: Rizzoli, 1980, p.196.

[72] Ibid.

[73] D. Porphyrios, *Sources of Modern Eclecticism: Studies of Alvar Aalto*, London: Academy Editions, 1982, p.2.

[74] Le Corbusier, *My Work*, London: Architectural Press, 1960, p.147.

Nature Relations and the Heart of Architecture

Through the course of this book many aspects of the attitudes towards nature held by Le Corbusier and Aalto have come to light, expressive of their early life experiences and their subsequent personalities. These have then been shown to imbue the heart of their work.

In the *Encyclopedia Britannica* it can be seen that 'Nature is a term of very uncertain extent'.[1] A subject that has taxed philosophers for generations, the word defies definition. In this conclusion we will attempt to define the various meanings of nature for Aalto and Le Corbusier. Broadly speaking, nature was, for the two men, the environment, the earth, sun, water and stars that make up the cosmos. In its ideal form it was also a system of order (flexible, in Aalto's mind) with divine origins. Nature also stood for a way of working, of creating things that would fit into that wider system. Nature could be accessed through love and the act of making love. Nature could also be terrible, unforgiving and indeed fatal. The cycles of life and death were in her thrall. The two men do not however seem to have been in total agreement on the meaning and significance of nature. There are a number of subtle differences between their attitudes to the subject, differences that we will now attempt to highlight.

Growth and Incessant Creativity

That both Le Corbusier and Aalto had common childhood experiences of being immersed in nature, and that both wove into these intuitions a detailed knowledge of biology and natural processes of growth, has been established. Having been vital in their youth, nature continued to be a model for their creative work, especially that which was concerned with provision for human habitation and, at a more fundamental level, human fulfilment.

It has been seen that Le Corbusier, the alpine youth, grew to have mountainous aspirations. Indeed, Jencks suggests that he was determined to

[1] *Encyclopedia Britanicca*, 11th Edition, Cambridge: Cambridge University Press, 1911, p.274.

face the demon of constant change through his incessant creativity.[2] The conclusion here does not oppose this, but suggests both reasons for and the character of this need for continual change and revolution. If more details of Le Corbusier's life were in the public domain this could be explicated more fully.[3]

Aalto the dramatist seems to stand akimbo, somehow disguising and protecting his more precarious self. We have sought to avoid denial of the personal past of a creative legend and indeed attempts to promote a nostalgic view of architect-heroes growing in the backwoods, as if in arcadia. The truth must have been so tragically different, since what was at best repeated bouts of hypochondria and depression (and at worst virtually psychotic behaviour that punctuated his otherwise manically creative life) can by no standards be without cause, nor without painful human effect.

From an Ancient World-View to Modern World-Building

Intrinsically bound to their interest in ancient Greek thought, nature provided a model for harmony and synthesis that both architects aspired to recreate (or facilitate) in their designs to the last. Le Corbusier and Aalto both grasped the ancient world-view or the notion of the cosmos, with nature ebbing and flowing, meandering towards a forever difficult and therefore perhaps more real harmony.

It is important to reiterate the Hellenic etymology, since it relates the metaphysical notion of harmony to the physical morphology of a 'joint' (harmos in Greek). Thereby there is on offer an idea that may be translated into a formal compositional technique for unifying the disparate, used incessantly by Aalto (Fig. 8.13), rather than being an abstract philosophical tenet alone.

Le Corbusier was almost literally struck down by this world-view during his 'Journey to the East'. Infected by the germs from Ancient Sophists, he was deeply unsettled until, in 1911, a philosophical crisis caused him to shed his formative mantle and orientate himself, again to the East, allowing consequent cosmic preoccupations to imbue his inevitable subsequent revolutions. These preoccupations have been demonstrated to have been active in his earliest Modernist experiments.

Although it may be applicable to his earliest use of the form, the suggestion by one commentator that Aalto felt his Classicism 'was more a style than an outlook on the world', and that 'it was Functionalism that was his first deeply internalised architectural ideology' is erroneous, since it misses the depth of vitality of Aalto's understanding of the Greek world-view.[4] The line drawn by St. John Wilson between Aristotle's Practical Art and the notion of function is useful.[5] Functionalism was attractive to Aalto's pragmatism, and remained something of a nemesis against which he cut his compositional teeth, but nevertheless the deeper ideology was one that connected with his need to recompose aspects of himself.

Similarly the notion that there was a severance of their dialogue with their nature-ridden past when Le Corbusier relinquished and Aalto declined the stylistic mantle of Art Nouveau is flawed. Abstracted natural growth underpins

2   C. Jencks, *Le Corbusier and the Continual Revolution in Architecture*, New York: Monacelli, 2000, p.13.
3   Nicholas Weber is currently writing a biography of Le Corbusier, utilising a number of previously inaccessible sources.
4   T. Koho, *Alvar Aalto: Urban Finland*, Helsinki: Rakennustieto, 1995, p.157.
5   C. St John Wilson, *Architectural Reflections*, London: Butterworth, 1992, pp.29–31.

Le Corbusier's conception of the Domino frame, as much as ritualistic Orphism flows through Villa Savoye. Aalto's flirtation with an unrooted Modernism was brief, but nevertheless nature was connoted in the embryonic entrance wave at Paimio, and the wooden wave at Viipuri.

Norberg-Schulz suggests that although Le Corbusier desired to recreate the plastic presence and intelligibility of Greece, he exchanges the classical 'organic' approach for something more abstract and removed.[6] Such suggestions of detachment have been cited here too in our discussions of Le Corbusier's stance towards nature. Yet his buildings invite their inhabitants to engage with both nature and one another, but in a rather different way to Aalto's. In form they are less evocative of organic fluid and erratic natural spaces than those of Aalto. 'Natural' materials are used, but in a way that distances them from their original antecedents – concrete, for example, instead of stone. Le Corbusier relied far more heavily on symbolism and geometry to evoke nature than did his counterpart. Light, for example, is used symbolically or for dramatic purposes. It is rarely used with the delicate and evocative touch of Aalto, who seems to have been more comfortable with the vagaries of nature. Le Corbusier seems to have wanted to frame and control his subject, organising it into fixed patterns, seeing it as a microcosm of a larger whole. It may even be said that Le Corbusier sought to frame nature – epitomised by his approach to the altar-like windows with tables that he created in the Villa Savoye (Plate 21) and the Petite Maison on Lake Geneva for his mother (1935),[7] and translated later into the balconies of the Unités (Plate 30). Nature is at the heart, but simultaneously outside and beyond. Le Corbusier wrote of the need for man to learn 'how to live', expressing the need to address the problem that 'man dwells badly'.[8] Possibly articulating an awareness of his own difficulty with wholeheartedly embracing nature, he wrote in *When the Cathedrals were White*: 'Knowing how to live is the fundamental question before modern society, everywhere, in the whole world. An ingenuous question and one that could be considered childish. How to live? Do you know reader? Do you know how to live soundly, strongly, gaily, free of the hundred stupidities established by habit, custom and urban disorganization?'[9]

The problem of dwelling, addressed by both men, was for Le Corbusier the deep and real reason for the problems of his time. In consequence he set out to counter the horrors of the industrial city with the garden city ideal, this time vertical. In this way man would follow 'the organic development of existence' and of everyday human activity, from the basic process of dwelling onwards.[10] For this reason Le Corbusier attempted to create an architecture which would act as a reminder to those who lived within it of the importance of balance and harmony in their lives. This was done symbolically, through the framing of views, through materials, through the creation of inside/outside spaces and through the inclusion of artworks and natural objects and through geometry. Aalto's second wife Elissa recalls that,

> Certainly nature had an effect on him. It might have been something he admired, something specific that didn't have any direct effect on architecture, but it did however enter the subconscious, and later such

6   C. Norberg-Schulz, *Genius Loci: Towards a Phenomenology of Architecture* New York: Rizzoli, 1980, p.76. He is referring to Le Corbusier's call for 'the masterly, correct and magnificent play of volumes brought together in light'. Le Corbusier, *Towards a New Architecture*, London: Architectural Press, 1982, p.31.

7   The Petite Maison on Lake Geneva was pronounced to be 'a crime against nature' by the local authorities in 1951. Le Corbusier, *Une Petite Maison*, Zürich: Aux Éditions d'Architecture, 1993, p.80.

8   Le Corbusier, *La Maison des Hommes*, Paris, 1942, p.5. Cited in Norberg-Schulz, *Genius Loci*, p.191.

9   Le Corbusier, *When the Cathedrals were White: A Journey to the Country of the Timid People*, New York: Reynal & Hitchcock, 1947, p.xvii.

10 Le Corbusier, *Towards a New Architecture*, p.268.

natural experience proved of use in design. When painting at Muuratsalo Alvar would sometimes sign: 'Oh, how all this nature disturbs me!' But he was clearly dependent on nature in many ways.[11]

Aalto sought to draw nature into his architecture, breaking down the notion of a boundary between the dwelling and outside. There is a constant materialising of a longing for engagement, and an invitation therein, and indeed encouragement to ruin and age, for nature to engulf both the dwelling and civilisation. In this sense there is an aura of immanence in Aalto's work, of participation in a process of human living, but within a broader natural context.

A deeper, more controversial reason for this difference between the compulsion to recreate engagement or detachment, addressed above, may be the different nature of the two architects' relationships with their mothers. In outline, Aalto's relationship with his mother had been deeply affectionate but cruelly severed; Le Corbusier's seems to have been more problematic, but lasted a lifetime.

Mania, Multivalency and the Ecology of Imagination

The character of the inner drive that called Le Corbusier to invest all in the development of his vision for humankind is important. It appears selfless, demanding huge amounts of time and energy, and it may be said to have prevented him having children and a family life. Yet it was always his choice – the acting out of the life of a Nietzschean Superman, the life of Zarathustra. When he first experienced Paris, in 1908, before his real toil and struggle began, he wrote, 'I want to fight with truth itself. It will torment me. But I am not looking for quietude, or recognition from the world. I will live in sincerity, happy to undergo abuse.'[12] This indicates a degree of expectation of rejection and lack of appreciation that has the air of a self-fulfilling prophecy. Much later, in 1947, after years of real struggle, he complained, 'Sometimes I despair. Men are so stupid that I'm glad I'm going to die. All my life people have tried to crush me ... Luckily, I've always had an iron will. Though timid as a youth, I've forced myself to cross Rubicons. Je suis un type boxeur.'[13] After his great plans were floored by the Vichy regime, Jencks suggests that the poet in Le Corbusier began to dominate the technocrat.[14] Such a life of perpetual struggle involved him in constant reassessment of his principles and the direction of his vision. At each turn, his determination to let nature, in the broadest sense, inform his work seems to have grown.

Aalto drew attention to the way in which his 'subconscious' instincts led him to design solutions.[15] Porphyrios suggests that 'By utilising associational richness of already operative and socially legitimate iconographic types ... Aalto achieves the ultimate poetic aspect of language: that of polysemy (the manifold levels of signification; the profusion of secondary and tertiary meanings)'.[16] Aalto claimed he intuitively distilled these many associations into new, composite manifestations. This process would have demanded from him skill and great strength in negotiating a myriad of ideas, forms and, inevitably, feelings, an

[11] Elissa Aalto in L. Lahti, *Ex Intimo*, Helsinki: Rakennustieto, 2001, p.25.

[12] Le Corbusier, letter to L'Eplattenier, 22 November 1908, cited in Jean Petit, *Le Corbusier lui-même*, Paris: Forces Vives, 1970, p.34.

[13] C. Jencks, *Le Corbusier and the Continental Revolution*, New York: Monacelli, 2000, p.26.

[14] C. Jencks, *Continual Revolution*, pp.228–41.

[15] Aalto, 'The Trout and the Stream', 1947; repr. in G. Schildt, *Alvar Aalto in his Own Words*, New York: Rizzoli, 1997, p.108.

[16] D. Porphyrios, 1979, 'The Burst of Memory: An Essay on Alvar Aalto's Typological Conception of Design', in *Architectural Design*, 49, 5/6, 1979, p.144.

ecology (a web enabling diversities to collaborate) reminiscent of Cobb's notion of the ecology of imagination. The notion put forward here is that it was from the 'gap' that both architects gained their strength, or more realistically their drive, and from nature that they gained their basic model of negotiation.

Aalto's determination to overcome an alienation he saw in the environment of modern buildings may have been a direct transference of the alienation that he felt at heart. That this was overcome at a creative level by his production of buildings that address the needs of both human and geographic nature and circumstance is laudable. Yet his personal tragedy remained for family and close friends to survive and mourn. Imagination may have been the key in Aalto's general stability, being a vehicle of exchange, a potential space in which to negotiate between inner and outer reality – what might be called an ecological field of mutual influence.[17]

Although often controlled by it, Aalto was, at some level, aware of his own tragedy. He believed that 'True architecture exists only where man stands in the centre. His tragedy, and his comedy, both.'[18] Indeed, his personal yearning for 'proximity to nature'[19] became professional in his deep architectural agenda of manifesting nature, 'a symbol of freedom';[20] 'there is a deeper, perhaps mystical domiciliary right for thought and work which builds upon the popular psyche and on purely geographic conditions.'[21]

Realism or Idealism: A Growing Sense of Architecture

A clear image of the two architects' differing conceptions of nature is offered by their basic approaches to the development of towns. One commentator characterises Aalto's town-planning schemes as being small, but growing and human in scale, and Le Corbusier's as being finite and scaleless, particularly the early ones.[22] These are incomplete critiques, but hold a kernel of truth about the notion of nature as either a dynamic process or a more static phenomenon. Le Corbusier referred to biology as the inspiration for his town-planning schemes, but not because he was interested in the way that organisms grow. He was more interested in the idea of a cellular structure binding all things together (Fig. 8.4)[23]. Aalto meanwhile, was concerned with the way that biological organisms evolve and mutate, allowing variety in essence (Fig. 8.5). At best Aalto's view aspired to allow for growth from a small beginning, giving as much power to the client to change the direction of the growth as possible (in his type houses), and encapsulated a nuance of formal expansion into modest, gestating wholes. Le Corbusier, on the other hand, used nature to conceive the principles behind complete systems – sun, air, greenery.

This difference may be implicit in the two natural philosophies that are said to have interested the two men, as Pallasmaa suggested in a comment about Villa Mairea. He positions Aalto as 'a Bergsonian sensory realist' rather than 'a Cartesian idealist', surreptitiously drawing Le Corbusier to mind.[24] Yet this should not allow the identification of Le Corbusier with his didactic Cartesian dialectic alone, since this was only one of his many personas.

[17] S. McNiff, Foreword to E. Cobb, *The Ecology of Imagination in Childhood*, Dallas: Spring Publications, 1993, p.xi.

[18] Aalto, 'Instead of an Article', 1958; repr. in G. Schildt (ed.) *Alvar Aalto: Sketches*, Cambridge, MA: MIT Press, 1985, p.161.

[19] Aalto, 'Experimental House, Muuratsalo', 1953, ibid., p.116.

[20] Aalto, 'National Planning and Cultural Goals', 1949, ibid., p.102.

[21] Aalto, 'Art and Technology', 1955, ibid., p.129.

[22] H. Wesse, 'Alvar Aalto', in *ARK*, 7–8, 1976, p.46.

[23] For a discussion of Le Corbusier's response to the more chaotic and disturbing sides of nature see, Colli, L., 'La Couleur qui cache, La Couleur qui Signalle', in J. Jenger (ed.), *Le Corbusier at la Coleur*, paris: FLC 1992, pp.24-5.

[24] J. Pallasmaa, *Villa Mairea*, Helsinki: Mairea Foundation and Alvar Aalto Foundation, 1998, p.86.

Sacred (In)Security and Life's Quarrelling Sub-problems

Far, it would seem, from Cartesian preoccupations, Le Corbusier's work began to comprise non-Euclidean forms. This drew some to write of the 'crisis of rationalism', of the 'conscious imperfectionism',[25] and the 'new irrationalism'.[26] In Ronchamp the overarching world-view is such as to suggest that Le Corbusier was confident of a sacred security that would unite the fluid forms – and offer metaphysical confidence to ameliorate the loss of a purely rational hold on life.

Exploring Le Corbusier's use of nature to offer a symbolic structure for life, Katherine Fraser Fischer writes:

> The combination of the curved and natural with the rectilinear and machined within a common context entails a further conclusion: architecture, like the body or vessel, is a container, and a qualified environment within a larger, more inchoate context. In this respect, it is significant that these objects, despite their naturalistic allusions, remain artificial tools for structuring a world from nature.[27]

The same writers who found imperfection and confusion in Ronchamp accepted Aalto's equally anti-rectilinear offerings, perhaps because a doctrine had not grown up around these. Indeed, from Viipuri Library ceiling onwards, Aalto explored the relationship of waving and straight lines as expressions of the diverse but allied functions in buildings and, concomitantly, of life's activity and experience. In common with many of his works, at Vuoksenniska Aalto manifests a dialogue between free-form expression and the control of the anchoring episode of the long, geometric wall. Here the wall roots the dynamic of the undulating wave. Aalto may have been less secure in the spiritual realm than Le Corbusier, ensuring his metaphysical hold by relating 'his swarming free line rhythms'[28] to Euclid's hand. For any notion of harmony to preside (in either life or architecture), Aalto had to hold fast to his theme of synthesis amid the complexity of his basic pattern of creative borrowing from a wide realm of influences (including history, contemporaries, place and people). It seems that his psyche was, after all, probably the more vulnerable.

In joining the disparate in this way Aalto may be describing his own life. He wrote of 'a kind of universal substance which helps me to bring the numerous contradictory components into harmony'.[29] An earlier translation, cited in Chapter 4, offers the words 'quarrelling sub-problems', which is a useful nuance in helping to decipher Aalto's meaning.[30] This is of great import, epitomising Aalto's mantra – that it was rational to drive for synthesis between otherwise dislocated elements of life and, in this case, matter – especially when your very sanity depends on it. He had an extremely important point here, one that anchored the 'organic line'[31] and seems to have become something of an insurance mechanism. Despite his dislike of limited rationalism, Aalto's sometimes manic fantasy needed to be rooted in such objectivity. This expanded view of rationalism (which allowed for the natural process of growth and change) was bred, not just from the bio-centrism that held currency with others in Europe (through his friends such as Moholy Nagy and Gropius) but, we argue, from his own psychological vulnerability.

25 J. Stirling, 'Ronchamp: Le Corbusier's Chapel and the Crisis of Rationalism,' *Architectural Review*, 119, March 1956, pp.155-61.

26 N. Pevsner, *An Outline of European Architecture*, London: Pelican, 1982, p.429.

27 K. Fraser Fischer, 'A Nature Morte', *Oppositions*, 15-16, 1979, pp.156–65.

28 R. Pietilä, 'Influences', in M.-R. Norri, R. Connah, K. Kuosma and A. Artto, *Pietilä: Intermediate Zones in Modern Architecture*, Helsinki: Museum of Finnish Architecture, 1985, p.10.

29 Aalto, 'The Trout and the Stream', 1947, in Schildt, *Sketches*, p.108.

30 Ibid., p.97.

31 Aalto, letter to Gropius, autumn 1930. Cited in Schildt, *Alvar Aalto: The Decisive Years*, New York: Rizzoli, 1986, p.66.

Others further from the Modernist fold celebrated the freedom of Le Corbusier's formal gestures at Ronchamp. Indeed, Venturi opened *Complexity and Contradiction in Architecture* by comparing Aalto and Le Corbusier with other architects, and praising both for their capacity to avoid simplification by promoting 'complexity within the whole'.[32] This complexity demonstrates a concern with both the cosmic and the particularly personal. Both men flipped between the two realms with ease – as they did between the present and the past, at both personal and architectural levels. Le Corbusier wrote that disbelieving in 'absolute truths' we should 'involve' our 'own self in every question'.[33] He infused nature into his work by simultaneously addressing the essentials of human living (sun, air and greenery), the minutiae of ergonomics and his own Platonic aspirations. They all came together in the Modulor, steeped as it was with Pythagorean principles and cosmological mythology.

Nature and Potential Space: The 'Gap' and the Power of Creativity

To recap, Winnicott's notion of the 'natural' growth process inherent in human life has provided the framework for the enquiries here, the basic tenet being that disturbance of the earliest environment has been shown to result in a primal 'gap' – a failure of the infant's environment and a disturbance of the process of 'primary' psychic creativity.[34] In a 'good enough environment' (in other words, that which facilitates rather than prevents primary, pre-sexual creativity) there should be no 'gap'. The first environment, Winnicott believed, is the experience of being held, starting before birth and progressing through the nursing period, facilitating psycho-somatic integration and 'natural' growth processes.[35]

Winnicott argued that the 'gap' interferes with the growth of the individual, and with the 'Potential Space' the individual might occupy.[36] This may be extrapolated into the phenomena of creativity in adulthood where play and creativity are linked in the transitional world (between subjectivity and objectivity). Indeed, independently Cobb describes how the child may grasp hold of a system of order from beyond their unpredictable environment, internalise it, and use it to seek to bring some order to the interior chaos: seeking to 'structure a world' through creative evolution.[37] This acts like a refuge, and can be an important ingredient in the future direction of a creative journey.

We may conclude that Aalto's aspirations for architecture had a mystical dimension that was intricately inspired by his own experiences of life's joys and agonies,[38] that he sought to imbue architecture with different aspects of the natural realm, through formal detail and symbolic phenomena, binding these together with 'a philosophy of geographical localism'.[39] 'The purpose of a building is to act as an instrument that collects all the positive influences in nature for man's benefit, ... we must also understand that a building cannot fulfil its purpose if it does not itself possess a wealth of nuances equal to that of the natural environment to which it will belong as a permanent ingredient.'[40]

[32] R. Venturi, *Complexity and Contradiction in Architecture*, New York: Museum of Modern Art, 1977, pp.18–19.

[33] Le Corbusier, *Precisions on the Present State of Architecture and City Planning*, Cambridge, MA: MIT Press, 1991, p.32.

[34] D. Winnicott, *Collected Papers: Through Paediatrics to Psycohanalysis*, London: Tavistock, 1958, p. 145.

[35] D. Winnicott, *Home is Where We Start From: Essays by a Psychoanalyst*, London: Pelican, 1987, pp. 142–9.

[36] D. Winnicott, *Playing and Reality*, Harmondsworth: Penguin, 1971, pp. 2–10.

[37] Cobb, *Ecology of Imagination in Childhood*, p.17.

[38] Aalto, 'Instead of an Article', 1958 in Schildt, *Sketches*, p.161.

[39] R. Pietilä, 'Architect's Approach to Architecture', in Norri, Connah, Kuosma and Artto, *Pietilä*, p.116.

[40] Aalto, 'The Reconstruction of Europe is the Key Problem for the Architecture of Our Time' in Schildt, *Own Words*, pp.150 and 152.

Generally speaking Aalto's aspirations were made earthy early in a design, as his 6B sketches evince, being drenched with richness of form and material through the sensuality of his details. This immediacy was personal as well as creative, and may explain why many associate more easily with Aalto the man than with Le Corbusier. Interestingly Von Moos argues that Le Corbusier was always battling so hard, his life so full of tensions and contradictions that his work never achieves the 'serene, familial and social' character of Aalto's.[41] Equally, many associate Aalto with nature more readily than Le Corbusier. Nevertheless this book has sought to make explicit the depth to which nature underpinned the lives and work of both. At the end of his life, months before he died, Le Corbusier recalled: 'I did have an excellent teacher who opened my eyes to the spectacle of nature ... he would help us draw from nature, not landscapes, but elements of plants. He would push us towards an understanding of how things go together.'[42] Through rigorous distillation and crystallisation this process transformed itself into a philosophy wherein nature and architecture were virtually synonymous. In 'Mise au Point' Le Corbusier wrote, 'I brought back the temple to the family, to the home. I restored the conditions of nature to the life of man'.[43]

[41] S. Von Moos, *Le Corbusier: L'architecture et son mythe*, paris: Horizons de France, 1971, p.299.

[42] Le Corbusier, in his last interview with Hugues Desalle, 15 May 1965, 'The Final Year' in I. Žaknić, *The Final Testament of Père Corbu*, New Haven: Yale University Press, 1997, p.105.

[43] Le Corbusier, 'Mise au Point', in ibid., p.96.

Bibliography

Aalto, A., (under pseudonym of Ping), 'Benvenuto's Christmas Punch', Kerberos, 1–2, 1921.

— 'Painter and Mason', *Jousimies*, 1921. Repr. in G. Schildt, *Alvar Aalto in his Own Words*, New York: Rizzoli, 1997, pp. 30–2.

— 'Motifs from the Past', *Arkkitehti*, 2, 1922. Repr. in G. Schildt, *Alvar Aalto Sketches*, Cambridge: MIT Press, 1985, pp. 1–2 and as 'Motifs from Times Past' in G. Schildt, *Alvar Aalto in his Own Words*, New York: Rizzoli, 1997, pp.32–5.

— 'The Hill Top Town', 1924. Repr. in G. Schildt, *Alvar Aalto in his Own Words*, New York: Rizzoli, 1997, p.49.

— 'Urban Culture', Sisä-Suomi, 12 December 1924. Repr. in G. Schildt, *Alvar Aalto in his Own Words*, New York: Rizzoli, 1997, pp. 19–20.

— 'Finnish Church Art', *Käsiteollisuus*, 3, 1925. Repr. in G. Schildt, *Alvar Aalto in his Own Words*, New York: Rizzoli, 1997, pp.37–8.

— 'The Temple Baths on Jyväskylä Ridge', Keskisuomalainen, 22 January 1925. Repr. in G. Schildt, *Alvar Aalto in his Own Words*, New York: Rizzoli, 1977, pp.17–19.

— 'Abbé Coignard's Sermon', 6 March 1925. Repr. in G. Schildt, *Alvar Aalto in his Own Words*, New York: Rizzoli, 1997, pp.56–7.

— 'Architecture in the Landscape of Central Finland', Sisä-Suomi, 28 June 1925. Repr. in G. Schildt, *Alvar Aalto in his Own Words*, New York: Rizzoli, 1997, pp.21–2.

— 'From Doorstep to Living Room', Aitta, 1926. Repr. in G. Schildt, *Alvar Aalto in his Own Words*, New York: Rizzoli, 1997, pp. 49–55.

— 'Armas Lindgren and We', *Arkkitehti*, 10, 1929. Repr. in G. Schildt, *Alvar Aalto in his Own Words*, New York: Rizzoli, 1997, pp.241–2.

— 'Housing Construction in Existing Cities', *Byggmästaren*, 1930. Repr. in G. Schildt, *Alvar Aalto Sketches*, Cambridge: MIT Press, 1985, pp. 3-6.

— 'The Dwelling as a Problem', *Domus*, 1930. Repr. in G. Schildt, *Alvar Aalto Sketches*, Cambridge, MA: MIT Press, 1985, pp. 29–33, and as 'The Housing Problem', 1930, G. Schildt, *Alvar Aalto in his Own Words*, New York: Rizzoli, 1977, pp.76–84.

— 'The Stockholm Exhibition I and II', 1930. Repr. in G. Schildt, *Alvar Aalto in his Own Words*, New York: Rizzoli, 1997, p.716.

— 'Letter from Finland', *Bauwelt*, 1931. Repr. in G. Schildt, *Alvar Aalto Sketches*, Cambridge, MA: MIT Press, 1985, pp. 34-5.

— 'The Geography of the Housing Question', 1932. Repr. in G. Schildt, *Alvar Aalto Sketches*, Cambridge, MA: MIT Press, 1985, pp. 44-6.

— 'Rationalism and Man', Speech to the Swedish Craft Society, 1935. Repr. in G. Schildt, *Alvar Aalto in his Own Words*, New York: Rizzoli, 1997, pp. 89–93.

— 'The Influence of Construction and Materials on Modern Architecture', 1938. Repr. in G. Schildt, *Alvar Aalto Sketches*, Cambridge, MA: MIT Press, 1985, pp. 60–3, and as 'The Influence of Structure and Materials on Modern Architecture', 1938, G. Schildt, *Alvar Aalto in his Own Words*, New York: Rizzoli, 1997, pp.98–101.

— 'An American Town In Finland', 1940. Repr. in G. Schildt, *Alvar Aalto in his Own Words*, New York: Rizzoli, 1997, pp.122–31.

— 'E.G. Asplund Obituary', *Arkkitehti*, 11–12, 1940. Repr. in G. Schildt, *Alvar Aalto in his Own Words*, New York: Rizzoli, 1997, pp. 242–3 and G. Schildt, *Alvar Aalto Sketches*, Cambridge, MA: MIT Press, 1985, pp. 66–7.

— 'The Architecture of Karelia', 1941, *Uusi Suomi*. Repr. in G. Schildt, *Alvar Aalto Sketches*, Cambridge, MA: MIT Press, 1985, pp.80–3, and as 'Karelian Architecture', in G. Schildt, *Alvar Aalto in his Own Words*, New York: Rizzoli, 1997, pp.115-19.

— ' The "America Builds" Exhibition, Helsinki, 1945', *Arkkitehti*, 1, 1945. Repr. in G. Schildt, *Alvar Aalto in his Own Words*, New York: Rizzoli, 1997, pp.131–6.

— 'Building Height as a Social Issue', *Arkkitehti*, 1946. Repr. in G. Schildt, *Alvar Aalto in his Own Words*, New York, Rizzoli, 1997, p.208, and as 'Building Heights as a Social Problem' in G. Schildt, *Alvar Aalto: Sketches*, Cambridge, MA: MIT Press, 1985, pp. 166–7.

— 'Culture and Technology', *Suomi-Finland – USA*, 1947. Repr. in G. Schildt, *Alvar Aalto Sketches*, Cambridge, MA: MIT Press, 1985, pp. 94-5.

— 'The Trout and the Mountain Stream', *Domus*, 1947. Repr. in G. Schildt, *Alvar Aalto Sketches*, Cambridge, MA: MIT Press, 1985, pp. 96–8, and G. Schildt, *Alvar Aalto in his Own Words*, New York: Rizzoli, 1997, pp.107–9.

— 'Finland as a Model for World Development', 1949. Repr. in G. Schildt, *Alvar Aalto in his Own Words*, New York: Rizzoli, 1997, pp.167–71.

— 'National Planning and Cultural Goals,' *Suomalainen-Suomi*, 1949. Repr. in G. Schildt, *Alvar Aalto Sketches*, Cambridge, MA: MIT Press, 1985, pp. 99–102, and as 'Finland as a Model for World Development' in G. Schildt, *Alvar Aalto in his Own Words*, New York: Rizzoli, 1997, pp. 167–71.

— 'Finland Wonderland', Architectural Association London, 1950. Repr. in G. Schildt, *Alvar Aalto in his Own Words*, New York: Rizzoli, 1997, pp. 184-90.

— 'Senior Dormitory M.I.T.', *Arkkitehti*, 4, 1950, p.64.

— 'Experimental House, Muuratsalo', *Arkkitehti – Arkitekten*, 1953. Repr. in G. Schildt, *Alvar Aalto Sketches*, Cambridge, MA: MIT Press, 1985, pp.115-16.

— 'Experimental House at Muuratsalo', *Arkkitehti*, 9, 9–10, 1953. Repr. in G. Schildt, *Alvar Aalto in his Own Words*, New York: Rizzoli, 1977, pp. 234-5.

— 'Art and Technology', Inauguration into Finnish Academy, 1955. Repr. in G. Schildt, *Alvar Aalto Sketches*, Cambridge, MA: MIT Press, 1985, pp.125-9, also in G. Schildt, *Alvar Aalto in his Own Words*, New York: Rizzoli, 1997, pp.171–6.

— 'Between Humanism and Materialism', 1955. Repr. in G. Schildt, *Alvar Aalto Sketches*, Cambridge, MA: MIT Press, 1985, pp.130-3.

— 'Form as a Symbol of Artistic Creativity', 1956. Repr. in G. Schildt, *Alvar Aalto in his Own Words*, New York: Rizzoli, 1997, pp. 181–3.

— 'Wood as a Building Material', *Arkkitehti – Arkitekten*, 1956. Repr. in G. Schildt, *Alvar Aalto Sketches*, Cambridge, MA: MIT Press, 1985, p.142.

— 'The Architect's Concept of Paradise', 1957. Repr. in G. Schildt, *Alvar Aalto Sketches*, Cambridge, MA: MIT Press, 1985, pp. 157–9.

— 'The Architectural Struggle', RIBA, 1957. Repr. in G. Schildt, *Alvar Aalto Sketches*, Cambridge, MA: MIT Press, 1985, pp. 144-8, and as 'Enemies of Good Architecture', in G. Schildt, *Alvar Aalto in his Own Words*, New York: Rizzoli, 1997, pp.201–6.

— 'Instead of an Article', 1958, *Arkkitehti – Arkitekten*. Repr. in G. Schildt, *Alvar Aalto Sketches*, Cambridge, MA: MIT Press, 1985, pp. 161-2, and G. Schildt, *Alvar Aalto in his Own Words*, New York: Rizzoli, 1997, pp.263-4.

— 'Speech for the Centenary of Jyväskylä Lycée', 1958. Repr. in G. Schildt, *Alvar Aalto Sketches*, Cambridge, MA: MIT Press, 1985, pp.162–4.

— 'Vuoksenniskan Kirkko', *Arkkitehti-Arkitekten*, 12, 1959, p.201. Repr. as *The Church of the Three Crosses*, Vuoksenniska, Parish Leaflet, 2001.

— 'Town Planning and Public Buildings', 1966. Repr. in G. Schildt, *Alvar Aalto Sketches*, Cambridge, MA: MIT Press, 1985, pp. 166–7.

— 'Riola Church', *Domus*, February 1967, p.447.

— 'The Relationship between Architecture, Painting and Sculpture: Discussion with Karl Fleig, 1969', in B. Hoesli (ed.), *Alvar Aalto, Synopsis: Painting Architecture Sculpture*, Zürich: Birkhäuser, 1980, pp.24-6. Also repr. in G. Schildt, *Alvar Aalto in his Own Words*, New York: Rizzoli, 1997, pp. 265-9.

— 'Interview for Finnish Television', July 1972. Repr. in G. Schildt, *Alvar Aalto in his Own Words*, New York: Rizzoli, 1997, pp.269–75.

— 'Centenary Speech of Helsinki University of Technology, 5 December 1972. Repr. in G. Schildt, *Alvar Aalto in his Own Words*, New York: Rizzoli, 1997, pp.281–5.

— 'Introduction' to A. Christ-Janer, *Eliel Saarinen*, Chicago: Chicago University Press, 1979 (orig. pub. 1948).

— 'Conversation', in G. Schildt, *Alvar Aalto Sketches*, Cambridge, MA: MIT Press, 1985, pp.170–2.

— 'The Human Factor' (undated), in G. Schildt, *Alvar Aalto in his Own Words*, New York: Rizzoli, 1997, pp.280–1.

Aalto, A. and A., 'Alvar Aalto's Own House and Studio', *Arkkitenti*, 8, 1937. Repr. as *Alvar Aallon Oma Talo ja Toimisto, Heslinki* (Alvar Aalto's Own House and Studio), Jyväskylä: Alvar Aalto Museo, 1999, p.2.

Aalto, A. and A., 'Mairea – Introduction', *Arkkitehti*, 9, 1939. Repr. in *Villa Mairea*, Jyväskylä: Alvar Aalto Museum, 1982, p.2.

Aalto, E., 'Contacts', in T. Hihnala and P.-M. Raippalinna, *Fratres Spirituales Alvari*, Jyväskylä: Alvar Aalto Museum, 1991, pp.6–11.

Agrest, D., *The Sex of Architecture*, New York: Harry N. Abrams, 1996.

Anderson, S., 'Aalto and Methodical Accommodation to Circumstance', in T. Tuomi, K. Paatero and E. Rauske (eds) *Alvar Aalto in Seven Buildings*, Helsinki: Museum of Finnish Architecture, 1998, pp.143-9.

Apollinaire, G., *L'Esprit nouveau et les poètes*, Paris: Jacques Haumont, 1946.

— *Le Bestiaire ou Cortège d'Orphée* in M. Décaudin, (ed.), *Oeuvres Complètes de Guillaume Apollinaire*, Paris: André Balland et Jacques Lecat, 1966.

Bacon, M., *Le Corbusier in America*, Cambridge, MA: MIT Press, 2001.

Baker, G.H., *Le Corbusier: The Creative Search*, London: Spon, 1996.

Belot, M. le Chanoine, Curé de Ronchamp. *Manuel du Pelerin*, 1930 p.13 in FLC.

Benevolo, L., *History of Modern Architecture* 2, Cambridge, MA: MIT Press, 1971.

Benton, T. (ed.) *Le Corbusier Architect of the Century*, London: Arts Council of Great Britain, 1987.

Bergson, H., *Creative Evolution*, London: Macmillan, 1911.

— *Mélanges*, Paris: Presses Universitaires de France, 1972.

Birkerts, G., 'Aalto's Design Methodology', *Architecture and Urbanism*, May 1983, Extra Edition, 12. pp. 13-14.

Blake, P., *No Place like Utopia*, New York: Norton, 1996.

Brookes, H.A., *Le Corbusier's Formative Years*, Chicago: Chicago University Press, 1997.

Buchanan, S. (ed.), *The Portable Plato*, Harmondsworth: Penguin, 1997.

Carl, P., 'Ornament and Time: A Prolegomena', *AA Files*, 23, 1992, pp.55-7.

Carrel, A., *Man the Unknown*, New York: Harper, 1935.

Christ-Janer, A., *Eliel Saarinen*, Chicago: Chicago University Press, 1979.

Cobb, E., *The Ecology of Imagination in Childhood*, Dallas: Spring Publications, 1993.

Cohen, J.-L., 'Le Corbusier's Nietzschean Metaphors', in Alexandre Kosta and Irving Wohlfarth (eds), *Nietzsche and 'An Architecture of Our Minds'*, Los Angeles: Getty, 1999, p.311.

Coll, J., 'Structure and Play in Le Corbusier's Art Works,' *AA Files* 31, summer 1996, pp.3-15.

Colli, L.M., 'La Coleur qui Cache, La Couleur qui Signale', in J. Jenger (ed.), *Le Corbusier et la Couleur*, Paris: FLC, 1992, pp.24-5

Colomina, B., 'Le Corbusier and Photography', *Assemblage*, 4, 1987, pp.12–13.

Connar, R., *Aaltomania*, Helsinki: Rakennustieto, 2000.

Constant, C., 'The Nonheroic Modernism of Eileen Gray', *Journal Society of Architectural Historians*, 53, September 1994, p.275.

Curtis, W., *Le Corbusier, Ideas and Forms*, London: Phaidon, 1986.

— *Modern Architecture Since 1900*, London: Phaidon, 1996.

de Rougemont, D., *Passion and Society*, London: Faber & Faber, 1958.

Durkin, T., *Hope in our Time: Alexis Carrel on Man and Society*, New York: Harper & Row, 1965.

Eisenstadt, J. M., 'Parental Loss and Genius', *American Psychologist*, 1978, 33, pp.211–23.

Eliel, C. S., *Purism in Paris*, New York: Harry N. Abrams, 2001.

Eriksen, E., *Insight and Responsibility*, New York: Norton, 1964.

Evans, R., *The Projective Cast*, Cambridge, MA: MIT Press, 1995.

Fagan-King, J., 'United on the Threshold of the Twentieth Century Mystical Ideal', *Art History*, 11, 1 1988, pp.89–113.

Fairbairn, W. R. D., *Psycho-Analytical Studies of the Personality*, London: Tavistock, 1952.

Fenichel, O., *The Psycholanalytical Theory of Neurosis*, London: Routledge Kegan Paul, 1947.

Fleig, K. (ed.) *Alvar Aalto Vol. 1*, 1922–62, Zürich: Verlag für Architecktur Artemis, 1990.

— *Alvar Aalto Vol. 2, 1963-70*, Zürich: Verlag für Architecktur Artemis, 1990.

— *Alvar Aalto Vol. 3, Projects and Finland Buildings*, Zürich: Verlag für Architecktur Artemis, 1990.

Foucault, M., *The Order of Things*, Bristol: Arrow Smith, 1977.

Frampton, K., *Modern Architecture; A Critical History*, London: Thames & Hudson, 1997.

— *Le Corbusier*, London: Thames & Hudson, 2001.

Ghyka, M., *Nombre d'or: rites et rhythmes Pythagoriciens dans le développement de la civilisation Occidental*, Paris: Gallimard, 1931.

Giedion, S., 'Space, Time and Architecture', Cambridge, MA: MIT Press, 2nd edn, 1949.

Griffiths, G., *The Polemical Aalto*, Datutop 19, Tampere: University of Tampere, 1997.

Grisleri, G., *Le Corbusier, il viaggio in Toscana, 1907*, exhibition catalogue, Florence: Palazzo Pitti, 1987, p.17.

Guthrie, W.K.C., *Orpheus and Greek Religion*, London: Methuen, 1935.

Häring, H., 'Wege zur Form', in *Die Form*, 1, 1925, pp.3-5.

Heinonen, R.-L., *Funktionalism läpimurto Suomessa*, Helsinki: Museum of Finnish Architecture, 1986.

Hellman, G.,'From Within to Without', *New Yorker Magazine*, 26 April and 3 May 1947.

Hervé, L., *Le Corbusier The Artist/Writer*, Neuchatel: Éditions du Grifon, 1970.

Hihnala, T., and Raippalinna, P.-M., *Fratres Spirituales Alvari*, Jyväskylä: Alvar Aalto Museum, 1991.

Hinz, B., 'Die Malerei im deutschen Faschismus', *Kunst und Konterrolution*, München: Carl Hanser Verlag, 1974.

Illingworth, R.S., *Lessons from Childhood*, London: Livingstone, 1966.

Infinitum Publications and Fondation Le Corbusier (eds), *Le Corbusier architecte artiste*, CD Rom Fondation le Corbusier, 1996.

Jaeger, W., *The Theology of the Early Greek Philosophers*, Oxford: Oxford University Press, 1947.

Jencks, C., *Le Corbusier and the Continual Revolution in Architecture*, New York: Monacelli, 2000.

Jenger, J., *Le Corbusier: Architect of a New Age*, London: Thames & Hudson, 1996.

John, A., 'Creativity and Intelligibility in Le Corbusier's Chapel at Ronchamp', *Journal of Aesthetics and Art History*, 163, March 1958, pp. 293-305.

Jones, O., *The Grammar of Ornament*, London: Dorling Kindersley, 2001. Orig. pub. in 1856.

Jormakka, K., Gargus, J. and Graf, D., *The Use and Abuse of Paper*, Datutop 20, Tampere: Tampere University, 1999.

Klein, E., *A Comprehensive Etymological Dictionary of the English Language*, London: Elsevier, 1971.

Koho, T., *Alvar Aalto – Urban Finland*, Helsinki: Rakennustieto, 1995.

Krustrup, M., *Porte Email*, Copenhagen: Arkitektens Forlag, 1991.

Labasant, J., 'Le Corbusier's Notre Dame du Haut at Ronchamp', *Architectural Record*, 118, 4, 1955, p.170.

Lacey, A. R., *Bergson*, London: Routledge, 1989.

Lahti, L., *Ex Intimo*, Helsinki: Rakennustieto, 2001.

Lahti, M., *Alvar Aalto Houses: Timeless Expressions*, Tokyo: A&U, 1998.

Lake, F., *Tight Corners*, London: DLT, 1981.

— *Clinical Theology*, London: DLT, 1986.

— *The Dynamic Cycle*, a Lingdale Paper no. 2, Oxford: CTA, 1986.

Langer, S. K., Mind: An Essay in Human Feeling, abridged edn, Baltimore: John Hopkins University Press, 1988.

Le Corbusier, *Une Maison – un palais: A la recherche d'une unité architecturale*, Paris: Crès, 1928.

— *The City of Tomorrow*, London: Architectural Press, 1946.

— *When the Cathedrals were White: A Journey to the Country of the Timid People*, New York:

Reynal & Hitchcock, 1947. Orig. pub. as *Quand les cathédrales étaient blanches*, Paris: Plon, 1937.

— *A New World of Space*, New York: Reynal & Hitchcock, 1948.

— *Modulor*, London: Faber, 1954. Orig. pub. as *Le Modulor*, Paris Éditions d'Architecture d'Aujourd'hui, 1950.

— *Modulor 2*, London: Faber, 1955. Orig. pub. as *Le Modulor 11*, Paris Éditions d'Architecture d'Aujourd'hui, 1955.

— *The Chapel at Ronchamp*, London: Architecural Press, 1957.

— *Le Poème électronique*, Paris: Les Cahiers Forces Vives aux Éditions de Minuit, 1958.

— *My Work*, London: Architectural Press, 1960.

— *Le Corbusier Talks with Students*, New York: Orion, 1961. Orig. pub. as *Entretien avec les étudiants des écoles d'architecture*, Paris: Denoel, 1943.

— *Mise aus Point*, Paris: Éditions Forces Vives, 1966.

— *The Radiant City*, London: Faber, 1967. Orig. pub. as *La Ville radieuse*, paris: Éditions de l'Architecture d'Aujourd'hui, 1935.

— *Urbanisme*, Paris: Editions Arthaud, 1980. Orig. pub. 1925.

— *Sketchbooks Volume 1*, London: Thames & Hudson, 1981.

— *Sketchbooks Volume 2*, London: Thames & Hudson, 1981.

— *Sketchbooks Volume 3, 1954–1957*, Cambridge, MA: MIT Press, 1982.

— *Sketchbooks Volume 4, 1957–1964*, Cambridge, MA: MIT Press, 1982.

— *Towards a New Architecture*, London: Architectural Press, 1982. Orig. pub. as *Vers une Architecture*, Paris: Crès, 1923.

— *The Decorative Art of Today*, London: Architectural Press, 1987. Orig. pub. as *L'Art decoratif d'aujourd'hui*, Paris: Crès, 1925.

— *Journey to the East*, Cambridge, MA: MIT Press, 1987. Orig. pub. as *Le Voyage d'Orient*, Paris, 1966, 1987.

— *Le Poème de l'angle droit*, Paris: Éditions Connivance, 1989. Orig. pub. 1955.

— *Precisions on the Present State of Architecture and City Planning*, Cambridge, MA: MIT Press, 1991. Orig. pub. as *Précisions sur état present d l'architecture et de l'urbanisme*, Paris: Crès, 1930.

Le Corbusier and De Fayet, 'Bauchant,' Esprit Nouveau, 17, 1922.

— and Jeanneret, P., *Oeuvre Complète Volume 2, 1929–34* Zürich: Les Éditions d'Architecture, 1995. Orig. pub. 1935.

— and Jeanneret, P., *Oeuvre Complète Volume 1, 1910–1929*, Zürich: Les Éditions d'Architecture, 1995. Orig. pub. 1937.

— and Jeanneret, P., *Oeuvre Complète Volume 3, 1934-1938*, Zürich: Les Éditions d'Architecture, 1995. Orig. pub. 1938.

— *Oeuvre Complète Volume 4, 1938–1946*, Zürich: Les Éditions d'Architecture, 1995. Orig. pub. 1946.

— *Oeuvre Complète Volume 5, 1946–1952*, Zürich: Les Éditions d'Architecture, 1995. Orig. pub. 1953.

— *Oeuvre Complète Volume 6, 1952–1957*, Zürich: Les Éditions d'Architecture, 1995. Orig. pub. 1957.

— *Oeuvre Complète Volume 7, 1957–1965*, Zürich: Les Éditions d'Architecture, 1995. Orig. pub. 1965.

Liddell, H.G., and Scott, R., *A Greek–English Lexicon*, Oxford: Clarendon, 1961.

Loach, J.,'Le Corbusier and the Creative use of Mathematics', *British Journal of the History of Science*, 31, 1998, pp.185-215.

— 'Jeanneret becoming Le Corbusier: Portrait of the Artist as a Young Swiss', *Journal of Architecture*, 5, 2000, pp.91–9.

McEwan, I.K., *Socrates Ancestors*, Cambridge, MA: MIT Press, 1993.

McLeod, M. 'Urbanism and Utopia: Le Corbusier from Regional Syndicalism to Vichy', Dphil Thesis, Princeton, 1985, p.245.

Mahler, M., *On Human Symbiosis and the Vicissitudes of Individuation*, New York: International Universities Press, 1968.

Menin, S., *Relating the Past: Sibelius, Aalto and the Profound Logos*, Unpub. PhD thesis, University of Newcastle, 1997.

— 'Aalto and Sibelius, 'Children of the Forest's Mighty God'', in A. Barnett, (ed.), *The Forest's Mighty God*, London: UK Sibelius Society, 1998, pp. 52–59.

— 'Soap Bubbles Floating in the Air', in *Sibelius Forum, Second International Jean Sibelius Conference 1995*, Helsinki: Sibelius Academy, 1998, pp.8–14.

— 'Fragments from the Forest: Aalto's Requisitioning of Forest Place and Matter', *Journal of Architecture*, 6, 3, 2001, pp.279–305.

— 'Aalto, Sibelius and Fragments of Forest Culture', *Sibelius Forum, Third International Jean Sibelius Symposium*, Helsinki: Sibelius Academy, 2002.

Mikkola, K., 'Aalto the Thinker', *Arkkitehti*, 7/8, 1976, pp.20–5.

— *Aalto*, Jyväskylä: Gummerus, 1985.

Miller, W., 'Thematic Analysis of Alvar Aalto's Architecture', *A & U*, October 1979, pp.15-38.

Milner, M., *On Not Being Able to Paint*, London: Heinemann Educational, 1950.

Moholy-Nagy, L., *The New Vision*, Chicago: Institute of Design, 1947. Orig. pub. in 1930.

Mosso, L., *Alvar Aalto. Catalogue 1918–1967*, Helsinki: Otava, 1967, p.129.

Naegele, D., 'Photographic illusionism and the New World of Space' in M. Krustrup (ed.) *Le Corbusier, Painter and Architect*, Aalborg: Nordjyllands Kunstmuseum, 1995.

Norberg-Schulz, C., *Genius Loci: Towards a Phenomenology of Architecture*, New York: Rizzoli, 1980.

Ochse, R.E., *Before the Gates of Excellence: The Determinants of Creative Genius*, Cambridge: Cambridge University Press, 1990.

Ott, R., 'Surface and Structure', in M. Quantrill and B. Webb (eds), *The Culture of Silence, Architecture's Fifth Dimension*, Texas: A & M University Press, 1998.

Paatero, K., 'Vuoksenniska Church', in T. Tuomi, K. Paatero and E. Rauske (eds) *Alvar Aalto in Seven Buildings*, Helsinki: Museum of Finnish Architecture, 1999, pp.113-15.

Pallasmaa, J.,'The Art of Wood', in *The Language of Wood*, Helsinki: Museum of Finnish Architecture, 1989, p.16.

— *Villa Mairea*, Helsinki: Mairea Foundation and Alvar Aalto Foundation, 1998.

Pauly, D., 'The Chapel of Ronchamp', *AD Profile* 55, 7/8, 1985, pp.30–7.

Petit, J., *Le Corbusier Lui-Même*, Paris: Forces Vives, 1970.

Pevsner, N., *An Outline of European Architecture*, London: Pelican, 1982.

Phillips, A., *Winnicott*, London: Fontana, 1988.

Pianizzola, C., 'Sole e Tecnologia per una Architettura della Luce', unpublished thesis, Istituto Universitario Architettura Venezia, 1996.

Pico della Mirandola, G., *On the Dignity of Man*, Indianapolis: Hackett, 1998. Written in 1486.

Pietilä, R., 'A Gestalt Building', *Architecture and Urbanism*, May 1983, Extra Edition, 12.

— 'Architect's Approach to Architecture', in M.-R. Norri, R. Connah, K. Kuosma and A. Artto, *Pietilä: Intermediate Zones in Modern Architecture*, Helsinki: Museum of Finnish Architecture, 1985.

— 'Influences', in M.-R. Norri, R. Connah, K. Kuosma and A. Artto, *Pietilä: Intermediate Zones in Modern Architecture*, Helsinki: Museum of Finnish Architecture, 1985.

Plato, *Symposium*, in S. Buchanan (ed.) *The Portable Plato*, Harmondsworth: Penguin, 1997.

— *The Republic III*, in S. Buchanan (ed.) *The Portable Plato*, Harmondsworth: Penguin, 1997.

Porphyrios, D., 'The Burst of Memory: An Essay on Alvar Aalto's Typological Conception of Design', *Architectural Design*, 49, 5/6, 1979, p.144.

— *Sources of Modern Eclecticism: Studies of Alvar Aalto*, London: Academy Editions, 1982.

Pottecher, F., 'Que le Fauve soit libre dans sa cage', *L'Architecture d'Aujourd'Hui*, 252, 1987, pp. 58–66.

Provensal, H., *L'Art de Demain*, Paris: Perrin, 1904.

Rabelais, F., *Oeuvres Complètes*, Paris: Gallimard, 1951 in FLC.

Reed, P.,'Alvar Aalto and the New Humanism of the Postwar Era', in P. Reed, (ed.) *Between Humanism and Materialism*, New York: Museum of Modern Art, 1998, pp.110–11.

Renan, E., *The Life of Jesus*, London: Watts, 1947.

Reunala, A., 'The Forest as an Archetype', special issue of *Silva Fennica*, 'Metsä Suomalaisten Elämäss', 21, 4, 1987, p.426.

— 'The Forest and the Finns', in M. Engman *et al.*' *People, Nation, State*, London: Hurst, 1989, pp. 38–56.

Richards, J.M., *Memories of an Unjust Fella*, London: Weidenfeld & Nicholson, 1980.

Riikinen, K., *A Geography of Finland*, Lahti: University of Helsinki, 1992.

Rosenblum, R., *Modern Painting and the Northern Romantic Tradition*, London: Thames &

Hudson, 1994.

Rüegg, A. (ed.) *Le Corbusier Photographs by René Burri: Moments in the Life of a Great Architect*, Basel: Birkhäuser, 1999.

Samuel, F.,'Le Corbusier, Women, Nature and Culture', *Issues in Art and Architecture*, 5, 2, 1998, pp. 4-20.

— 'Le Corbusier, Teilhard de Chardin and the Planetisation of Mankind', *Journal of Architecture*, 4, 1999, pp.149–65.

— '*Orphism in the Work of Le Corbusier with Particular Reference to his Scheme for La Sainte Baume*,' PhD thesis, Cardiff University, 1999.

— 'The Philosophical City of Rabelais and St Teresa: Le Corbusier and Édouard Trouin's Scheme for St Baume', *Literature and Theology*, 13, 2, 1999, pp.111–26.

— 'A Profane Annunciation: The Representation of Sexuality in the Architecture of Ronchamp', *Journal of Architectural Education*, 53, 2, 1999, pp.74-90.

— 'Le Corbusier, Teilhard de Chardin and La planétisation humaine: spiritual ideas at the heart of modernism', *French Cultural Studies*, 11, 2, 32, 2000, pp.163-288.

— 'Le Corbusier, Rabelais and the Oracle of the Holy Bottle', *Word and Image*, 17, 4, 2001, pp. 325-38.

Schildt, G., *Alvar Aalto: The Early Years*, New York: Rizzoli, 1984.

— *Alvar Aalto Sketches*, Cambridge, MA: MIT Press, 1985.

— *Alvar Aalto: The Decisive Years*, New York: Rizzoli, 1986.

— 'Alvar Aalto's Artist Friends', in T. Hihnala and P.-M. Raippalinna, *Fratres Spirituales Alvari*, Jyväskylä: Alvar Aalto Museum, 1991.

— *Alvar Aalto: The Mature Years*, New York: Rizzoli, 1992.

— *Alvar Aalto: The Complete Catalogue of Architecture, Design and Art*, London: Academy Éditions, 1994.

— *Alvar Aalto in his Own Words*, New York: Rizzoli, 1997.

Scully, V., *The Earth, the Temple and the Gods*, New Haven: Yale University Press, 1962.

Seiveking, A., *The Cave Artists*, London: Thames & Hudson, 1979.

Spate, V.,'Orphism', in N. Stangos (ed.) *Concepts of Modern Art*, London: Thames & Hudson, 1997.

St. John Wilson, C., *Architectural Reflections*, London: Butterworth, 1992.

— *The 'Other' Tradition of Modern Architecture*, London: Academy Editions, 1995.

Standertskjöld, E., 'Alvar Aalto's Standard Drawings 1929–1932' in R. Nikula, M.-R. Norri, and K. Paatero (eds) *The Art of Standards, Acanthus*, Helsinki: Museum of Finnish Architecture, 1992, pp.89–111.

— 'Alvar Aalto and Standardisation', in R. Nikula, M.-R. Norri, and K. Paatero (eds) *The Art of Standards, Acanthus*, Helsinki: Museum of Finnish Architecture, 1992, pp.74-84.

Stirling, J., 'Ronchamp: Le Corbusier's Chapel and the Crisis of Rationalism', *Architectural Review*, 119, 711, March 1956, pp.155-61.

Storr, A., *The Dynamics of Creation*, Harmondsworth: Penguin, 1991.

— *Solitude*, London: Harper Collins, 1997.

Teilhard de Chardin, P., *L'Énergie Humaine*, Paris: Éditions du Seuil, 1962.

— *The Future of Man*, London: Collins, 1964.

— *The Appearance of Man*, London: Collins, 1965.

Treib, M.,'Aalto's Nature', in P. Reed (ed.) *Alvar Aalto Between Humanism and Materialism*, New York: Museum of Modern Art, 1998, pp.46–67.

Tuomi, T., Paatero, K. and Rauske, E. (eds) *Alvar Aalto in Seven Buildings*, Helsinki: Museum of Finnish Architecture, 1998.

Tuovinen, E. (ed.) *Alvar Aalto: Technology and Nature*, dir. Y. Jalander, New York: Phaidon Video, PHV 6050.

Turner, P., *The Education of an Architect*, New York: Garland, 1977.

Udovickl-Selb, D.,'Le Corbusier and the Paris Exhibition of 1937', *Journal of the Society of Architectural History*, 56, 1, March 1997, pp.42–63.

Venturi, R., *Complexity and Contradiction in Architecture*, London: Architectural Press, 1983.

Vernant, J.-P., *Mythe et Pensée chez les Grecs*, Paris: La Découverte, 1985.

Vogt, A.M., *Le Corbusier: The Noble Savage*, Cambridge, MA: MIT Press, 1998.

Walden, R. (ed.) *The Open Hand*, Cambridge, MA: MIT Press, 1982.

Weisberg, R.W., *Creativity: Beyond the Myth of Genius*, New York: W.H. Freeman & Co., 1993.

Wesse, H., 'Alvar Aalto', in *ARK*, 7–8, 1976, p.46.

Weston, R., *Alvar Aalto*, London: Phaidon, 1995.

Winner, E., *Invented Worlds*, Cambridge, MA: Harvard University Press, 1982.

Winnicott, D.W., 'Primitive Emotional Development', 1945, in *Collected Works*, London: Tavistock, 1958.

— 'Transitional Objects and Transitional Phenomena' 1951, in Winnicott, *Playing and Reality*, Harmondsworth: Penguin, 1971, p.26.

— *Collected Papers: Through Paediatrics to Psychoanalysis*, London: Tavistock, 1958.

— 'Cure', 1970. Repr. in D.W. Winnicott, *Home is Where We Start From: Essays by a Psychoanalyst*, Harmondsworth: Penguin, 1986.

— *Playing and Reality*, Harmondsworth: Penguin, 1971.

— 'The Concept of a Healthy Individual', in D.W. Winnicott, *Home is Where We Start From: Essays by a Psychoanalyst*, Harmondsworth: Penguin, 1986.

— *Home is Where We Start From: Essays by a Psychoanalyst*, Harmondsworth: Penguin, 1986.

Wogenscky, A., *Les Mains de Le Corbusier*, Paris: Éditions de Grenelle (no date).

I. Žaknić, *The Final Testament of Père Corbu*, New Haven: Yale University Press, 1997.

Index

Page numbers in *italics* refer to illustrations in the main text (Plates are referred to separately). Notes alongside the text are denoted by suffix "n" followed by the note number (e.g. "39n[96]" means note 96 on page 39). Abbreviations: "AA" means "Alvar Aalto" in this index: and "LC" is "Le Corbusier".